Policing

Policing
The Essentials

MICHAEL E. BUERGER
Bowling Green State University

JOHN LIEDERBACH
Bowling Green State University

STEVEN P. LAB
Bowling Green State University

New York Oxford
OXFORD UNIVERSITY PRESS

Oxford University Press is a department of the University of Oxford.
It furthers the University's objective of excellence in research, scholarship,
and education by publishing worldwide. Oxford is a registered trade mark of
Oxford University Press in the UK and certain other countries.

Published in the United States of America by Oxford University Press
198 Madison Avenue, New York, NY 10016, United States of America.

© 2022 by Oxford University Press

CIP data is on file at the Library of Congress
978–0–19–092197–2

Printing number: 9 8 7 6 5 4 3 2 1
Paperback printed by Marquis, Canada

CONTENTS

PREFACE

◆○

W riting a succinct introductory text on any topic is a challenge, especially when the topic of the text has a wealth of information and material upon which to draw. Policing has a well-developed body of research, and there are numerous well-regarded books available for class use. Most of the books have grown into lengthy tomes complete with pictures, tables, and graphs (which we know many, if not most, students ignore or gloss over), and they come with a high cost to students. In a time when colleges and universities are pushing for more economical alternatives to the traditional large introductory text, we have found that there is a need for a book like the one you are holding right now.

Trying to take the wide amount of available information on policing and paring it down while maintaining a book that covers the essential range of topics needed in introductory courses is not an easy task. In this book, we have attempted to produce an overview of policing in the US that includes discussion of the major issues facing policing without all the costly frills of other texts. We have successfully used this approach on other "Essentials" texts. The primary audience for this book is those students who have little academic knowledge of policing and those who need a refresher on policing.

We have incorporated several features with this book to aid students and instructors. First, we have attempted to cite relevant scholarship throughout the book and suggested additional readings for each chapter. Second, there are "Web Activities" that point the reader to additional materials that supplement and expand on chapter topics. Third, "Critical Thinking Exercises" pose scenarios and questions that ask readers to apply their knowledge and expand their thoughts on issues. Finally, we have placed some material on the book's website rather than include it in the book in order to hold down the book's cost. Our intent is to continue to add to the website as new topics and issues emerge and the book is revised.

The successful completion of a book relies on input from a wide array of individuals. One important group is the manuscript reviewers who raise new ideas and insights that inevitably lead to changes and that challenge the authors to question their work. In the preparation of this book one reviewer opined that we are not "pro-law enforcement" and clearly "biased" against law enforcement. This took us by surprise since all of us have spent our careers either working as police officers, working with the police, studying policing, and/or researching police and policing topics, all in concert with police agencies. One of us worked as a police officer in two adjoining states, and all of us have worked with police in multiple jurisdictions as they worked to improve their effectiveness. An important part of improving any organization is to talk about the good, the bad, the promising, and the challenges they are facing. In an introductory text it is important to try to provide a balanced presentation. As we double-checked our work in light of the reviewers' comments, we believe we have provided both positives and negatives of policing. Policing is an admirable profession, and the people on the job face difficult situations on a daily basis, and largely do the job well. We would be remiss in our attempt to educate students (and police) if we did not discuss the problems and challenges that need to be addressed.

We want to thank everyone who provided input. Steve Helba and the staff of Oxford University Press have been nothing but supportive, and their guidance and assistance are greatly appreciated. Thanks also go to the following reviewers, who offered important comments and insights to the book:

Michael D. Brooks—Dyersburg State Community College
Robert M. Clark—Pennsylvania Highlands Community College
Kelly Fisher—Indiana University Kokomo
Jonathon Fredericks—SUNY Rockland
Xiaochen Hu—Fayetteville State University
Michael J. Jenkins—University of Scranton
Michael Patrick Mendenhall—Ferris State University
Nabil Ouassini—Prairie View A&M University
Louis A. Reeves—St. Mary-of-the-Woods College
Bonnie Semora—Dalton State College
Kenneth Whitman—Alabama A&M University

We have incorporated many of their suggestions, although the goal of keeping the book a manageable length and reasonable cost prohibited us from including them all. We have started a list of ideas they provided for use in future editions. We also need to thank the many police officers, departments, agencies, and researchers with whom we have worked over the years for their valuable support, knowledge, and insights that have helped shape our careers and our understanding of policing in the United States.

CHAPTER 1

Introduction

CHAPTER OUTLINE

Introduction and Overview

Defining Police

Role of Police

Balancing Freedom and Public Order

Police as Gatekeepers within the Criminal Justice System

A Uniquely American System of Policing

Policing as a Multivariate Phenomenon

Chapter Summary

After reading this chapter, you should be able to:

- Describe the job of police in a democratic society in terms of balancing freedom and public order
- Describe the specific role of police within the criminal justice system
- Understand the operation of the larger criminal justice system using the analogy of a funnel
- Explain how and why the American system of policing is unique among nations
- Define American policing as a *decentralized* rather than centralized system
- Define the term *multivariate* and explain the various influences on police behavior in terms of individuals, organizations, community, and situational factors
- Understand coercion as a central feature of police work

INTRODUCTION AND OVERVIEW

This chapter introduces some basic concepts about American policing that serve as an introduction and overview for the rest of the text. There are four main sections of the chapter. The first section covers issues associated with defining police as an occupational group. It presents some basic deficiencies within both popular conceptions of police and those derived from dictionaries. The main point of the section is to identify the use of coercion as the central and defining feature of police work. The second section of the chapter describes the role of police along two dimensions. The first dimension involves the role of police within a democratic society in terms of a balancing of freedom and public order. This dichotomy is defined as a zero-sum game wherein police must decide on a daily basis between maintaining public order and protecting individual liberties. The second dimension more specifically involves the police role in terms of the American criminal justice system using the popular analogy of the criminal justice funnel. The section explains the analogy of the funnel and the police's gatekeeper role at various points in which the funnel narrows, which results in a reduction of criminal cases in the system. The third section of the chapter defines the American system of policing as unique among nations. It describes American policing as a decentralized system using various examples to explain both the unique features of the system as well as some of the associated advantages and disadvantages. The final section of the chapter defines policing as a multivariate phenomenon in which a multitude of factors may potentially influence police decision-making. These factors include those from several different contexts, including individuals, the police organization, community, and factors unique to each police–citizen encounter.

DEFINING POLICE

Students taking an introductory course on law enforcement who are asked to provide a definition of police tend to focus on the role of police as crime-fighters. These attempts to define police often center on the street-level act of an arrest and/or the investigation of crimes by detectives or criminal investigators. This focus on the crime-fighting role of police is a popular conception among introductory students—and indeed members of the general public—for a couple of reasons. People tend to emphasize their own experience in any attempt to understand the world around them, including police. Anyone who has ever been arrested is not likely to forget the experience. Even if we ourselves have not been arrested, most of us know or are familiar with someone who has been arrested at some point in time. We also tend to remember to a lesser degree our interactions with police involving less serious infractions such as the issuance of a traffic citation. These interactions involve problems that are less serious but nonetheless associated with the law enforcement role of police. The conception of police as primarily crime-fighters is also portrayed quite prominently within the popular media. Movies and television programs emphasize the manner in which police investigate crime scenes and eventually "catch the bad guy." Media depictions of police in this way reinforce our own conceptualizations of police that center almost exclusively on the police's role as crime-fighters.

The popular conceptualization that emphasizes the police role as crime-fighters is of course not wrong. Police do indeed fight crime. But that understanding is more incomplete than inaccurate. Police do all sorts of things in addition to their law enforcement duties. *Black's Law Dictionary* (2018) defines *police* as "the function of that branch of the administrative machinery of government which is charged with the preservation of public order and tranquility, the promotion of public health, safety, and morals, and the prevention, detection, and punishment of crimes." The *Merriam-Webster Dictionary* (2018) similarly defines *police* as "2(a) the department of government concerned primarily with maintenance of public order, safety, and health and enforcement of laws . . . 2(b) the department of government charged with prevention, detection, and prosecution of public nuisances and crimes." These definitions recognize several responsibilities or goals of police other than law enforcement, such as crime prevention, the maintenance of public order, and the promotion of health and morals. So at this point, our definition of police includes the popular conception that emphasizes law enforcement, but also several other duties that collectively encompass the sorts of things we expect police to do. Our definition combines the popular conception of police with the dictionary definitions to more accurately describe the sorts of things police are supposed to do.

The task of defining police, however, should arguably involve more than popular conceptualizations or even an exhaustive listing of duties derived from some dictionary. A more valid understanding of policing needs to focus less on goals—or what police are supposed to do, or what they are trying to do—and more on *how* police do what they do. Put another way, our understanding of police should focus on the means of their work—*how* they do what they are supposed to do—rather than just the ends or goals of the job. We focus on *how* police do their work because the manner in which police do their work more effectively encompasses the wide variety of jobs that police perform and distinguishes their work from the work involved in any other occupation.

The prominent police scholar Carl Klockers (1985) defined *police* as "institutions or individuals given the general right to use coercive force by the state" (12). His definition builds on the earlier work of another prominent police scholar Egon Bittner (1978), who recognized the importance of what he termed **coercive force** in defining the police and understanding how they do their work. For these and other police scholars, the distinguishing and most important aspect of police work is their use of coercion:

> In sum, the role of the police is to address all sorts of human problems when and insofar as their solutions do or may possibly require the use of force at the point of their occurrence. This lends homogeneity to such diverse procedures as catching a criminal, driving the mayor to the airport, evicting a

drunken person from a bar, directing traffic, crowd control, taking care of lost children, administering first aid, and separating fighting relatives. (Bittner 1978, 38)

The term *coercive force* within this context involves pretty much everything that the police do in their work. Students are sometimes reluctant to accept any definition of police that focuses almost exclusively on the importance of coercive force, most likely because we commonly limit our understanding of force to those acts that involve the use of physical force including pushes, punches, kicks, or even the actions of swinging a club or shooting a firearm. Students know that police sometimes engage in the use of physical force, but what about all of the other aspects of police work that do not involve the use of physical force? How do those fit into a definition of police that emphasizes the use of coercion?

The above definition of police and a recognition of coercion as the distinguishing feature of police work demands that we alter our way of thinking about coercion and expand it beyond acts of physical aggression. *Coercion* within this expanded understanding includes the actual commission of all of the above acts of physical force, but it also encompasses all sorts of behaviors police employ to otherwise accomplish the goals of their work, such as threats, verbal commands, and other nonviolent behaviors intended to address a wide variety of situations.

Consider the example of police action at a traffic accident. Police must secure the scene before they investigate fault or even render medical aid to those involved. They must walk out into the road, put their hand up, and direct other drivers to stop in order to prevent further collisions. A line of stopped vehicles quickly forms in the road. The police action in this example is obviously not one of physical force, but police have clearly used some form of coercion in order to secure the scene. Oncoming drivers are coerced into stopping, mostly because they know they cannot simply ignore a police command to stop. The other drivers might not have stopped if anyone other than a police officer had stood in the road and put their hand up. Consider another example of police exiting their patrol car and approaching the front door of the location of a loud party involving underage drinkers. Those underage drinkers who view the police approach the front door quickly exit out of the back door. They leave before the police perform any action other than to walk toward the front door. The police issue no verbal commands to leave or perform any acts of physical aggression. The underage drinkers certainly would not have left in the presence of anyone other than police. The mere presence of police has coerced them to leave the party.

The threat or use of some form of coercion is involved in virtually everything that the police do during the course of their work. Police are not merely crime-fighters, and their work involves much more than the goals proscribed by governments and/or those listed within dictionary definitions. Aside from those working within correctional agencies, police are the only individuals in society allowed—or even expected—to use coercion in some or all of its forms to accomplish the goals of their job. A definition of police that recognizes the importance of coercion in some ways forces students to understand the essence of police work in all of its forms—and to understand more completely why we need police in the first place. The next section considers the role of police more specifically in terms of the demands of a democratic society and within the context of the American criminal justice system.

ROLE OF POLICE

The following section describes the role of police along two dimensions. The first dimension is that of balancing freedom and public order, wherein the police are charged with protecting two integral but competing interests within a democratic society. This involves a discussion of issues that students may perceive to be more philosophical than practical in nature; however, balancing freedom and public order is fundamental to the work of police in resolving both routine, everyday human problems as well as those involving the safety and security of entire communities. The second dimension describes the role of the police within the context of the entire criminal justice system that includes both the courts and corrections. This second dimension is pragmatic in nature and involves a straightforward description of how police fit into the larger governmental bureaucracies designed primarily to suppress crime and process lawbreakers.

Balancing Freedom and Public Order

One issue in regard to the role of police in a democratic society involves **freedom versus public order**. The goal of *freedom* within this context can be defined as individual liberty to act as one chooses. The goal of *order* refers to the need for some type of authority or civility in society (Langworthy and Travis 1999; Lundman 1980). The accomplishment of both of these societal goals involves the work of police in a democratic society. The overarching job of police includes (1) maintaining a degree of public order in the community and (2) protecting individual liberties.

Students should recognize that the interests of freedom and public order are competing rather than complementary. That is, in any given situation, an increase in the degree of freedom provided to individuals presents increasing risks of disorder. The opposite is also true: The imposition of increasing levels of order reduces the degree of freedom available to individuals. The situation is what some refer to as a "zero-sum game," wherein one person or a group can gain something only by causing another person or group to lose something.

Let's run through a couple of examples to demonstrate the point. The first involves a relatively minor, everyday problem all too familiar to students. University police are called to a dorm room in which a large party is generating significant noise and disruption to other dorm residents. The police arrive on the scene and are confronted with some discretionary choices. The police can choose to command the hosts to turn down the music and disperse the party. This choice involves a reduction of liberty to the hosts of the party and an increase in the orderliness of the dorm. There really is no scenario that involves an increase in the liberty of the party hosts and a corresponding increase in the orderliness of the dorm. Police can provide more freedom or more public order, but they cannot provide more of both freedom and public order at the same time.

A second example is perhaps more descriptive of the issue's importance for police, individual citizens, and entire communities. A large group of protesters holds a public march after having secured a permit from the city. The protest eventually spills onto a public highway, mostly because the leaders of the protest are interested in garnering public attention and these tactics have worked in the past to generate media exposure to their issues of concern. Vehicles traveling the highway are forced to slow down and eventually stop in the road to avoid striking the protesters. Police are summoned to the scene by angry motorists stopped on the highway. Police must choose to either increase public order and shut down the protest or maintain the protesters' freedom to publicly assemble and voice their collective position on the issues of concern. The choice confronted by police involves an increase of public order at the expense of freedom or vice versa. There are no two ways around the issue. Indeed, 2020 included a series of events that galvanized social opposition to the police in ways that exemplify inherent difficulties in balancing freedom and public order and the job of police more generally. This opposition involved large-scale protests in the aftermath of several recent highly questionable and deadly police citizen encounters including the death of George Floyd in Minneapolis, Breonna Taylor in Louisville, and Jacob Blake in Kenosha (WI). Recent protests and calls to reform (or even "defund") the police call into question the fundamental ways in which police commonly balance these interests, particularly within communities of color.

Critical Thinking Exercise

Freedom versus Public Order and the Militarization of Local Police Agencies

Most scholars agree that local police agencies in the United States have become increasingly militarized over time, particularly since the 9/11 terror attacks in 2001. **Militarization of policing** refers to the tendency of local law enforcement agencies to adopt military-style tactics and equipment in order to maintain public order and enforce the law. These trends have recently culminated in strategies to transform police agencies into intelligence-led organizations that employ paramilitary tactics and hardware such as mine-resistant ambush-protected (MRAP) vehicles. The recent dramatic rise in the deployment of police paramilitary units (PPUs) among both large and small police agencies provides additional clear evidence of the trend toward militarization (Balko 2014; Kraska and Cubellis 1997; Kraska and Gaines 1997). Increased militarization of local police forces in the United States should not be viewed solely as a response to the current threat posed by international terrorism, but rather as only the most recent phase within a long-term shift in the organizational, strategic, and tactical character of local policing in the United States (see Chapter 2).

How do you believe the rise of militarized police in the United States has influenced the job of balancing freedom and public order? Does militarization in any way threaten how police perform this fundamental balancing act in the United States? Can you think of any recent examples wherein local police have tended to increase order at the expense of liberty? Do these situations involve police agencies that have become increasingly militarized?

Policing in a democratic society often involves this street-level balancing of freedom and public order. Police perform an intricate balancing act between these two interests on a minute-by-minute basis. As Langworthy and Travis (1999) point out, "policing serves to balance the tension between freedom and order in society" (9). But balancing freedom and public order is not an easy task. Students may liken the situation of police to that of a football referee. The referee must make difficult choices within the context of rules that are in many cases quite vague. How much contact needs to occur, for example, between a receiver and a defensive back in order to justify a ruling of pass interference? No matter what the referee decides—to throw or not throw a penalty flag—the fans of one of the two competing teams will not be happy. In fact, when the football referee properly does their job, the fans of one of the competing teams will almost certainly be upset. Such is the case for the police in a democratic society: They oftentimes must choose between two competing interests within the context of situations that are ambiguous or not clear. How "disorderly" does one need to act in order to be charged with the crime of disorderly conduct? Under what circumstances do police need to formally arrest neighbors engaged in a dispute? No matter what the police officer decides, one or more people are likely to be unhappy about the result.

Perhaps one of the primary goals of any introductory course on law enforcement should be acquiring an appreciation for the difficulties faced by police in the continual balancing of freedom and public order in a democratic society. Students should recognize that for police in non-democratic societies, imposing public order is much easier: Those forces need not worry about the protection of individual liberties. Policing free citizens is necessarily more difficult and messy provided the zero-sum game that involves balancing fundamental but competing interests. It is the job of police in a democracy to do so successfully.

POLICE AS GATEKEEPERS WITHIN THE CRIMINAL JUSTICE SYSTEM

The second dimension describes the role of the police in a more pragmatic and less philosophical way. This role involves the police acting as **gatekeepers** within the criminal justice system. The term *gatekeepers* is used here because police officers are usually the first point of contact between citizens and the rest of the criminal justice system that also includes the court system and the system of corrections. Taken together, police, courts, and corrections comprise the three main parts of the larger criminal justice system. The police role as gatekeepers in this system involves their decisions concerning when and how to intervene in citizens' lives on behalf of the criminal justice system. This role has more recently been expanded as police have increasingly become the first point of contact for most social services.

Introductory courses on the functions of the larger criminal justice system often characterize the processing of individuals or criminal cases as analogous to the shape of a funnel, whereby a comparatively large number of individuals or criminal cases enter the system. Then, the number of individuals or criminal cases are significantly reduced at various points as they progress through the system. Figure 1.1 depicts this funnel analogy and the sequence of events as individuals or criminal cases progress from one part of the criminal justice system to the next (Bureau of Justice Statistics 1997).

Figure 1.1 depicts the **criminal justice funnel** in terms of five primary points: (1) entry into the system, (2) prosecution and pretrial services, (3) adjudication, (4) sentencing and sanctions, and (5) corrections. Police are the primary actors in the system at point 1 (entry) and also to some degree during point 2 (prosecution). Police involvement at entry into the system includes the reporting of crimes to law enforcement. Police may detect and observe crimes themselves, but more commonly citizens report crimes to police. Thus, the work is generally referred to as **reactive policing**—police usually act on information from citizens about crimes that have already occurred. The ability of police to mitigate crime is obviously more limited than many people realize because of this obvious but often overlooked fact.

Police then investigate the observed or reported crime. The investigation is performed either by patrol officers, who are commonly the first responders to a crime scene, or by specialized detectives or criminal investigators who investigate the crime circumstances retrospectively, or after the fact. The police then either arrest or release the suspect, depending on whether they can gather enough evidence to legally implicate the suspect as the criminal perpetrator. In the case of a criminal arrest, police essentially hand over the case to the court system and prosecutors, who choose to either pursue a criminal conviction or drop the case, usually for lack of evidence. If the case goes to trial, the police will commonly appear in court to testify as witnesses on behalf of the prosecution.

Students need to recognize certain realities about the police role within the criminal justice system that are perhaps not easily discerned in Figure 1.1. The number of criminal cases is significantly reduced at two points that are important to understanding the nature of police work. The first point occurs at the far left of the figure, between the stages labeled "Crime" and "Reported and observed crime." A very large portion of crimes committed are not reported to police—ever. This fact was recognized as early as the 1970s as scholars began to refer to the vast number of unreported criminal acts as the **dark figure of crime**. We know that roughly one-half of all crimes are not reported to police. The number of crimes that go unreported varies to a large degree depending on the type of criminal activity. Citizens are much less likely to report crimes that they perceive to be less serious, or those committed by someone they know. Citizens sometimes do not report crimes because they do not believe the perpetrator will ever be identified or apprehended, much less punished. Victims in some cases do not report very serious crimes such as sexual assaults because they feel uncomfortable doing so. No matter the reason, police have absolutely no chance to apprehend perpetrators and solve the very large percentages of crimes that never come to their attention.

The second point at which the number of cases is significantly reduced occurs between the points of investigation and arrest (the next two steps in

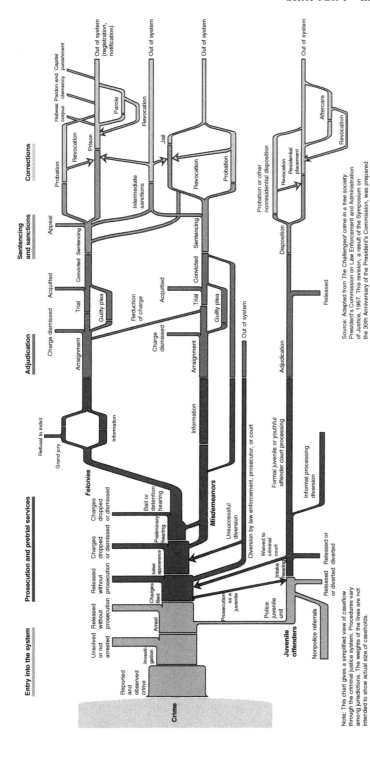

Figure 1.1 Criminal Justice Funnel

SOURCE: bureau of justice statistics, 1997.

Note: This chart gives a simplified view of caseflow through the criminal justice system. Procedures vary among jurisdictions. The weights of the lines are not intended to show actual size of caseloads.

Source: Adapted from *The Challenge of crime in a free society.* President's Commission on Law Enforcement and Administration of Justice, 1967. This revision, a result of the Symposium on the 30th Anniversary of the President's Commission, was prepared by the Bureau of Justice Statistics in 1997.

Figure 1.1). A relatively large percentage of the crimes reported to police do not result in a criminal arrest. Again, the number of crimes that eventually result in a criminal arrest—an event referred to by police as a **case clearance**—varies to a large degree depending on the type of criminal activity. For example, close to two-thirds of all murders are typically cleared by an arrest, but only about 1 in 10 burglaries reported to police typically results in a criminal arrest (FBI 2010). Crimes do not result in a criminal arrest for a number of reasons. There is sometimes simply a lack of sufficient evidence. Victims in some cases do not cooperate with police. Police investigators often do not devote much time or effort to solving less serious crimes. The takeaway for students in an introductory law enforcement class is that police very often fail to apprehend the criminal perpetrator, something that almost never occurs within the context of popular media depictions of police work.

A UNIQUELY AMERICAN SYSTEM OF POLICING

Another thing that students in an introductory course on policing should know is that the structure and organization of policing in the United States is unique among nations. We as a nation are clearly an outlier in terms of how policing is set up in comparison to other countries. This comes as a surprise to most students—and indeed, most American citizens—probably because we usually tend to believe that our own experiences and knowledge base can be generalized to other people and situations. This is clearly not true in relation to the structure and organization of American policing compared to other nations. Let's provide some rough data in terms of how policing is set up in several other industrialized democracies, and then we'll compare this information to the situation in the United States in order to demonstrate the point.

Canada is our neighbor to the north and is often described as our closest ally. Based on 2017 data, Canada has an estimated population of 36,710,000 persons scattered comparatively thinly across the nation, roughly 4 persons per square kilometer. Policing in Canada is administered on the municipal (local), provincial (roughly equivalent to our state level), and federal (national) levels. There are 141 municipal police agencies plus 36 agencies that have jurisdiction within First Nations areas inhabited primarily by aboriginal Metis and Inuit populations. The provinces of Newfoundland, Ontario, and Quebec employ provincial police agencies. The Royal Canadian Mounted Police (RCMP) have original law enforcement jurisdiction at the federal level and also within the remaining provinces (Conor 2018). So there are roughly 181 separate law enforcement agencies in Canada, or about 1 police agency for every 202,817 persons.

The United Kingdom is one of the primary democracies of Western Europe and another close ally to the United States. It is comprised of the nations of England and Wales and, based on 2017 data, has an estimated population of 66,020,000. It is much more densely populated than Canada, with roughly 272 person per square kilometer. Policing is centrally administered by the Home Office in a system that includes 43 local police agencies and 3 more specialized police agencies with jurisdiction across the United Kingdom (Office of the Health and Safety Executive 2018). So there are roughly 46 separate law enforcement agencies in the United Kingdom, or about 1 police agency for every 1,435,217 persons.

Sweden is the third largest nation of the European Union (EU) by land area and based on 2017 data has an estimated population of 9,980,000. The population is more thinly dispersed than within the United Kingdom at roughly 230 persons per square kilometer. The Swedish Police Authority (SPA) is the central administrative unit for policing across the nation. The national police commissioner is appointed by the central government to lead the SPA. The SPA administers 7 different police regions and 8 national-level departments, but it is essentially the only distinct police agency in the country (Swedish Police Authority 2018). So Sweden has a single police organization with numerous geographical subunits organized at the national level to police a population of over 9 million.

Japan is among the world's most modern, developed, and industrialized nations and has been a US ally since the end of World War II and the restructuring of its governmental institutions during and after the occupation of Allied forces. Based on 2017 data, Japan has an estimated population of 127,185,000. The country is densely populated, with roughly 340 persons per square kilometer. The national government established a centralized police organization—the National Police Agency (NPA)—to administer police organizations at the prefectural level (roughly equivalent to our state level). The NPA has primary jurisdiction at the national level and operates 7 regional police bureaus that operate out of major cities. On the local level, each of Japan's 45 prefectures has its own autonomous police agency (National Police Agency 2017). So Japan has a police organization for roughly every 2,764,891 persons.

We included only four countries, and the statistics may not encompass every single independent law enforcement agency in each country; however, a sampling of any number of additional modern industrialized countries would not significantly change the picture presented here, particularly in terms of the most important point of comparison: the manner in which policing is structured and organized.

Taken collectively, this small sampling and rough overview provides some idea about how policing is normally organized at the national level. Students can see that the number of separate police organizations ranges from a single agency (Sweden) to roughly 181 in Canada. The number of police agencies per person is lowest in Canada at just over 200,000, but the other three nations have a police agency for every 1.4 million, 2.7 million, and 9 million persons. Most nations have some type of centralized, national-level governing body that either polices the nation as a whole or, more commonly, in conjunction with up to a couple hundred other police agencies that derive their authority at the local- (in most cases only very large cities) or state-level equivalent.

Based on 2017 data, the United States has an estimated population of 325,700,000. The population density is roughly 35.6 persons per square kilometer, which is much less than that of the United Kingdom or Japan and about equivalent to that of Sweden. There are an estimated 17,965 autonomous police agencies in the United States, or roughly 100 times as many police agencies as the nation with by far the most police agencies described in our small sample above (President's Task Force on 21st Century Policing 2015). The United States has a **decentralized police system**, whereby police powers are distributed locally throughout the nation rather than subsumed under a single agency or small number of federal-level agencies. There is a police agency for every 18,090 persons in the United States, many more agencies per person than in any of the nations in our sample (1 police agency for every 202, 817 in Canada; 1,435,217 in the United Kingdom; 9,980,000 in Sweden, and 2,764,891 in Japan).

This tremendous disparity in the number of autonomous police agencies cannot be explained by population size, density, or even crime levels. But perhaps it can be explained at the state level. Maybe one or two of the US states are driving national-level disparities in the number of police organizations? Let's examine a couple of states. Connecticut is a comparatively small state on the eastern seaboard. The estimated population in 2017 was 3,588,000, or roughly one-third the population of Sweden. Connecticut has 143 police agencies, and Sweden has 1. Ohio is a comparatively large Midwestern state that in 2017 had an estimated population of 11,658,000, or less than one-tenth the population of Japan. Ohio has 831 police agencies, and Japan has somewhere between 45 and 50. Texas, obviously a very large state, in 2017 had an estimated population of 28,304,000. This is less than one-half the population of the United Kingdom, which has roughly 46 separate police agencies. Texas has 1,913 separate police agencies. The national-level disparities between the United States and other nations persists no matter which individual states you seek to examine in terms of the number of autonomous police organizations.

Why would the United States ever want or need close to 18,000 autonomous police agencies, when every other nation on the globe gets by just fine (or arguably better with regard to the mitigation of rates of crime) utilizing a single police agency, or a couple dozen, or even several hundred?

The simple answer is that America has thousands upon thousands of autonomous police agencies lacking any sort of centralized or national-level authority because that is the way that we, as Americans, prefer it. One of the bedrock principles of American government is federalism, in which government power is divided among national- and state-level institutions. The entire American experiment, beginning with the Revolutionary War in opposition to the British monarchy, involves the imposition of local rather than national control over government functions. We, as Americans, are all about local control. The idea is that an autonomous local or municipal police agency will be much more responsive to and reflective of the local community. For example, policing in America could have been structured in a manner much more similar to other nations, whereby a centrally controlled single police agency (perhaps something like the "National Police Agency of the United States") would administer several hundred or even thousands of local "precincts" or "districts." Would the leadership of such a national police agency—or even commanders at the district level—necessarily understand and appreciate local problems and issues of concern to local residents?

The structure of American policing and the logic of thousands upon thousands of autonomous police organizations rest upon the assumption that locally controlled agencies are much more responsive to the problems and concerns of local communities. Think of your own hometown and the issues of primary concern: traffic on local roads, criminal activity specific to each neighborhood, patrol visibility within certain blocks and intersections, problems with local juveniles or particular property owners, and so on. Your hometown's local police force should recognize and at least be in a position to most effectively respond to these concerns. So, too, municipal police agencies in the United States most often recruit and hire officers from within the immediate geographic area. These officers presumably recognize and understand local concerns and community-level norms much better than any "outsider." Finally, the local police chief is usually hired and fired by the locally elected mayor. Any local police chief who fails to recognize and respond to problems of local concern cannot last long on the job, and local mayors who fail to hire and/or retain a police chief favored by most of the local residents clearly risks losing the next election. This in essence embodies the logic of police who are locally controlled, and so we end up with thousands upon thousands of autonomous police agencies in the United States. We have done the same in primary and secondary education: There are approximately 13,800 local independent school districts in the United States for no other reason than a preference for schools that are controlled locally.

The logic of local control seems clear, at least from what most scholars would describe as a uniquely American perspective. The lack of any definitive centralized control and the existence of close to 18,000 autonomous police agencies does engender some problems, however. First, the decentralized system of policing in the United States creates obstacles to the formulation of standardized policies and procedures, particularly in the areas of police education and training. There are hundreds of separate police training academies across the nation; the state of Ohio has 60 training academies alone. Each of the 50 states administers its own separate rules and requirements. There is no reasonable way to ensure the effectiveness of police training and the qualifications of police officers within this context. Some training academies are better than others.

The decentralized system of policing also presents challenges in terms of tackling national problems. The United States has long struggled to formulate and implement effective policies to mitigate rates of illegal drug use and sales

---

Critical Thinking Exercise

The Opioid Crisis: A National Problem for 18,000 Autonomous Police Agencies

The opioid addiction crisis is one of the most important problems that currently confronts the United States. Opioids are a class of drugs that includes prescription pain medications such as oxycodone, morphine, and fentanyl, as well as the illegal drug heroin. There are over 20 million Americans who have a substance abuse disorder, including 2 million who are addicted to prescription pain relievers including opioids and more than 1 million persons addicted to heroin. There were 52,404 drug overdose deaths in the United States in 2015, with most involving an opioid (American Society of Addiction Medicine 2016). The opioid crisis is a major problem across the United States: in rural communities, small towns, suburbs, and the largest urban centers. No American jurisdiction has been spared the ravages of the current opioid crisis.

The United States struggles to mitigate this crisis, and most of the thousands of local police agencies are directly involved. For example, local police, who are commonly the first responders to an overdose incident, are saving thousands of lives administering naloxone, the nasal spray medication that can reverse the effects of heroin overdose. Local police are increasingly concentrating enforcement strategies on street-level dealers (Police Executive Research Forum 2017).

Do you believe that this continued struggle is at least in part due to the highly decentralized nature of policing in the United States? Do you think that effective policies to mitigate the current national-level crisis can be devised and implemented with 18,000 different autonomous law enforcement agencies? Would more centralized authority within the structure of American policing produce more effective policies in this case? Why or why not?

---

and/or gun control. These and other national issues cross jurisdictional boundaries and involve the authority of hundreds if not thousands of individual police chiefs. Finally, the decentralized system of policing in the United States sometimes gives rise to disagreements involving jurisdictional authority and which of the many possible agencies will assume control over criminal investigations and other matters in cases where more than one agency may have legal jurisdiction.

Students need to recognize that the structure of American policing is unique among nations. We've erected a highly decentralized system that involves close to 18,000 autonomous police organizations, which makes it difficult to compare policing within the United States to that found anywhere else in the world. No other nation comes close in terms of the number of autonomous police agencies, and this unique situation creates both strengths and problems in terms of how policing works that are unique to American law enforcement.

POLICING AS A MULTIVARIATE PHENOMENON

The American system of policing is indeed unique among nations; however, there are other aspects of the job and profession that are clearly within the experience and performance of law enforcement officers no matter where they are employed.

This section of the chapter covers one of the more universal aspects of police work, which describes policing as **multivariate**. Introductory students are not likely to be familiar with this term, but it is commonly used by social science researchers and police scholars to describe the nature of any observable event or phenomenon. We need to take a quick step back before we specifically explain our use of the term *multivariate* and consider first some of the goals of scholars and any student taking an introductory course on law enforcement. Then, we can return to it and explain why it is important to understanding some truths about police work.

Police scholars are essentially interested in understanding how and why police officers do what they do on the job. This is also the primary goal of any introductory college-level course concerning law enforcement. Students take the course because it is commonly required within criminal justice degree programs, but also presumably because students themselves are interested in learning about why and how police do their job. Perhaps students want to someday be a police officer, or maybe they want to understand the work of police because they plan to establish a career elsewhere within the criminal justice system. Students taking an introductory law enforcement class—no matter the reason—should be familiar with the things that contribute to how and why police officers do what they do on the job.

We can in this way describe police work as observable events or phenomena. Police do all sorts of things as part of their work. They arrest criminal suspects; they issue citations; they settle arguments; they break up fights; they conduct patrols; they provide emergency medical services; they investigate; they give directions and provide advice to confused citizens. These and all other actions of police can be observed and ultimately explained and understood. So police work can be described as an observable event or phenomenon that can be explained and understood.

Students—and indeed most other everyday citizens—commonly attempt to understand and explain police work in ways that are less rigorous but more or less similar to the research conducted by police scholars. You may recall the last instance in which you were issued a speeding ticket by a police officer. Your initial reaction was likely annoyance or even anger, but then most people subsequently try to make sense of the event in their own mind. *Yes, I was going over the speed limit, but just about everyone else driving on this road was going over the speed limit. Why did I get a ticket, and why now?* You may conclude based on some superficial consideration that you were just unlucky that day, or that the officer was in a bad mood or did not like you, or that the officer needed to satisfy some sort of monthly quota of speeding tickets determined by his or her department.

You are in some ways doing the exact same thing that police scholars do when trying to understand what factors influence the work of police—in this case, the issuance of a speeding ticket to you. We can take this or any other police action—whether it be an arrest, the issuance of a verbal command, a physical fight, handcuffing—observe it, and then analyze it in various ways in order to determine what caused it.

All of the different factors we consider to explain police actions—in the above example, why the officer issued you a speeding ticket—researchers commonly define as variables, or more generally things that can change from one context to another. In terms of our speeding ticket scenario, for example, the officer's mood could vary from angry to happy; he or she could have liked or disliked you; the police department could have or not have some type of ticket quota. Other potential variables might include how many miles per hour you were driving over the speed limit, your reaction and nature of communicating to the officer after you were pulled over, weather conditions, and so on. These and many other factors or variables could help to explain why you were issued a speeding ticket in this particular instance.

Now we are in a position to more effectively consider use of the term *multivariate* in the section header. A **variable** as described above is any one factor that can change from one context to another. We can even number possible variables individually within the context of our speeding ticket example: (1) officer mood, (2) officer opinion of you, (3) department ticket quota, (4) miles per hour driving over the speed limit, (5) nature of your reaction, (6) weather conditions, and so on. Ultimately, the variable we are trying to understand is the cause for issuance of the speeding ticket. The ticket can either be issued or not in any particular instance.

People quite often focus on the impact of any single variable or associated groups of variables in an attempt to understand and make sense of the world. There may be many different factors or variables to explain poor performance on a test, but students sometimes tend to focus exclusively on those external to themselves, such as their perception that the test questions themselves were not valid or were in some why unfair. Citizens also tend to similarly attribute the cause of any particular police action to a single factor or closely associated group of factors. You may, in the case of our speeding ticket example, tend to identify officer mood or any of other single variables as *the* reason why you were issued a ticket: "He didn't like me from the beginning," or "She picked me out because I am driving an old rusty car," or "He would not have given me the ticket had it not been the last day of the month!"

Our tendency to focus on any single factor to explain the issuance of the speeding ticket—or indeed any other social phenomenon—probably has more to do with wanting to simplify our understanding of things so we can move on with our lives than with anything else. This tendency to focus on single-factor explanations makes things easier to understand or "explain it to ourselves," or even to allow us to comprehend any present event in ways that are consistent with our existing understanding of similar past events: "This cop acted just like the last one who gave me a speeding ticket!"

The problem with single-variable explanations is that they most often do *not* accurately explain how and why things occur in the real world. Most real-world phenomena—including the work of police—cannot be accurately explained by any single variable. Police work instead needs to be understood as a multivariate phenomenon. That is, we need to consider many different types of factors or variables in order to understand how and why police officers do what they do on the job. Many factors—not just one or a couple—explain any particular police action. Students need to let that reality sink in, because it is a way of understanding that is both contrary to our natural human tendency to focus on single-factor explanations and absolutely necessary to acquiring a more accurate and meaningful understanding of police work.

The task of understanding policing as a multivariate phenomenon is complicated by the sheer number of single variables or closely associated groups of potential variables to be included within any explanation of police behavior. Langworthy and Travis (1999) provide what seems to be the most efficient conceptual framework to begin to understand policing as a multivariate phenomenon, or what they refer to as a "balance of forces" (24–29). Their organizational scheme draws from the various existing lines of research on police and groups a multitude of variables to be considered in terms of (1) people, (2) organization, and (3) community. We would also consider a fourth category of variables that is probably most appropriately labeled as "situation." So the recognition of policing as a multivariate phenomenon involves a consideration of many different factors or variables such as those that fall into the categories of people, organization, community, and situation.

Let's return to our speeding ticket example to demonstrate the point. What factors may have contributed to the police action of issuing you a speeding ticket on this particular occasion? The *people* involved include both the police officer and you as the driver. Things to perhaps consider with regard to the officer include gender, age, race/ethnicity, and/or years of experience on the job. You also brought certain individual characteristics to the encounter including gender, age, and race/ethnicity. *Organization* in this context refers to the features of the employing police department, including its size in terms of the number of sworn officers as well as the department's policies and procedures. *Community* in this context includes the size of the population, the form of government, the degree of support provided to the police department, and the number and the types of roads within the community. *Situation* includes things like the weather, time of day, and day of the month. These and potentially many other variables may have influenced the police decision to issue you a citation for speeding in this particular instance.

We can use this sort of framework to discern the reasons for police actions in many contexts other than the issuance of a speeding ticket, including those that are clearly more important than traffic enforcement. For example, what contributes to a police decision to arrest someone involved in a domestic dispute or in possession of illegal drugs, or to take an unruly juvenile into custody, or to provide emergency medical assistance in the case of an opioid overdose, or even to shoot a dangerous criminal suspect?

The very large take-home for students is that policing is complex and perhaps much more difficult to understand than it may initially seem to be, at

Critical Thinking Exercise

Research on Racial Profiling and the Multivariate Nature of Policing

Racial profiling endures as an important public and political issue. Within the context of police work, it can be defined as a law enforcement–initiated action based on an individual's race, ethnicity, or national origin rather than on an individual's behavior or information identifying them as having engaged in criminal activity. Public and scholarly concern over the issue has focused predominantly on police decisions during traffic stops, in part because data shows that within many jurisdictions minority drivers are stopped, searched, and/or arrested at rates that are disproportionate to their relative numbers in the population.

The research designed to measure the occurrence of racial profiling during traffic stops provides one of the best examples to demonstrate the multivariate nature of policing. One of the authors of this book was involved in a project to develop and implement improved strategies for the collection and analysis of traffic stop data in Texas (Liederbach, Trulson, Fritsch, Caeti, and Taylor 2007). The state of Texas passed a law with the goal of identifying and eliminating racial profiling. The law required every police agency in the state to collect data for all traffic stops. Police were required to collect data on any detained persons, including their race/ethnicity, whether a search was conducted, whether any search conducted was a consent search or probable cause search, and whether there was an arrest. These data were then routinely compared with statistics on the racial/ethnic composition of the local jurisdiction to discern the degree to which racial profiling may have occurred.

The enactment of this law seemed to inflame rather than lessen public debate regarding the racial profiling issue, despite legislators' best intentions. Many of the problems with the law can be traced to a failure to recognize policing as a multivariate phenomenon. The required data were largely limited to detainee race/ethnicity and variables associated with common police actions including searches and arrests. The law as proscribed largely failed to consider the impact of factors *other than race* on police decisions to stop, search, and/or arrests motorists. Charges of racial profiling seem quite difficult to uphold when organizational rules and state codes compel police to stop and/or search regardless of an individual's race/ethnicity. These situations include stops made on the basis of a discovery of an outstanding warrant or a mandatory search conducted incident to an arrest.

No one denies the existence of racial profiling, but data collection and analyses need to take into account the multitude of factors involved in police decisions to stop, search, and/or arrest in order to be valid. The goal of these sorts of studies needs to be to discern the influence of race/ethnicity on officer actions *relative to other factors* such as organizational rules, state codes, or even other extralegal or situational factors such as socioeconomic status, weather, vehicle condition, and the demeanor of the officer and detainee. In the end, the research team on this project created a data collection instrument that included 21 additional variables to consider in regard to why police may have stopped, searched, and/or arrested a motorist. This is what we mean when we describe policing as a multivariate phenomenon.

What sorts of factors do you think are important in determining the underlying reasons for police actions in terms of the decision to (a) stop a motorist for speeding, (b) arrest someone involved in a neighbor dispute, and (c) shoot a dangerous criminal suspect? Does the number of important factors in each case confirm that policing is indeed a multivariate phenomenon?

least to many citizens. The goal going forward both within this book and more generally within the larger context of understanding our interactions with law enforcement officers is to incorporate the view of policing as a multivariate phenomenon and to resist the adoption of more narrow points of view that are limited to a single or group of closely associated factors. Policing is multivariate!

CHAPTER SUMMARY

This chapter identified and described some of the most basic concepts involved in understanding American policing. The overriding goal was to set up the rest of the text through the introduction of these basic concepts. Four basic ideas were covered. First, we defined police in terms of one central concept—coercion. Students were asked to expand their understanding of coercion to include just about every tool used by police to solve all sorts of human problems. The policing occupation is unique, mostly because officers are allowed and expected to use coercion as necessary to accomplish whatever we as citizens need them to accomplish. Second, we described the role of police along two dimensions. The first dimension required students to consider police work as a balancing of two competing interests: freedom and public order. Police perform this balancing act every day and within the context of each of their decisions. The freedom versus public order dichotomy virtually ensures that some segments of the American populace will not be happy with the work of police as a result of any particular police decision. The second dimension was a more straightforward description of the police role within the criminal justice system using the popular analogy of a funnel: The police play a role as gatekeepers within the system and at various points in which this funnel narrows to reduce the number of criminal cases. The third idea required an understanding of the unique character of the American system of policing. The fact is that the American system has many more autonomous police agencies than any other nation on earth. We outlined some important advantages and disadvantages of this uniquely decentralized system of policing. The fourth and final idea in the chapter involved an introduction of the term *multivariate* to describe the wide variety of factors that potentially influence police decisions on the street. The point of the discussion was to understand policing as a complex interaction among these various factors and to dissuade the adoption of simple one-factor explanations of police behavior.

KEY TERMS

case clearance

coercive force

criminal justice funnel

dark figure of crime

decentralized police system

freedom versus public order

gatekeepers

militarization of police

multivariate

reactive policing

variable

FURTHER READING

Bittner, E. (1978). "The Functions of Police in Modern Society." In *Policing: A View from the Street*, edited by P. K. Manning and J. Van Maanen, 32–50. New York: Random House.

Klockers, C. B. (1985). *The Idea of Police*. Beverley Hills, CA: Sage.

Langworthy, R. H., and L. F. Travis (1999). *Policing: A Balance of Forces*. 2nd. ed. Upper Saddle River, NJ: Prentice Hall.

President's Task Force on 21st Century Policing (2015). *Final Report of the President's Task Force on 21st Century Policing*. Washington, DC: Office of Community Oriented Policing Services.

CHAPTER 2

History and Development of the Police

After reading this chapter, you should be able to:

- Understand that modern policing developed in what scholars have identified as three distinct phases
- Define the differences between three phases in the development of modern policing: the avocational or informal phase, the transitional phase, and the formal phase

- Identify and describe selected forms of policing that directly influenced modern American policing including vigilante groups, slave patrols, bounty hunters, the American sheriff, and London "bobbies"
- Identify and describe the three eras of modern policing in America: the political era, the professional/reform era, and the community policing era
- Identify and describe problems in the political era of policing that led to the emergence of the professional era of policing
- Identify and describe problems in the professional/reform era of policing that led to the emergence of the community-oriented policing era
- Identify and describe the dominant policing functions in the three eras of modern American policing
- Define and understand various modern patrol strategies including hotspots of crime and data-driven police tactics

INTRODUCTION AND OVERVIEW

This chapter provides an overview of the history of policing in three primary sections. The first section of the chapter presents a discussion of "phases" in the development of modern police. Students should use this section of the chapter to organize their thoughts on the topic and as a framework for understanding how modern full-time professional police emerged over time. The development of modern full-time, professional policing occurred in stages rather than all at once. The informal or avocational phase describes periods wherein policing was accomplished on a temporary basis by average citizens using methods such as kin policing and/or the hue and cry method. The transitional phase involved individuals or groups that performed the policing function on a part-time or voluntary basis, including citizen watch programs and vigilante groups. The third phase involves the eventual emergence of full-time police forces much as we know them today. This section of the chapter concludes with an identification of the social and political forces that drove these shifts in the nature and character of the development of policing over time.

The second section of the chapter focuses more closely on how policing developed in the United States and covers selected historical developments that served as a bridge from the earlier forms of policing to the typical modern American municipal police force. Groups such as vigilantes and "bounty hunters" proliferated within the American frontier, while the American sheriff developed from early English origins to become the forerunner of modern police forces in many parts of the United States. The London Metropolitan Police, largely considered the first modern police force, provided an impetus for the creation of the first formalized professional police agencies in the United States shortly thereafter.

The third and perhaps most important section of the chapter traces the history of modern policing in the United States. Students need to recognize and understand the three eras of modern policing in the United States—the political era, the reform/professional era, and the community policing era—as well as the contexts within which these eras arose and then declined. This discussion is not merely historical or a look back on some bygone eras; the history of modern policing and these three eras should provide students with an understanding of how some of the current problems in policing came to be, as well as the basis of some ideas on how to fix them. Students should recognize that each successive era begins with a recognition of the problems of the previous era and a plan to fix them. Often, we as a society succeeded in fixing the problems of an earlier era only to confront new and often unanticipated problems—some of which emerged as a direct result of our intended fixes. The chapter concludes with an outline of modern patrol strategies that are driving the nature and character of American policing today.

PHASES IN THE DEVELOPMENT OF MODERN POLICE

Students of the history of policing often approach the subject as if full-time, professional police as we recognize them today have always been the norm. The modern full-time, professional police force, however, is a comparatively recent phenomenon that dates only to the 19th century. That is, there were no full-time professional police for the vast majority of recorded history. This reality is sometimes difficult for students to comprehend because Americans from a very early age are taught to recognize particular individuals as police officers and the specialized purposes of the modern police organization. The development of police as we know them today has instead been comparatively recent. The historical evolution toward modern policing was also no accident. Modern policing developed in response to a variety of specific social and political conditions. This section provides a review of the scholarship on the development of modern police, as well as an identification of the forces influential in shaping the nature and character of police as we know them today.

Scholars generally identify three phases in the development toward modern policing (Lundman 1980). The first phase has been labeled the **informal or avocational phase of policing**. The term *avocational* refers to something that one does when they are *not* engaged in their full-time occupation. There were no full-time police officers during this phase of history. Instead, the job of "policing" fell to ordinary citizens who were otherwise employed in other activities. This type of informal policing involved every member of a group sharing responsibility for accomplishing the police function of social control (Langworthy and Travis 1999). Avocational or informal policing occured within preindustrial communities in which people generally did not perform specialized occupational roles. Everyone within these types of communities, for example, farmed, fished, and/or hunted and gathered for their own subsistence. These types of societies were not organized to promote or support the creation a sole occupation in policing or any other specialized occupation. One example of informal or avocational policing was known as **kin policing**, which dates to about 900 AD, wherein the responsibility for social control was in the hands of "people" who were responsible for their families or "kin." Another example included **hue and cry**, which dates at least to the 13th century, whereby citizens who witnessed a crime would make a "hue and cry" or public announcement of the crime and identification of the perpetrator so as to eventually lead to the apprehension of the fleeing criminal (National Law Enforcement Museum 2012).

The second phase in the development of modern police, the **transitional phase of policing**, involves individuals and/or groups that perform the policing function on a part-time or voluntary basis. The **watch system**, or "the watch," one of America's first known systems of law enforcement, was established during the early 1600s in colonial Boston. The watch was typically comprised of citizens who served as volunteer "watchmen" who patrolled the streets at night looking for crimes. New York (then known as New Amsterdam) developed its own watch system in 1652 (National Law Enforcement Museum 2012). **Vigilante policing** another example of transitional forms of policing that involves organized extralegal movements comprised of individuals who take the law into their own hands. America has a long tradition of vigilante policing, which is detailed in the section below with other prominent early forms of American policing.

The third phase in the development of modern police, the **formal phase of policing**, involves the creation of organized groups of people who act as full-time professional police officers. This chapter describes the origins of London's Metropolitan Police as well as the three eras of modern policing in the United States. The transition from the second transitional phase to the third formal phase is of utmost importance for students interested in understanding the nature and character of modern policing. This shift is particularly important because it illustrates how and why we have modern full-time professional police forces, at least within Western industrialized societies. The institution of modern full-time police forces is a response to specific societal and political trends.

This shift toward the formal phase of policing involves at least three factors (Lundman 1980; Silver 1965). The first factor involves **changing patterns of social organization**. As societies become more complex and specialized in terms of their organization, the need for occupational specialists increases, including the need for specialists in social control or law enforcement. In Britain and the United States, the shift toward more specialized patterns of social organization occurred most obviously during the Industrial Revolution. During this period there was a large-scale shift from hand production methods to machines and the rise of the factory system that began to impact British society during the mid-1800s and the United States some decades later (Horn, Rosenband, and Smith 2010). The shift toward increasingly complex societies like the one that occurred during the Industrial Revolution seems to be a precursor for the development of modern full-time professional police forces within democratic societies.

The second factor in the shift toward the formal phase of policing is **rising perceptions of criminality**. The shift toward formalized police forces becomes more likely in societies wherein people feel less safe and believe there is more crime than previously was the case. This factor seems intuitive. People are more likely to perceive the need for more formalized social control and law enforcement within the context of a perceived rise in criminal activity. These perceptions of rising criminality may be associated with actual increases in real crime, or they may also be associated with changing perceptions about what constitutes "criminal" activity. This distinction involves shifts in societal perceptions between behavior that is deemed to be "unseemly" or simply "deviant" versus behavior that is defined as "criminal." Societal definitions of behaviors such as public drunkenness or "loitering," for example, seem to shift over time. We define these behaviors as deviant but largely harmless or "criminal" depending on the social and political context. The shift toward more formalized, full-time police seems to be hastened during periods in which people perceive more criminal behavior, whether real or perceived.

The third factor in the shift toward the formal phase of policing is **elite interests**. Societal elites are generally defined in Western industrialized societies as including political leaders, high-ranking military officers, and corporate or business executives (Mills 1956). Societal elites are at the top of the ladder in terms of political influence and wealth, and so they are typically interested in maintaining their societal position. Formalized, professional full-time police forces are viewed by societal elites as an instrument to maintain the status quo and mitigate threats posed by groups lower on the ladder, sometimes referred to as "dangerous classes," who have been defined at various points in history to include the poor, immigrants, juveniles, and members of ethnic minority groups (Crosby 1883). Societal elites are in a position to advocate for and lead the establishment of formalized, professional full-time police and are more likely to do so when their interests and the status quo appear to be threatened in some way.

TOWARD MODERN POLICE

The preceding section underscored that the emergence of modern policing did not occur all at once. Modern policing is a result of changes in how policing is accomplished that unfolded in stages over time. These developments include phenomena that clearly represent some sort of direct transition from the earliest informal or avocational sorts of policing to what we all recognize as the typical full-time professional police forces of today. The next section covers three forms of policing that exerted more direct influences on the nature and character of modern American policing: vigilante groups and "bounty hunters"; the institution of the American sheriff; and the London Metropolitan Police, commonly referred to as "bobbies."

Vigilantes and Bounty Hunters

A vigilante is a member of a volunteer group organized to suppress and punish deviant and/or criminal behavior, usually in situations where the vigilante group members believe the normal processes of law are inadequate (Brown 1969). Vigilantes and bounty hunters should be considered as part of a transitional stage between informal and formal policing in America. Vigilante groups are not regular formalized police, but rather they are an organized committee of citizens who together intend to "take the law into their own hands" through crude methods such as flogging, expulsion from a designated territory, or even killing. Other names for vigilante groups include "regulators" or "committees of safety." The first vigilante group recorded within what is now the United States was the South Carolina Regulators in 1767. The San Francisco Vigilance Committee originated in 1856 and was likely the largest vigilante group in the United States, with a membership between 6,000 and 8,000. These and other vigilante groups were an "almost constant factor in American life" through the turn of the 18th century (Brown 1969, 121).

Brown (1969) conducted one of the most comprehensive studies of vigilante policing in America. He considers these groups different than the more informal "lynch mobs" sometimes highlighted within popular movies in that vigilante groups emerged repeatedly and over the course of a defined period of time. Vigilante movements typically arose in the absence of law and order in frontier regions of the country. They were usually led by the "frontier elite" as a means to protect their own interests. Leaders included businessmen and wealthy landowners. Middle-class individuals filled out the rank-and-file membership. Brown (1969) in his research divides documented American vigilante movements in terms of 116 Eastern groups and 210 Western groups. Eastern groups were found mostly from the Appalachian Mountains to the Mississippi River during the first half of the 19th century. Brown recorded 202 killings at the hands of these groups, including 35 within the state of Louisiana. Western groups were found from the Great Plains to the Rocky Mountains primarily during the latter half of the 19th century following the movement of settlers on the North American continent. There were 729 deaths associated with these groups, including 140 in the state of Texas.

Vigilante groups are defined by scholars as either "constructive" or "destructive" based on several factors. For example, Brown (1969) relates that vigilante groups can be considered constructive or in some ways positive when they represent the consensus of the community and their actions are short-lived. Vigilante groups can be considered destructive when they are largely opposed by the larger community and/or their existence leads to lawlessness or even wars between rival vigilante movements. More generally, the vigilante movement in the United States often led to long-term negative consequences, because they often eroded public confidence in the law and often promulgated extremist and discriminatory actions against racial and ethnic minority groups including Jews, immigrants, African-Americans, and political radicals (Brown 1969).

Law enforcement persons commonly referred to as **"bounty hunters"** could also be considered as part of a transitional stage between informal and formal policing in America. Bounty hunters are more formally referred to as bail

---

Web Activity

Students interested in a more detailed presentation of the role and activities of vigilante groups in the American West are encouraged to visit the Legends of America website at https://www.legendsofamerica.com/we-vigilantelist/. The website provides detailed summaries of 16 different vigilante groups from this period.

enforcement agents or bail recovery agents (http://nabea.org). The Eighth Amendment to the United States Constitution establishes bail as a right of the American people. The system of bail in the United States usually involves court issuance of a bail bond, or money or some form of property that is pledged to the court by an arrestee in exchange for that person's release from pre-trial detention. Many arrestees cannot afford to pay for their own pre-trial release, so a bail bondsman or bond dealer pledges the necessary funds or property to the court, usually in exchange for a fee of 10 percent of the total amount of the bond. In case the arrestee does not appear for their court date, the bail is forfeited and the suspect can be charged for the crime of failing to appear. This sort of system resembles processes that originated in England prior to 1000 AD (Burns and Kinkade 2005). The job of the bounty hunter or bail enforcement agent is to locate and apprehend defendants who flee or "bail jump" and do not return for trial. The early American frontier provided ample opportunities to jump bail and hide from the authorities, so the courts granted significant rights and privileges under the law for bail recovery agents to effectively "hunt down" and catch bail jumpers (Burns and Kinkade 2005). The most recent available data indicate that there are over 14,000 licensed bail recovery agents in the United States. They work within the bail bond business, which generates over $4 billion annually (Parenti 1997).

Critical Thinking Exercise

Slave Patrols as a Forerunner to Modern American Police

Slave patrols operated from the early 18th century through the Civil War and comprised one of the earliest forms of policing within the southern American colonies. The first slave patrols were formed in South Carolina in 1704 (Hansen 2019). The primary purpose of slave patrols was to apprehend and return runaway slaves to their owners. These patrols also served to deter both potential runaway slaves and the possibility of larger-scale slave revolts that threatened to destabilize the political and social foundations of the American South that depended on the operation and maintenance of institutional slavery. Members of formalized slave patrols were sometimes selected from the ranks of local militias and included both lower- and upper-class whites in the ranks (Hansen 2019). Slave patrols have often not been included in texts devoted to the early history of American policing and criminal justice, but scholars have increasingly recognized slave patrols as a precursor of modern American policing (Turner, Giacopassi, and Vandiver 2006). Hadden (2001), for example, suggests parallels between the operation of slave patrols and the discrimination and systemic violence of vigilante groups that operated in the American South during the period of Reconstruction (1863–77).

More recently, scholars have suggested that the legacy of slave patrols and associated history of racial discrimination and violence forms the basis of ongoing problems in modern American policing including racial profiling and pervasive mistrust between police and communities of color. Students are encouraged to consider the ways in which pre–Civil War slave patrols may exert lasting influences on American policing. How might the legacy of slave patrols contribute to racial discrimination and/or profiling within the context of modern American policing? How does the legacy of slave patrols form a context for understanding the origins of the Black Lives Matter movement and recent large-scale protests designed to reform American policing?

The American Sheriff

The institution of the American **sheriff**—an arm of law enforcement with jurisdiction at the county level of government—predates the inception of modern municipal or "city" police agencies in the United States. Most of what is recorded in terms of the history of policing in the United States involves the development of municipal police forces, so the institution of the American sheriff is often ignored or at least downplayed within the scholarship. The office of the county sheriff, however, is a mainstay of the American law enforcement industry and should be understood within the context of any discussion on the history of policing in the United States. Many students, for example, reside in places where the county sheriff maintains primary law enforcement jurisdiction.

County-level policing through the office of the sheriff employs over 350,000 total personnel, including roughly 200,000 sworn officers (Brooks 2019). The importance of this popularly elected office within the American policing institution stems not only from the number of officers these organizations employ, but also from the sheriff's inherently political nature, their broad scope of legal authority, and the large geographic jurisdiction patrolled by sheriff's deputies. These unique organizational features differentiate the office from their more commonly studied municipal counterparts, so much so that the office of the sheriff has been described as a "distinctive policing modality" separate from the typical municipal police agency (Falcone and Wells 1995: 123).

The office of the American sheriff can be traced from over 900 years of tradition with roots that originate all the way to medieval England. These historical traditions have shaped three primary differences between county-level offices of the sheriff and municipal police organizations. First, the county sheriff is popularly elected by the people and derives authority directly through public election rather than administrative appointment. Historical accounts document the development of the roles and powers of the sheriff's office through the centuries in England, where the office had to adapt to the impact of ongoing struggle between royal authority and local powers for political control (Struckhoff 2003). These struggles for power continued as the office of the sheriff was successfully transferred to the American colonies. The selection of the county sheriff became a "right of the people" immediately following the American Revolution. The sheriff became a popularly elected office early on and remains overwhelmingly so today (Falcone and Wells 1995). Because American sheriffs are directly elected by the public, they are presumably more responsive to the concerns of local citizens than perhaps a local police chief who has been appointed by a mayor or city manager.

The second primary difference between sheriffs and municipal police organizations can also be traced to historical traditions. The office of the American county sheriff has always been granted a broader range of responsibilities than that of municipal police organizations, similar to the scope of responsibilities granted to the office's predecessor, the medieval English office of the shire-reeve. The **shire-reeve** had wide-ranging duties, including local law enforcement, tax collection, and heading the local judiciary (Falcone and Wells 1995). After the Norman Conquest in 1066, the office of shire-reeve became more of a political position that the king sold to the highest bidder, who then assumed the right to keep taxes collected over the royal quota. Similar to the historical shire-reeve of medieval England, the modern American sheriff usually performs several functions in addition to law enforcement such as court services; civil process and writs, including the serving of criminal warrants; and the administration of local jails (Brown 1978). The third common difference between county sheriffs offices and municipal (or city) police agencies is that sheriffs' deputies typically patrol a much larger geographic area (i.e., county). More generally, students of the history of policing should recognize the American sheriff as a unique entity that in many ways has developed separately and apart from the more commonly studied municipal counterparts.

London "Bobbies"

London's Metropolitan Police force is recognized as the first modern, full-time police agency. The Metropolitan Police were created through legislation passed by the British Parliament in 1829. The purpose of the bill was to replace the existing unorganized system of informal citizen police groups with an organized body of highly trained professional police (LaGrange 1998). The legislation and resulting formation of the Metropolitan Police was largely a response to regular street crimes, but also a rising tide of political violence and crises associated with working-class protests and class conflicts between the wealthy and poor citizens of London (Miller 1977). Thus, the formation of the first modern police force is consistent with the notions of Lundman (1980) that organized police are a response to societal changes and class conflicts.

Sir Robert Peel introduced the legislation that created the Metropolitan Police. Peel was acting British home secretary, a cabinet-level position within the British government. Peel appointed Charles Rowan (an Army officer) and Richard Mayne (a prominent attorney) to lead the new police force. Peel is an important historical figure within this context and is generally considered the "father of police" (LaGrange 1998). British police officers are commonly referred to as "bobbies" due to the influence of Peel. Peel and others confronted significant challenges in gaining public acceptance of the new police force. Citizens were understandably concerned that an organized full-time police force would ultimately infringe on individual liberties. Peel needed to somehow develop the "bobbies" in ways that encouraged public support and legitimacy, so he enacted a list of important guiding principles. "Peel's Principles," as they came to be known, have stood the test of time and can be viewed as important doctrines for police agencies even today. These principles define what Peel believed to be the framework of democratic policing and can be summarized in terms of four points. First, the primary function of police is crime control. Second, police need to be well trained, professional, and properly restrained in their use of force. Third, the government and citizens need to provide oversight over the police. Fourth, the police need to be accessible to the public.

London's Metropolitan Police by all accounts quickly succeeded in earning legitimacy and public confidence. The "bobbies" on the street were tough enough to maintain public order, but restrained enough to ease fears of repression

(Miller 1977). They wore blue uniforms that distinguished them from the military and were identified by number to facilitate organization and public accountability. Officers were originally not permitted to vote so as to limit political influence and corruption, and they were recruited from outside London to maintain a professional but impersonal relationship with citizens. The organization closely monitored officers' use of force, and they did not normally carry firearms on duty. The success of London's "bobbies" paved the way for the creation of formalized full-time police forces elsewhere, including eventually the United States.

MODERN POLICE IN THE UNITED STATES

The advent of modern policing in the United States occurred between the 1830s and the 1850s, when several East Coast cities developed formalized police forces, including Boston, Philadelphia, and New York City. The next several sections of this chapter focus on the history of modern policing in the United States from this point of inception to the present day; however, students need to be aware of several important considerations before proceeding to the details.

Overview and Important Considerations

First, scholarship on the history of modern policing in the United States has focused almost exclusively on the development of large urban municipal (or "city") police departments rather than county sheriffs and/or state- and federal-level law enforcement agencies (see, e.g., Struckhoff 2003). Second, because policing in the United States developed in a highly decentralized way, there are about 15,000 unique police agencies, each with its own history and development. Third, most police scholars recognize and describe the history of modern police in the United States in terms of three distinct periods: the (1) political, (2) professional/reform, and (3) community policing eras.

These three considerations work to present a somewhat distorted view of the development of modern policing across the United States. For example, students who grew up in a small town or under the primary jurisdiction of a rural county sheriff may have a difficult time squaring what they know about their own local police forces with the history as it is described in this chapter. There is, of course, no way to accurately describe the history of policing across thousands of unique places. Policing developed in different ways across various points in time across these different agencies and places. However, the history described here should be considered a fairly accurate description of the development and operation of police within the larger urban cities of the United States. Keeping these important considerations in mind, we proceed with the history of modern policing in the United States using the common framework of three distinct eras previously identified by scholars.

The Political Era: Machine Politics, Community Ties, and Service

The **political era** of modern policing spans from roughly the mid-1800s, with the development of the first American municipal police departments, through the early decades of the 1900s (Fogelson 1977). The key to understanding this era is the concept of the **political machine,** which is an organization derived from a political party headed by single leader or "boss" who earns enough votes to control the administrative functions of a city. These political machines emerged during the 19th century as large waves of foreign immigrants and native migrants from rural places moved into the cities of the East Coast of the United States. The machines were organized down to the neighborhood level, where local representatives of the machine, or "ward bosses," responded to neighborhood problems and issues in ways that ensured that local residents would vote to elect political candidates aligned with the machine. The political machine at the local level, for example, granted "favors" to individuals, families, and/or neighborhoods—a job, a referral to a doctor, or favorable interpretations of the local ordinances—in exchange for votes on election days. Recently arrived immigrants and migrants often lacked the skills and/or experience necessary to "make it" in the big city, so political machines filled these needs in order to gain or maintain political power.

The operation and dominance of political machines within most large American cities during this period meant that they had enormous influence on the historical development and operation of American policing. Municipal police departments—as agencies of local government—were organized and operated primarily to satisfy the goals of the dominant political machine. Police agencies, for example, were organized down to the neighborhood level in much the same way as the political machine so as to satisfy the desires and needs of local citizens and garner votes on election day. The boundaries of local political "wards" often paralleled those of the local police "precincts" across various sections of the city (Miller 1977). Ward bosses worked with police precinct commanders to respond to the concerns and needs of local citizens and neighborhoods (Fogelson 1977; Kelling and Moore 1988).

The effects of this system on police were primarily two-fold. First, the most important function of police during this era was the provision of services rather than crime control or even the maintenance of public order. Police departments became "one-stop shops" for the provision of all sorts of local services, including housing, meals to the homeless or destitute, selective enforcement of local ordinances, and the provision of police jobs as political "favors" to local residents willing to serve the interests of the political machine. The emphasis on service delivery as a dominant law enforcement function is unique to this era of policing. Second, an emphasis on service delivery during this era also helped to create close ties between local communities and the police who patrolled within them. Officers of particular ethnic backgrounds were commonly assigned to neighborhoods occupied exclusively by residents of the same ethnic background (Haller 1976). In many cases, police were recent immigrants themselves, so they easily established connections with local citizens largely because in many ways they were "one of them." As a result, the political era of policing is most notable for (1) an emphasis on service delivery and (2) the establishment and maintenance of close ties between police and local communities (Langworthy and Travis 1999).

Problems of the Political Era: Crime Control, Corruption, and Civil Rights

The dominance of political machines and their resulting control over the operation of municipal police departments created some obvious problems. First, police agencies during the political era did not effectively control crime. This fact should not be surprising given that officers lacked any sort of qualifications or training in law enforcement. They generally obtained their job through relations with someone tied to the dominant political party rather than because of any expertise, education, or other qualification. Police also lacked any sort of technologies to help them control crime. Police typically walked a beat—no patrol car, no radio, and no readily available backup—and there was certainly no crime measurement or analysis designed to mitigate crimes. Perhaps more importantly, police agencies did not effectively control crime simply because they were not set up to do so. The political machines that controlled the operation of local police departments were much more intent on the provision of services and the garnering of votes than crime control.

The second problem was corruption, both of individual police officers and entire police agencies. Police of this era commonly engaged in the "shakedown," or robbing of arrestees, and collected "fees" in exchange for the selective non-enforcement of organized crimes such as prostitution and gambling. Indeed, the entire system of municipal policing during this era could be defined as one gigantic case of political corruption wherein politics controlled the management and operation of departments and the day-to-day decision-making of officers.

The third problem was that the police violated citizens' civil rights regularly. Police officers and organizations during this period have often been described as "non-legalistic" (Haller 1976; Kelling and Moore 1988). They were not trained in the law, and they commonly used excessive force and engaged in brutality against criminal suspects in violation of their civil rights. One form of brutality was the **"third degree,"** whereby police used techniques of physical and mental torture to extract criminal confessions. Other forms of common police violence during the period were more informal, including the regular and approved "roughing up" of unruly juveniles to keep them in line.

The Progressive Era Reform Movement and Push for Police Professionalism

The period of US history between the 1890s and the 1920s would come to be known as the Progressive Era. The **progressive reform movement** during this period was a response to problems stemming from rapid changes in American cities associated with large-scale industrialization, urbanization, and immigration. Progressive reformers sought to regulate businesses and the operation of local governments to improve the lives of citizens, particularly the poor immigrants and rural migrants who had recently flocked to the large urban centers. Progressive Era reformers were mostly societal elites, college-educated urban residents who advocated for wide-scale changes in the social, political, cultural, and economic spheres of American society. These reformers also attempted to change the organization and operation of municipal police agencies as part of this larger societal movement (Alpert and Dunham 1988; Fogelson 1977; Lundman 1980).

Reformers believed that most of the problems in American policing resulted from the link to politics and the political machines that promoted corruption, incompetence, and inefficiency. They sought to improve American policing by mitigating the strong and corrupting influences of politics that were the defining feature of the political era; they wanted to sever the ties between politics and policing.

The reformers identified at least three primary ways to mitigate the influence of politics and thereby improve the operation of large urban municipal police agencies (Fogelson 1977; Kelling and Moore 1988). One goal of reformers was to centralize police operations and increase the power and prestige of the police chief. During the political era, police departments were decentralized to reflect the organization of the political machines, and much of the power was vested in precinct commanders who worked directly with neighborhood ward bosses to accomplish the political goals of the machines. Reformers advocated a shift toward centralized, hierarchical, and top-down organizations led by a powerful and influential police chief who was not beholden to the interests of the political machines. A second goal of reformers was to upgrade the quality of police personnel through more rigorous selection processes, training, and the establishment of higher salaries. A third goal of reformers was to narrow the function of police to focus more exclusively on crime control as the most important objective. Reformers sought to eliminate many of the service functions promoted by political machines and promote police as "experts" in crime-fighting in much the same way that doctors and lawyers are established as experts in the respective fields of medicine and the law. These three goals became the cornerstone of efforts to alter and improve policing throughout most of the 20th century—a period that would come to be known as the **professional/reform era** of modern policing in the United States.

Police Reformers: August Vollmer And O. W. Wilson

Strategies to reform and professionalize police during the first half of the 20th century were developed and carried out by a multitude of police leaders and administrators; however, two individuals stand out as most influential to the success of these movements. **August Vollmer** (1876–1955) is generally regarded as the founder of modern policing in the United States because of his contributions to police professionalism and reform in the areas of police administration, training and education, and crime-fighting tactics (Oliver 2017). He spent 27 years as the police chief in Berkeley, California. He was among the first police administrators to adopt the latest managerial techniques and advocate for the application of scientific principles to control crime. Vollmer and other reformers believed that crime-fighting needed to become the police's primary function, and he created specific tactics to mitigate crime, such as motorcycle patrols and patrol cars with radios, lie detector machines, crime laboratories, and distinct units dedicated to the suppression of juvenile delinquency. Vollmer served as a professor of police administration and established police training classes and degree programs in criminology and law enforcement at the University of California at Berkeley.

O. W. Wilson (1900–1972), one of Vollmer's pupils, initially worked as a police officer in Berkeley, California, and later served as police chief in Fullerton, California; Wichita, Kansas; and finally Chicago, Illinois, during the 1960s. Wilson also served as the dean of the School of Criminology at UC–Berkley. Wilson's style of management was indicative of the movement to reform and professionalize police overall (Bopp 1977). He was the author of what has arguably been the most influential textbook on police administration. He advocated an institutionalized police organizational management structure that was highly centralized and focused on crime control as the primary function of modern police. In this way, Wilson's management style was indicative of the larger movement to more broadly transform police throughout the professional/reform era.

The Professional/Reform Era: Centralized Police Bureaucracy and Focus on Crime Control

Police reformers such as August Vollmer and O. W. Wilson worked well beyond the efforts initiated by progressives at the turn of the 20th century. Indeed, the professional or reform era is widely considered by most scholars to extend into at least the 1980s. Reformers by that time had largely succeeded in the transformation of municipal police agencies and the primary goals of the professional or reform movement, including the shift toward centralized top-down organizations run by a strong police chief, upgraded police personnel, and a more narrow focus on crime control as the most important police function. The reform movement helped to mitigate the influence of politics on policing such that police organizations derived their primary authority and legitimacy from law enforcement. Police became widely identified as professional "crime-fighters" and were increasingly judged on their ability to influence crime rates. Police executives developed core strategies to identify and reduce crime levels, including preventative motorized patrol, rapid response to service calls and the eventual 911 emergency communications system, and retrospective criminal investigations to solve crimes involving police detectives and increasingly complex forensic techniques. These and other tactics obviously improved the crime-fighting ability of local police, particularly in comparison to the rudimentary and inadequate methods of the earlier political era. The reforms also helped to lessen (but not eliminate) some of the most egregious problems of political corruption and police brutality. For the most part, police officers in most large urban jurisdictions obtained their job through civil service testing and lengthy training programs rather than political connections. In the bigger picture, the professional/reform movement had largely worked to transform local police by the latter decades of the 20th century. Police organizations were highly centralized, focused almost exclusively on crime control, and populated by police officers who were much more highly trained than their predecessors.

The police reform agenda had largely succeeded by the mid-20th century; however, problems in the movement to professionalize police clearly emerged during the turbulent decades of the 1960s and 1970s (Fogelson 1977; Rumbaut and Bittner 1979). First, crime rates in America's large urban cities rose quite sharply. Police, as a result of the professional reforms, had marketed themselves as "expert" crime-fighters. Scholars recognize that many factors influence crime rates of aside from police, but soaring crime rates were (and still are) defined largely as a problem for police to solve. Americans increasingly feared crime as rates continued to increase, and some citizens, at least in part, directly blamed police. Second, the costs of police reform in terms of dollars and cents became increasingly evident as the US economy began to falter in the early 1970s. Municipal governments and taxpayers scrutinized whether the costs of reforms—higher police salaries and benefits, lengthy training programs, and expensive crime-fighting equipment—were really worth it, particular since crime rates were rising sharply rather than falling. Third, and perhaps most important, a clear disconnect had developed between police and citizens. Surveys revealed that citizens in some segments of American society were increasingly dissatisfied and did not trust police. This phenomenon was particularly acute in minority communities that continued to experience rising levels of crime and police brutality—and became rather impossible to ignore by the late 1960s, particularly in American cities that experienced large-scale protests, and in some cases riots, associated with the civil rights movement and the Vietnam War. Americans could turn on their television sets and see the battle lines for themselves: police in riot gear on one side and citizen protesters on the other. Something within the movement to reform and professionalize American police had clearly gone wrong.

Community Alienation and the Need for Police-Community Collaboration

The movement to reform and professionalize police began with progressives and the goal of severing politics and police. Reformers recognized that politics had been the source of many of the problems of the political era, and so they undertook steps to reduce political influences. They created centralized police organizations led by strong police chiefs. They narrowed the function to crime control and reduced ancillary services. They promulgated training and strategies designed to promote police as expert crime-fighters. The reforms had largely succeeded over the decades, so why did so many Americans harbor negative attitudes toward and opinions of police? The movement to reform and professionalize police had produced one very negative consequence—**community alienation** (Fogelson 1977; Kelling and Moore 1988). Police had become separated and disengaged from the citizens they were sworn to protect and serve. The reforms were designed to separate police from politics, and they largely succeeded. But in so doing, these same reforms also "succeeded" in separating police from citizens and the general public. Police were no longer connected to the community in the ways that were common during the political era. Police, for example, no longer walked the beat and spoke directly to citizens; they rode in patrol cars and answered service calls. More broadly, police organizations devised and implemented crime control strategies and tactics without any input from community members or organizations. Police were "experts" at crimefighting, so why would they need input from regular citizens? Doctors do not need input from regular citizens to cure disease, and lawyers do not need input from regular citizens to understand the law. Police became increasingly isolated in their efforts to stop rising crime rates. Reformers had not set out to separate police from the public, but the movement to professionalize police and rid them of political influences had resulted in wide-scale community alienation by the end of the 1970s and into the 1980s.

Critical Thinking Exercise

Community Alienation, Urban Riots, and the Demise of the Professional/Reform Era

The major problem of the professional/reform era—police-community alienation—became readily apparent to average Americans within the context of numerous, large-scale urban riots and their aftermath during the latter 1960s. There were more than 150 riots in major American cities between 1965 and 1968. These riots involved the death of 83 individuals and more than $100 million in property damages during 1967 alone. The riots occurred in economically disadvantaged African-American urban neighborhoods.

President Lyndon Johnson appointed a National Advisory Commission on Civil Disorders in 1968 to investigate the causes of the riots. The commission identified numerous causes centered on widespread and enduring racial discrimination, including economic inequality, poor and inadequate housing, high unemployment, voter repression, and segregated housing. The commission also underscored the impact of long-standing repressive and violent police practices and misconduct within these neighborhoods, as well as cases in which police responses to the riots had exacerbated the violence (George 2018).

The footage of the urban riots broadcast to millions of American homes through television news reports and the problem of police-community alienation became obvious and impossible to ignore. This situation eventually contributed to the formulation of new ideas and the advent of what came to be known as the community-oriented policing movement during the 1970s and 1980s. The riots and their aftermath need to be understood by students today as an important historical artifact but perhaps more importantly in the context of more recent headlines, urban protests, and the series of notorious police–citizen encounters that have stoked anti-police sentiment and undermined police legitimacy in some communities. These recent events sparked protests in Baltimore, Chicago, New York City, and elsewhere that promoted slogans that have become familiar to most citizens: "Hands Up; Don't Shoot" and "Black Lives Matter" (Gambino and Thrasher 2014; Wisniewski and Madden 2015a, 2015b).

Do you believe we are in the midst of another paradigm shift in policing associated with the emergence of social unrest and anti-police movements among some segments of the American population? Why or why not?

The Community-Oriented Policing Era and the Idea of Co-production

The problem of community alienation from police prompted ideas and strategies that would eventually lead to a new era of American policing commonly referred to as the **community-oriented policing (COP) era**. The main idea is that police cannot operate successfully in isolation from the community and citizens. The police can produce no desirable outcome—low crime rates, the maintenance of public order, the provision of necessary services to citizens—without some sort of positive collaboration with the community (Banton 1964). The concept that underpins this era of policing is that citizens and communities need to become "co-producers" in crime control with the police. The efforts of police and citizens need to be integrated in order to succeed. Police cannot control crime all by themselves.

Students should be able to see some parallels in the shift in philosophy between the professional/reform and community policing eras and the earlier shift between the political and professional/reform era. Progressive Era reformers identified politics as the major problem in policing at the turn of the 20th century, and so they instituted reforms or changes in the way police operate to fix the major problems. Community-oriented policing reformers did the same thing seven or eight decades later. They identified community alienation as the major problem in policing and instituted reforms or changes in the way police operate to fix it.

The reforms associated with the COP movement can be summarized along three dimensions. First, reformers recognized the need to directly engage citizens as co-producers in crime control and community order. Police could no longer "go it alone" in their efforts to mitigate crime. Second, reformers supported the implementation of proactive crime control strategies aimed at mitigating the causes of crime. These strategies would require police to do more than simply answer service calls after a crime or other sort of problem had occurred. Third, reformers believed that police resources needed to be focused on solving the problems that specifically created the need for police services in the first place. Here, police would be expected to solve community problems in order to prevent future calls and crimes.

One driving force behind these ideas was the experimental implementation of **foot patrol** in some urban communities (Trojanowicz 1983; Wilson and Kelling 1982). Foot patrol had been the primary strategy during the political era. Officers "walked the beat" in order to deter crime and catch criminals on scene when they were able; but also foot patrol allowed police the opportunity to interact with citizens face-to-face and become familiar with their problems and concerns. Foot patrols seemed to be largely responsible for the establishment and maintenance of close ties between police and local communities during the political era, and community-oriented reformers investigated whether the reintroduction of foot patrols in some communities could work to re-establish these connections between police and citizens. They found that for the most part citizens preferred foot patrols to motorized patrols, and that foot patrols worked to mitigate citizens' fear of crime in some communities. Reformers more broadly believed that police could work together with the community to identify community problems and collaboratively devise tactics to mitigate them and fix "broken" communities. Foot patrols are not practical or appropriate in many jurisdictions simply because of the large geographic size of the patrol districts, but the foot patrol experiments supported the general idea that police needed to more directly engage citizens as co-producers in crime control and community order. This led to the implementation of foot patrols and other strategies to designed to support community collaboration, including community meetings between police and citizens, community surveys on problems and police tactics to solve them, block watch and other citizen-driven crime prevention tactics, programs designed to place police within community schools, and the creation of mini "storefront" police stations in specific neighborhoods to facilitate more street-level police–citizen contacts.

Another hallmark of the community-oriented era is a tactic that has commonly been referred to as **problem-oriented policing** (**POP**; Eck and Spellman 1987). POP was an effort to make police more proactive and focused on solving community problems. Police traditional answered calls for service reactively. That is, they responded to calls only *after* a crime had occurred or problem was evident. Then, police would handle that particular call as an isolated event. They would handle the particular call, then move on to the next call, and so on. The problem with this "incident-driven" approach common to the professional/reform era of policing is that the problem underlying these service calls never gets identified or solved, and so these problems tend to reoccur over and over again. POP encouraged police on the street to view every service call as an underlying "problem" to be solved rather than an isolated event. In this way, POP is best described as a proactive crime control strategy that focuses police efforts on solving community problems. For example, police within a particular community may repeatedly respond to the same address on the same day of the month to mitigate a domestic violence problem. Police responses under the old incident-driven approach would be limited to an arrest or at least a separation of involved individuals—and then doing the same thing next month after another domestic violence call comes in. POP demands that officers identify the cause of the problem in the first place. Perhaps the perpetrator has a substance abuse problem that occurs every month after payday. Police could "problem-solve" this situation by referring the perpetrator to substance abuse or anger management treatment, or by facilitating the removal of the victim from the home and into a domestic violence shelter. The idea is for police to become more proactive, solve the problem that underlies each and every call for service, and ultimately reduce crimes associated with the underlying problem.

The community policing paradigm held sway through the 1990s, and a majority of American police agencies subscribed to the model's basic principles. American police agencies today continue for the most part to adhere to the principle of community collaboration and co-production, so much so that "everybody" now seems to know that police cannot operate in isolation from the public and citizens. Similar to both the previous political and professional/reform eras, however, problems and limitations of the COP model eventually surfaced over time. One problem was a degree of rank-and-file opposition from police themselves. Some officers were reluctant to perform duties associated with the COP movement that they defined as perhaps not "real police work" or directly associated with crime-fighting, such as attending community meetings, going on foot patrol, and other initiatives to collaborate with the community. A second problem relates to the need for community involvement with the police. Studies showed that people in some communities were not interested in collaborating or were fearful of the police, particularly in some urban neighborhoods where police-community relations had long been strained. A third problem relates to crime rates. Crime across America had declined from the 1960s through the 1990s; however, pockets of high-crime rates continue to exist in many urban centers. Calls for community collaboration and co-production can be difficult to follow in places where high rates of violent predatory crimes persist. The community-oriented model is far from perfect, but the paradigm does represent a distinct and widely recognized "third" era of modern American policing following the political and professional/reform eras described earlier within this chapter.

Web Activity

The Office of Community Oriented Policing Services (COPS) is part of the US Department of Justice and is responsible for promoting community policing nationwide. Students are encouraged to visit the extensive website developed by COPS at https://cops.usdoj.gov. The website provides the public news associated with current community policing strategies, documents that describe grants awarded to local and state police agencies to perform community policing tactics, and resources and publications that provide detailed information on community policing as it is practiced in communities across the United States.

Critical Thinking Exercise

Issues in the Formation of Police-Community Partnerships

The primary goal of community-oriented policing proponents was to mitigate the problem of community alienation that emerged during the latter stages of the professional/reform era and forge stronger partnerships between police and the communities that they serve. The need for stronger police-community partnerships has been largely accepted by police executives, officers, and community leaders since the 1980s. A number of community policing programs, for example, depend to some degree on police-community collaboration in order to work, including community-based crime prevention programs, citizen police academies, and programs with problem-solving tactics that rely on citizens to assist in identifying and prioritizing problems for the police to address (Skogan 2004).

Policing scholars, however, provided clear evidence that the formation of these partnerships is more difficult than many had anticipated. Surveys have demonstrated that many citizens do not want to get involved in crime prevention efforts or otherwise work with police because they may be unaware of these strategies, they are fearful of the police, or they are simply apathetic (Buerger 1994). So, too, police and citizens often seem to differ in regard to what the most important community problems are and how to fix them (Liederbach et al. 2008). Community policing strategies also seem to be threatened by attitudinal shifts that have occurred in the aftermath of the September 11, 2001, terror attacks and growing concerns associated with homeland security and the ongoing war on terror.

Do you believe that community policing is a viable strategy going forward? Can police and communities work together effectively to identify and solve local neighborhood problems? Why or why not? If not, what changes need to be made to make these sorts of partnerships more effective?

Modern Patrol Strategies: Hotspots of Crime and Data-Driven Tactics

Policing over the last 20 years seems to have transitioned again in terms of the evolution of patrol strategies and the wide-scale implementation of data-driven tactics to reduce crime. This transition is justified on the basis of two observations. First, we know, based on decades of scholarship and crime statistics, that crime is nonrandomly distributed across geographic spaces. That is, the overwhelming majority of crimes occur in small geographic spaces known as "hotspots." Second, police executives and many scholars believe that police can reduce crime through proactive and focused patrol tactics based on crime data.

The first observation, the **nonrandom distribution of crime,** is based on criminological scholarship of urban crime. This research focuses on the importance of places in understanding the geographical dispersion of crime across cities. Criminologists since the early post–World War II period recognized distinctions in the crime rates across larger geographical units, such as neighborhoods; however, contemporary studies identify significant variations in the distribution of crime among much smaller geographic units, commonly referred to as "places." This "place-based" approach to criminology recognizes the nonrandom distribution of crime in which the occurrence of crime varies widely within specific neighborhoods and is often highly concentrated in particular "hotspots."

Research studies, for example, have consistently found that 3–5 percent of addresses citywide produce roughly 50 percent of all police service calls (Pierce, Spar, and Briggs 1988; Sherman, Buerger, and Gartin 1989; Weisburd, Maher, and Sherman 1992). These **hotspots of crime** are very small geographic areas often reserved for a narrow range of functions, perhaps controlled by a single owner, and separated from the surrounding area. Specific examples of these places include stores, homes, apartment buildings, street corners, and mass transit stations (Eck 2002). In sum, we *know* there is a significant clustering of crime concentrated within a relatively small number of geographic units or hotspots and that offenders choose these hotspots as targets of crime based on specific place characteristics. These truths generate obvious implications for police: Methods of patrol must be proactive and focused on crime hotspots in order to identify, apprehend, and/or deter criminal perpetrators.

The second observation, the need for proactive and focused patrol strategies, has resulted in some innovations designed to mitigate crime that occurs in hotspots. Research on police patrol and evidence on proactive and focused tactics paralleled criminological studies that identified the nonrandom distribution of crime within particular hotspots. The earliest studies during the 1970s repudiated traditional or routine patrols, whereby officers spent most of their time driving randomly around a comparatively large geographic space or "beat" waiting for a service call (Kelling et al. 1974). Research on what were referred to as "directed" patrols during the 1980s showed how police could more effectively reduce crime. These patrols directed officers to focus on specific locales and target them for purposive law enforcement based on rudimentary crime data (Cordner 1981). Patrol tactics were increasingly refined through the 1990s to include specific strategies that attacked chronic concentrations of crime. These studies demonstrated that crackdowns and "saturation" patrols could suppress crime and deter criminals without simply displacing them elsewhere (Fritsch, Liederbach, and Taylor 2009; National Research Council 2004). Sherman and Weisburd (1995), in probably the most widely cited study published during this period, were among the first to prove that patrols concentrated within small geographic spaces significantly reduced service calls and observed community disorder. Braga's (2005) analysis of nine randomized experiments provided results that were more definitive and generalizable and confirmed for many the effectiveness of what had become known as "hotspot patrols."

The adoption of hotspot patrols has accelerated as scholars focus on measuring crime within increasingly smaller geographical units of analysis such as clusters of addresses, block faces, or specific buildings. These places are much smaller than the typical police administrative unit such as a "beat," so police organizations require new tools to determine the effectiveness of patrol strategies (Mastrofski, Weisburd, and Braga 2010). This goal has been facilitated by the widespread adoption of newer computer mapping and crime analysis technologies, especially in the aftermath of the September 11, 2001, terror attacks.

Police organizations within this context have assumed additional responsibilities in the war on terror that demand improved response capabilities. **CompStat**—short for *compare statistics*—was developed by the New York City Police Department as a process that uses current crime data to analyze crime patterns and quickly allocate patrol resources to problem areas. Many large urban police agencies have implemented these strategies in some form or another: 56 percent of recently surveyed agencies use computers for crime mapping, 48 percent use computers for crime analysis, and 20 percent have a specialized unit with personnel assigned full time to crime analysis (Santos 2014). Research on crime analysis supports these tactical trends for reducing crime. Baltaci (2010), for example, examined the effect of crime analysis measured by 22 items on the crime and clearance rates of over 800 police agencies and found that broader crime analysis activities were correlated with lower violent crime rates and higher total clearance rates.

Police executives in some jurisdictions are pushing for the adoption of more comprehensive strategies known collectively as **intelligence-led policing (ILP)** (Ratcliffe 2007, 2008). Similar in some ways to Compstat, these strategies use real-time crime analysis and incorporate intelligence analysis in the deployment of both specialized units and regular patrol officers (Carter 2004). The reality is that police agencies—provided the necessary resources in terms of personnel and software—now have the capability to target patrol resources *each day* on the most serious and immediate threats. High-intensity police patrols often incorporate "real-time crime centers," wherein police agencies use many of the analytical capabilities of Compstat and ILP to focus specifically on incidents occurring *at the moment*. The real-time crime centers may gather data from a wide range of source, including—but not limited to—service-call data, real-time intelligence, and public and private surveillance camera video. These sources provide immediate crime data to field commanders, detectives, and ultimately patrol officers who can be deployed immediately. Put simply, contemporary intelligence-led patrol strategies put police on top of the most significant crime problems in real time using the best available information technology systems.

CHAPTER SUMMARY

This chapter presents a relatively brief history of policing in three parts. One goal was to communicate how modern policing developed over time, mostly due to changing social and political forces. The process included different phases, including the informal or avocational phase, the transitional phase, and the formal phase. Here, we see how policing originated as a "side" activity of normal everyday citizens, and then developed over hundreds of years into a full-time profession for a limited number of designated personnel. Another goal was to shed some light on the particular development of policing in America. The chapter provides an overview of several forms of policing that directly led to the emergence of modern policing in the United States, including vigilante groups, bounty hunters, the institution of the American sheriff, and London's "bobbies." A third goal was to provide more detail on the progression of modern policing in America. The chapter provides details on three eras of policing in the United States, including the political era, the professional/reform era, and the community policing era. The material underscores how problems in each particular era led to movements that altered policing to the extent that "new" eras of policing in America emerged over time. Lastly, the chapter provides some information on more modern police strategies and tactics that continue to influence changes in how American police operate.

KEY TERMS

bounty hunter
changing patterns of
    social organization
community alienation
community-oriented
    policing (COP) era
CompStat
elite interests

foot patrol
formal phase of policing
hotspots of crime
hue and cry
informal or avocational
    phase of policing
intelligence-led policing
    (ILP)

kin policing
nonrandom distribution
    of crime
political era of policing
political machine
problem-oriented
    policing (POP)
professional/reform era

progress reform
   movement
rising perceptions of
   criminality

shire-reeve
third degree
transitional phase of
   policing

vigilante policing
watch system

FURTHER READING

Eck, J., and W. Spellman (1987). "Who You Gonna Call? The Police as Problem Busters." *Crime and Delinquency* 33(1): 31–52.

Falcone, D. N., and L. E. Wells (1995). "The County Sheriff as a Distinctive Policing Modality." *American Journal of Police* 14: 123–49.

Fogelson, R. M. (1977). *Big-City Police*. Cambridge, MA: Harvard University Press.

Haller, M. (1976). "Historical Roots of Police Behavior: Chicago, 1890–1925." *Law and Society Review* 10(Winter): 303–24.

Ratcliffe, J. H. (2008). *Intelligence-Led Policing*. Portland, OR: Willan Publishing.

Roberg, R., K. Novak, G. Cordner, and B. Smith (2012). *Police & Society*. 5th ed. New York: Oxford University Press.

Skogan, W. G. (2004). *Community Policing: Can It Work?* Belmont, CA: Wadsworth.

Wilson, J. Q., and G. L. Kelling (1982). "Broken Windows: The Police and Neighborhood Safety." *The Atlantic Monthly* 249(3): 29–38.

CHAPTER 3

Roles and Responsibilities of the Police

After reading this chapter, you should be able to:

- Discuss the public perception of the police role in society
- Identify the three primary categories of police responsibilities and the relative time spent on each category
- Discuss the patrol function of the police and its effectiveness

- Demonstrate knowledge on police investigation, both reactive and proactive
- List and discuss various tools used in investigations with an emphasis on emerging tools
- Provide examples of the changing role and strategies related to police law enforcement functions
- Discuss order maintenance and give examples of proactive order maintenance
- Give examples of both reactive and proactive service functions of the police

When asked about the job of the police, the average person says that they enforce the law and arrest offenders. This view is certainly reinforced anytime someone looks at the media. News programs, fictional entertainment, and reality television offer a view of policing that focuses on law violation and police responses to specific events. The entertainment media portray policing as an exciting career of hunting criminals, thwarting robberies in progress, engaging in high-speed car chases, making dynamic entries, and apprehending desperate criminals. In truth, these events happen infrequently. These presentations paint a narrow picture of everyday police activity that is far from reality. This chapter looks at the many roles and responsibilities of the police and places them into the context of policing in modern society.

EARLY MANDATE FOR THE POLICE

An examination of the early history of modern policing reveals that there was no emphasis on making arrests or gathering evidence. Sir Robert Peel, in developing the first modern police force, the Metropolitan Police, set forth a number of guiding principles (see Table 3.1). One central, overriding principle was that the police role is to prevent crime . Sir Robert Peel and Charles Roman, the commissioner of the new organization, both saw crime prevention as the basic principle underlying police work (LaGrange 1993). Even earlier attempts at formal policing, such as that in 17th-century Paris, emphasized crime prevention through methods such as preventive patrol, increased lighting, and street cleaning (Stead 1983).

An inspection of the Peelian principles reveals that crime control was based on police presence and positive interaction with the citizenry. The police were to be easily accessible to the citizenry, act in ways to earn the citizens' respect, dress in a manner that would command respect, and earn the public's cooperation. Importantly, the police were to be able to control their temper and refrain from reacting with violence. Note that "the police are the public and the public are the police" (Crime Prevention Website 2019) rather than two different groups working at cross purposes, as often portrayed in today's media. Crime control was the outcome of working with the public to address crime and problems in the community.

MODERN PERCEPTION OF THE POLICE ROLE

The early emphasis on preventing crime and general orientation for crime control has not been lost in modern policing. What has emerged is a shift to a more overt interest in making arrests and solving crimes. This appears in surveys of

Table 3.1 The Peelian Principles

1. The basic mission for which the police exist is to prevent crime and disorder.

2. The ability of the police to perform their duties is dependent upon public approval of police actions.

3. Police must secure the willing co-operation of the public in voluntary observance of the law to be able to secure and maintain the respect of the public.

4. The degree of co-operation of the public that can be secured diminishes proportionately to the necessity of the use of physical force.

5. Police seek and preserve public favour not by pandering to public opinion but by constantly demonstrating absolute impartial service to the law.

6. Police use physical force to the extent necessary to secure observance of the law or to restore order only when the exercise of persuasion, advice and warning is found to be insufficient.

7. Police, at all times, should maintain a relationship with the public that gives reality to the historic tradition that the police are the public and the public are the police; the police being only members of the public who are paid to give full-time attention to duties which are incumbent on every citizen in the interests of community welfare and existence.

8. Police should always direct their action strictly towards their functions and never appear to usurp the powers of the judiciary.

9. The test of police efficiency is the absence of crime and disorder not the visible evidence of police action in dealing with it.

Source: Crime Prevention Website (2019).

the public and in both fictional and news presentations of crime and policing. The role of the media in molding public perceptions and expectations for the police cannot be overemphasized.

Crime accounts for a major portion of the written and broadcast media. Roughly 25 percent of all media entertainment programming deals with criminal activity and/or the operations of the criminal justice system (Reiner 2002). Indeed, the number of reality television programs targeting crime and criminal justice has grown since the late 1980s. One very important thing to note is that many of these programs appear as quasi-news reports focusing on sensational, unsolved crimes. Examples of these shows are *48 Hours, Dateline,* and *20/20.* In recent years, entire broadcasting channels—such as Investigation Discovery, Crime and Investigation, and A&E—have appeared that are either devoted to crime and criminal justice or have an extensive amount of crime-related shows. Crime news also focuses on criminal activity and responses to crime. Various studies put crime news at roughly 20 percent of all news in newspapers and on television (Dominick 1978; Graber 1977, 1980; Hofstetter 1976).

The media presentations have a great deal of influence on the public's view of crime, what the police do, and expectations for the police. Unfortunately, if you compare the media portrayal of crime and policing to the actual extent and types of crime and what the police face every day, there is a great deal of difference. The media distort the crime picture by focusing on selected types of crime, overemphasizing the level of crime, and failing to provide accurate or complete information about criminal incidents and what the police handle on a daily basis. First, there is a disproportionate focus on violence in both news and fictional accounts of crime (Chermak 1998; Chermak and Chapman 2007; Dominick 1978; Ferguson 2013; Gerbner et al. 1980; Greer and Reiner 2012; Higgins and Ray 1978; Jewkes 2011; Marsh 1991; Oliver 1994; Oliver and Armstrong 1998; Reiner et al. 2000; Robinson 2011; Surette 1992). The media's focus on rare and more serious crimes rather than the more typical street crime is what Surette (2015) calls the **backwards law**.

The overemphasis on violent offenses, particularly between strangers on the street, alters public expectations for the police. Viewers hold inaccurate images of crime and the criminal justice system. Gerbner et al. (1977, 1978, 1979) and Barrile (1980) note that survey respondents give answers that reflect "television reality" rather than the real-world information. People's beliefs and perceptions are influenced by and mirror the media presentations of crime and policing. Surette (2018) notes that the public has a great deal of control over what they watch on all of the emerging social media platforms (what he refers to as **new media**), and most presentations are unfiltered, and are offered in real time with little information on the context or background of the event,. Most of these focus on the more sensational crimes and events. Crime and policing, in the news, fictional media, and the new media, become spectacles that are amplified in the minds of the public.

THE REALITY OF THE ROLE AND RESPONSIBILITY OF THE POLICE

The reality of policing is not the same as it is portrayed in media presentations. While the police bear the majority of responsibility for addressing crime by making arrests and investigating offenses, they are called on for many other things. In broad terms, there are three primary responsibilities of police work: law enforcement, order maintenance, and service. These aspects were first explored by James Q. Wilson in his 1968 book *Varieties of Police Behavior*. **Law enforcement** reflects the public's typical view of the police role: specifically, responding to situations in which the police apply the criminal code, make an arrest, and do the follow-up necessary for a successful prosecution. **Order maintenance** involves situations where calls to the police can be handled through means besides making an arrest and invoking the legal processes. Included under order maintenance are loud noise complaints, arguments between family members or acquaintances, and landlord-tenant disputes. In all of these cases, it may be possible to make an arrest and invoke the legal process, but it is handled more informally. **Service** is exactly what it sound like. The police assist the community or individuals, such as by leading funeral processions, providing emergency treatment at accident scenes, providing information to citizens, checking properties when residents are on vacation, and helping someone who is locked out of his or her car. Today, the police also act as medics/first responders (offering first aid for injuries, Narcan for opioid overdoses, and other immediate care) and social workers (making referrals and providing assistance in suicide situations, domestic violence cases, and similar situations).

The amount of time spent on each category of police work has been the subject of a number of projects over the years. In one of the earliest assessments, Wilson (1968) claimed that law enforcement comprised roughly 10 percent of all police activity. This was based on detailed observations of police–citizen encounters in 20 communities. Similar claims have been found in other observational studies of police behavior (Bittner 1970; Reiss 1971). Webster (1970), in a study of police patrol, indicated that the police spend only 17 percent of their time fighting crime but 55 percent on social services and administrative activity. In a study of Kentucky police behavior, Lilly (1978) reports that patrol officers spend 60 percent of their time providing information and less than 10 percent working on violent and property crimes.

Scott (1981) presents evidence based on the Police Services Study, a project that analyzed over 26,000 calls to the police in 24 jurisdictions. Only 642 calls (2 percent) dealt with violent crime and 4,489 (17 percent) involved nonviolent crimes. The remaining 81 percent of calls fall into either order maintenance or service-related calls. Lab (1984) examined miscellaneous incident reports filed by the Charlotte, North Carolina, police department in 1983. These reports documented patrol activities when no crime was committed or when citizens decided not to file a formal complaint. Analysis of the reports revealed that 58 percent involved order maintenance functions and 26 percent were for service activities (Lab 1984). The remaining 16 percent involved some form of law enforcement–related activity (such as serving arrest warrants) or situations in which the caller could not be located when the officers arrived. The dominance of routine patrol, administrative functions, service issues, and interacting with citizens not directly related to enforcing the law also appears in more recent observational analyses and in studies of nonurban police departments (Liederbach and Frank 2003, 2006).

The generally accepted view is that the police spend roughly 20–25 percent of their time dealing with law enforcement issues. The remainder falls into the categories of order maintenance and service. It is important to note that the division between the roles and responsibilities is not always clear cut and the categories are not mutually exclusive. Many of the order maintenance situations have the potential to require law enforcement activity. For example, a loud noise complaint could turn into a fistfight when the parties are drinking and arguing. An arrest may become necessary to handle the situation even though the initial

---

Web Activity

The variety in daily police activity is evident in numerous sources. A detailed breakdown of activity based on the Scott (1981) and Lab (1984) projects can be found on the textbook website. You can also investigate local perceptions of police behavior by talking with police administrators in your community.

caller did not want anyone to be arrested. Similarly, many law enforcement activities may result in service functions. An example would be officers responding to a shooting who are then tasked with notifying next of kin about the death.

The crossover between the roles and responsibilities of the police is understandable when considering the more general mandate for policing. If you consider crime prevention and crime control as broader, more enveloping roles for law enforcement, it become easy to see the intermingling of law enforcement, order maintenance, and service. Preventing crime and controlling the community involves a wide array of actions and potential interventions. Legal responses to specific behaviors (i.e., imposition of the criminal code through arrest to prosecution) is certainly an appropriate method. Using alternatives besides law enforcement also makes sense in many situations, such as intervening in youthful misbehavior and family altercations.

Discussions of order maintenance and service typically include an explanation of why the police are called for actions that are clearly not, or marginally, criminal. Most explanations involve three factors:

- The police are visible and available in the community all day, every day.
- The public views the police as having the ability to take charge and the legal right to use force if necessary.
- The public has easy access to the police by phone and use of the universal 911 system.

It is not hard to understand why the public calls on the police for a wide range of behaviors in the community. Problems have to be dealt with; and the police are visible, have the training and right to invoke the legal system, and are easily contacted.

The balance of this chapter explores the law enforcement, order maintenance, and service roles of the police in more detail. Under each of these roles, the police may take a variety of actions in pursuit of solutions or successful conclusions to problems or situations. There are a wide range of techniques and studies that have been proposed, implemented, and undertaken that will illustrate the diversity in police responsibilities.

Critical Thinking Exercise

Given the levels of crime in society and the fact that many people are fearful of crime and victimization on a daily basis, it is not surprising that many communities lament the shortage of police officers and call for departments to hire more officers to protect them. It could be argued that officers could spend more time dealing with crime and offenders if they were not so busy with order maintenance and service functions. Should police continue handling order maintenance and service activities? Why or why not? If they do not handle those types of calls, who should take over for the police? How would this be funded? What problems or implications, if any, would arise if the police were no longer involved?

ENFORCEMENT OF THE CRIMINAL LAW

"Enforcing the law" by apprehending criminals after crimes occur is an important part of police work and the focus of most discussions of policing. As noted earlier, the image of the police is one that involves hunting criminals, thwarting robberies in progress, engaging in high-speed car chases, making dynamic entries, and apprehending desperate criminals. The public and the media typically think of police work as involving tense confrontations, takedown moves, and the use of an enticing array of high-tech weaponry and science. While these are evident in policing, by far the more common tools used by the police are patience, good communication skills, and knowledge of human psychology. Similarly, the public's willingness to cooperate with the police plays a large part in the police's ability to enforce the law by bringing criminals to justice (Black 1981; Mastrofski, Snipes, and Supina 1996). Not all interactions between the police and the public end with an arrest. This is true even when considering instances in which a crime has been committed and there is a victim/complainant involved.

When looking at the law enforcement functions of the police, some important elements are patrol, investigation, and arrest. At the same time, there are law enforcement activities that rely on more informal responses that do not lead to arrest and invoking criminal justice system processing. A bridge across all of these activities is the crime prevention and crime control. The underlying idea of law enforcement is ensuring the safety of the community by denying criminals the opportunity to commit crime and by defusing volatile situations before they reach the point of violence (Lab 2019).

Patrol

Police patrol is the most visible aspect of policing. Patrolling the community has been a staple of police work since before the establishment of formal police organizations and the Metropolitan Police. Early **watch and ward** (the watch system discussed in Chapter 2) required able-bodied men to keep watch over the community at night. These individuals would typically walk the community looking for problems. If they saw any, they were to raise the alarm. Patrol has been done on foot, on horseback, on bicycles, or in motor vehicles throughout the history of policing. This visible patrol is seen as a means of preventing crime by **deterrence**. The assumption is that potential offenders will be deterred from committing crimes due to presence of police patrolling the community. Active patrol raises the possibility that a criminal will be seen and apprehended. The impression that the police are always around and ever vigilant discourages criminals from committing crime: That is the essence of police deterrence. Often, the presence of authority, backed up by powers of arrest, will scatter potential troublemakers or quiet boisterous behavior.

There is an implicit belief that routine patrol enhances the ability of the police to observe crimes and criminal activity as it is taking place, thus allowing the police to intervene. In reality, patrol is a largely **reactive**. Most of the time the police on patrol are alerted to problems by the public, usually through calls to the department that are dispatched over the radio to a specific address. The police rarely see criminal acts in progress on their own. They mainly react to citizens' calls for assistance.

Patrol officers are the primary public face of the police department offering a range of services. They are the visible presence of the police throughout the community on a daily basis and the first to respond to crimes and calls for assistance on a wide array of issues and concerns. While they have the power to make arrests and invoke the criminal code, they also deal with order maintenance and service functions/requests. The patrol officer's workload is dictated by service calls from dispatch and direct requests from citizens over the course of the patrol.

The visible and ubiquitous nature of patrol suggests that it is an effective means for addressing problems in society. This assumption has been examined through several analyses looking at different facets or aspects of patrol. Three key topics that have been considered are the deterrent impact of patrol, the impact of response time, and the effectiveness of foot patrol.

The Kansas City Preventive Patrol Experiment

The deterrent potential of patrol was examined in one of the most well-known studies—the **Kansas City Preventive Patrol Experiment**. This study focused on the impact of routine patrol on levels of crime, arrests, citizen fear, service delivery, traffic accidents, and response time (Kelling et al. 1974). The experiment divided 15 patrol beats into three groups: proactive, reactive, and control. The proactive beats had two to three times more patrol than normal. The reactive beats had all patrol withdrawn from the area and patrol responded only to calls for assistance. The control beats had normal levels of patrol.

The project lasted a year, and the change in police patrol presence was assessed by comparing data from before the changes to data from the time of the change. The results showed that the level of patrol had no appreciable impact on crime, arrests, fear, or other outcomes. The beats with proactive patrol did not experience reduced crime, greater arrests, reduced fear, or other positive changes when compared to either the reactive or control beat conditions. The experiment did not reveal the expected deterrent impact or potential of police patrol. These results suggest that in terms of deterring or preventing crime, police patrol is not effective.

Some important caveats should be noted. The experiment did not have a zero-patrol condition. Every area received police coverage. The police continued to respond to calls for assistance, thus providing police presence in all areas. Specialized police units were not included in the project and were present and active in the beats without normal patrol (Larson 1975). Reactive beats also saw officers acting in a more proactive fashion than normal. It is also important to note that patrol is not ubiquitous even in areas with extra patrol (Larson 1975). The project demonstrates that enhanced patrol (the proactive beats) is not equivalent to better policing. Mere presence through random patrol does not have an impact over and above police availability.

Police Response Time

A common view of police patrol is that the speed at which they can respond to a call for service or a crime (i.e., the **response time**) is crucial for combatting and solving crime. It would be important, therefore, for the police to be spread throughout the community so they can get to the location of a crime as quickly as possible. Analyses of rapid response times have shown that police response speed has little impact on the police's ability to deal with the situations or to catch the offender (see, for example, Cordner et al. 1983; Spelman and Brown 1981; van Kirk 1978). This is primarily due to circumstances beyond the control of the police and their ability to get to the scene in a timely fashion.

These circumstances involve things that happen before the police are even alerted. First, many crimes (such as burglaries and thefts) are discovered hours or days after the actual crime, making the police response speed meaningless. Second, citizens often delay calling the police, possibly due to shock, not knowing exactly what to do, or an uncertainty about whether to call. A citizen's delay negates any impact of police speed. Interestingly, Spelman and Brown (1981) note that most citizens value knowing when the police will arrive over the actual speed of their response. Finally, when the offense is a personal crime in which the victim and offender are both present and aware of what is taking place, it is highly unlikely that the offender will stay around once they know the victim or a witness has called the police. The offender will most likely be gone, even if the police can be there in one or two minutes.

To say that response time is not at all important would be going too far, however. The evidence suggests that solving crimes is not a function of immediate, rapid response to the scene of a crime. Indeed, the most common factor in solving any crime is having a victim or witness who can identify the offender for the police to find and arrest. Rapid response time is more important in accidents or other situations in which an individual is in need of medical or other emergency aid. While the police may not have the training needed to fully address the situation, they are typically called and arrive at situations prior to other responders. Rapid response, therefore, is important in the police service role.

Foot Patrol

Criticism of the police over their apparent failure to stem the crime problem in the 1970s led to new strategies for police operations. One of the early movements was to reintroduce a very old approach to policing—namely, foot patrol. Foot patrol had almost disappeared in the mid-20th century with the advent of automobiles and the assumed need for rapid response. An important loss in the move to motorized patrol was the close, fact-to-face interaction between everyday citizens and police officers. The only time citizens would see the police out of their vehicles would be when the police were called to deal with a crime or were enforcing traffic laws, and that contact would almost always have a confrontational component. The movement to community-oriented policing was meant to build relationships between the police and the public. Foot patrol was considered a key aspect of building those relationships.

Foot patrols received a great deal of attention. A primary concern was the effectiveness of these patrols on curbing crime and enhancing police–citizen interactions. Two major analyses of foot patrol were undertaken in Flint, Michigan, and Newark, New Jersey. The Flint evaluation showed roughly a 9 percent drop in overall crime in the foot patrol areas when compared to the overall city crime rate (Trojanowicz 1983), but there was no impact on burglary, larceny, or nighttime crime. When considering other potential outcomes, foot patrol appeared to have a major impact. Citizens in foot patrol areas reported feeling safer (49 percent) and believed crime had fallen (48 percent), and 70 percent attributed the changes to the foot patrol in the area (Trojanowicz 1983). An evaluation of the Newark foot patrol did not find any reductions in crime, although the residents reported feeling safer and believed the crime problem was getting better (Police Foundation 1981).

Other studies have also reported similar mixed results or no impact from foot patrol. Esbensen (1987) found reductions in some crimes, such as prostitution and public drunkenness, but no impact on any Part I Index crimes (murder, rape, robbery, aggravated assault, burglary, larceny, motor vehicle theft, and arson). He also noted mixed attitudes toward the police. Similarly, Bowers and Hirsch (1987), in an analysis of foot patrol in Boston, and Epstein (1978), in a study in Winnipeg, Manitoba, found no impact on crime. Bowers and Hirsch (1987) also found no change in citizens reporting of crime to the police. Alternatively, Brown and Wycoff (1987) found lower levels of fear and greater feelings that crime was going down. This last study focused on "citizen contact patrol" in which officers actively stopped and met with residents in their areas. The positive perceptions may be due to the extra emphasis on citizen contact (Brown and Wycoff 1987).

These results on foot patrol offer some support to the concept of promoting more direct, non-crime-related contact between the police on patrol and the citizenry. While the results do not show any major impact on crime levels in foot patrol areas, they do suggest that the efforts can build more rapport and interaction between the two parties. This interaction has the further potential of aiding community-oriented policing initiatives and breaking down any perceived barriers between the police and the public.

Summary

Patrol has been an essential component of policing since the establishment of modern policing. Officers on patrol are the recognizable face of policing for the general public and respond to a wide array of requests that come through either direct contact with individuals or as dispatched calls for service. The fact that research on patrol does not show great impacts on crime rates does not mean that patrol is inessential to the overall mission of the police. Nor does it suggest that the police are inessential. Patrol participates in activities that relate to prevention initiatives, order maintenance, and service.

Investigation

A second major law enforcement function of policing, **investigation**, involves police officers (generally detectives) who specialize in addressing criminal events that require more attention in order to identify the offender and/or gather the evidence needed for prosecution. Most investigations take place after a patrol officer has responded to a call that does not end in an arrest and makes a report that indicates more attention is needed. Investigations may also take place in the absence of an initial call for service or crime. In these cases the police, or other source, identifies a potential problem or issue that involves possible criminal activity and needs to be looked at.

Effectiveness of Investigation

Detectives and investigations receive a great deal of attention in the media, leading to the assumption that investigating crime is an effective means of solving crimes and arresting offenders. Indeed, the many fictional police/crimes shows on daily television almost all focus on the investigative function and they almost always portray a positive outcome from the investigation. The same can be seen in reality crime shows, particularly those that focus on unsolved cases where good detective work is able to unravel what really happened and bring the fugitive to justice. The reality, however, often differs from the media presentations.

The effectiveness of investigation has been the subject of several studies. The RAND Corporation, under a grant from the Department of Justice, conducted one of the earliest evaluations of investigation. Greenwood and Petersilia (1975) surveyed 153 police departments in jurisdictions with a population of 100,000 or more and observed operations of 25 investigations units to assess the impact of investigations on crime rates, arrest rates, and clearance rates, as well as the operations of the units. Their findings indicated that the impact of the investigation units was minimal. Most serious crimes received only superficial attention and work by investigations (Greenwood and Petersilia 1975). Most of the information used in solving crimes came from the crime victims and was given to the initial patrol officers, with the victim identifying the offender in three-quarters of the cases. Greenwood and Petersilia (1975) also reported that most investigative time was spent reading prior reports and files and trying to find victims and witnesses. Relatively little time was spent on identifying the perpetrator. One of the study's recommendations was that departments could significantly reduce the number of detectives without having an appreciable impact on clearance rates.

The results from the RAND analysis were largely duplicated in a study of investigations in one medium-sized city. Willman and Snortum (1984) altered their focus from that of the RAND study, specifically from looking at only cleared crimes to all reported crimes. The authors report that investigations solve only a small percentage of all crimes. Most crimes are solved when a victim or witness at the crime scene tells the responding police officer. Investigators spend the majority of their time preparing the case and the files for processing, rather than identifying the offender and making the initial arrest (Willman and Snortum 1984).

The results of the RAND and Willman and Snortum studies, and other similar analyses, have formed the basis for calls to reduce the use of investigation units in policing. Some have argued that since most clearances are the result of information gathered by the initial responding officer, the investigation function could be incorporated with patrol by allowing the initial respondent to follow through with any further investigation or preparation of the case for further processing. Despite

Web Activity

Greenwood and Petersilia's (1975) study offers a wealth of information on investigation and its impact on crime, arrests, and clearance rates as well as the policy implications of the research. You can read the summary report at https://www.rand.org/pubs/reports/R1776.html.

the results and the possible policy implications, there has been relatively little change in the basic responsibilities and functioning of investigation units since 1980.

Focused/Proactive Investigation

Investigation is not always a reaction to events first addressed by patrol officers called to the crime scene. Many investigations focus on specific problems and take a more **proactive approach** to dealing with crime and potential crime in the community. In larger police departments, investigation falls into units that target specific problems and behaviors. Examples of these include gang units, vice (drugs, alcohol, prostitution, and/or sex offenses), domestic violence, and enterprise crimes (business crimes, organized crimes, etc.). These types of investigations often require the detectives to find ways to uncover and/or infiltrate the crimes and groups committing the crimes as a means of gathering evidence, building cases, and making arrests. These efforts can be very simple or very complex.

One type of focused/proactive investigative activity is a sting operation. Newman (2007) defines a **sting operation** as one in which there are several key elements:

- an opportunity or enticement to commit a crime, either created or exploited by police;
- a targeted likely offender or group of offenders for a particular crime type;
- an undercover or hidden police officer or surrogate, or some form of deception; and
- a gotcha climax when the operation ends with arrests.

In essence, investigators set up an opportunity for offenders to do what they would normally do—only, unwittingly, with law enforcement officers. Good examples of stings would be fencing operations, sales of alcohol to minors, and street prostitution sweeps.

Sting operations typically involve a decoy to lure offenders to take action thinking it is a normal, non-sting situation. Fencing operations typically involve the police setting up a store or pawn shop that will buy stolen goods. Burglars, robbers, and other offenders will bring in materials they have stolen in order to secure cash for the goods. Investigators will record and document the transactions and the property they recover for use in prosecutions and eventually arrest the offenders. To combat the sale of alcohol to minors, an underage decoy working with investigators will enter a bar or store to buy alcohol (often with fake identification). If the decoy is successful at securing alcohol, the business owner and/or person selling the alcohol will be arrested or receive a citation for the offense. The final example of a prostitution sting involves officers posing as either prostitutes (when they are targeting those who solicit sex) or customers/"Johns" (when they are targeting the prostitutes).

Another focused/proactive investigation approach involves undercover work. This approach has been used successfully in drug investigations. In this scenario, investigators will try to infiltrate the drug supply chain at various points in the process. This could mean that an investigator joins the drug operation as a member of the group distributing the drugs (either helping with manufacturing, importing, or selling the drugs) or as a purchaser of the drugs (typically as a repeat buyer) or in other ways. In any of these situations, the officer has to build close ties with the offenders and become accepted by them. This invariably has an element of danger associated with the work.

A variation on undercover investigations (drug or other offenses) involves the use of confidential informants. These individuals are not police officers, but they work with investigators to infiltrate the criminal operation. Informants can offer a range of information and services to investigators, such as the time and place of an offense, offender and witness names and locations, or evidence that can be used in investigations. Informants may also work undercover buying illegal goods and services on behalf of the police. This situation often includes a strong undercover surveillance operation in which the investigators can record and document multiple events in order to show that the criminal behavior is part of the offender's normal activity. These types of investigations can be both dangerous and require payments (either in terms of cash or promises of leniency) to the informants. These arrangements typically require approval and detailed documentation of every action undertaken by the informant on behalf of the investigation.

While focused and proactive investigations are common, they are not without controversy. One major concern often raised in relation to these efforts, and one that emerges in many legal proceedings based on them, is the issue of entrapment. **Entrapment** is the idea that the police enticed or induced an individual to act in a way that they would not normally act. For example, a person arrested for buying drugs could claim that they normally would not buy drugs and only did so in this event because of the pressure applied by the undercover police officer. If that is indeed what happened, entrapment becomes a legal defense to the action. On the other hand, if a person who has a history of buying and selling illicit drugs is arrested for buying drugs in an undercover sting, it will be difficult, if not impossible, to successfully claim entrapment. This is because the person normally does this behavior. The fact that it is the individual's normal behavior or activity negates a claim of entrapment.

Web Activity

The intricacies of sting and undercover operations can be examined in more detail in the *Sting Operations* response guide available at the Center for Problem Oriented Policing at https://popcenter.asu.edu/content/sting-operations-0.

Investigative Tools

Investigators have a wide array of tools and technology to aid in both proactive and reactive cases. Modern scientific advances have opened the door to more timely evidence collection and the testing of evidence gathered at the crime scenes (and after). Among these tools are surveillance methods, fingerprint and trace evidence collection and analysis, DNA analysis, and drug testing. These tools have enabled the police to improve their ability to uncover criminal events and to enforce the law.

Surveillance. One investigative tool that has a long history in investigations and policing is **surveillance**. The basic premise of patrol is to put eyes on the street in order to see what is taking place. Many media presentations in the past included scenes of police officers sitting in patrol cars or in a building "staking out" a person or location to gather information and evidence. The use of still cameras or movie/video cameras were used to capture images of what took place. This could also include audio recordings of the target subjects. Today, the police rely on closed-circuit television (CCTV) emplacements to do the same thing, and often to simply capture any behavior taking place in an area.

CCTV technology has grown from simple static cameras connected to devoted monitors to entire system that can include remote-controlled pan-and-tilt cameras, digital recordings, computer-aided object recognition, crowd analysis, facial recognition, and tracking of individuals (Davis and Velastin 2005). The number of CCTV cameras installed and used just by law enforcement is not known, although it is common in most larger cities for the police to employ extensive monitors and devices to record images. Based on 2014 data, there were 125 cameras for every 1,000 people in the United States (Statista 2018). At the end of 2016 there was an estimated 62 million cameras in use in the United States (SSI 2016). Manhattan (New York) alone has over 20,000 cameras, and Chicago has over 32,000 cameras (Draper 2018). Many of these are used by private companies and individuals, but the data demonstrate the ubiquitous use of surveillance equipment in the country.

The great growth of surveillance, particularly using CCTV and related technology, suggests it is an effective tool for law enforcement. Interestingly, there is an absence of evidence on its impact in policing and investigations. Most claims for its effectiveness are based on anecdotal evidence from successful investigations and prosecutions. Actual studies of the impact of surveillance typically look at CCTV and focus on changes in crime instead of on just investigation. The evidence shows that CCTV can impact crime, although the impact is not universal and the conditions for when it succeeds are not clear (Welsh and Farrington 2009). CCTV holds some promise as a tool for gathering evidence.

Fingerprints and Trace Evidence. The value of fingerprints in investigations has long been assumed by the general public. Fingerprints can be considered one type of trace evidence. **Trace evidence** is defined as materials that are left behind or could be transferred from the offender to the victim (or location) during the commission of a crime. Common types of trace evidence are hair, fibers, soil, fluids, and glass. Investigators will collect the various forms of trace evidence based on the type of crime and what they see as potentially important at each crime scene. In many cases the evidence will actually be collected by investigators with special training or by crime scene technicians who are called to the scene by investigators. The potential evidence is then transferred to a forensic crime laboratory for identification and analysis.

More than any other thing, victims typically expect the police to collect fingerprints to help identify the offenders. In the past, the inspection of collected prints involved actual visual examination by investigators making comparison to fingerprints collected by local law enforcement agencies. The development of the **Automated Fingerprint Identification System (AFIS)** in the 1970s greatly improved law enforcement's ability to search and compare fingerprints. The system identifies potential fingerprint matches warranting a visual inspection by a fingerprint examiner. Because most AFIS systems were localized and accessed only fingerprints on record at local agencies, the FBI established the **Integrated Automated Fingerprint Identification System (IAFIS)** in 1999. This system is a computerized, national storage system for fingerprints and other related information, such as photographs of individuals, name, and birthdate. While the electronic match of fingerprints has improved under IAFIS, a human examiner must still make a final determination of a match. It is also important to note that fingerprints and most trace evidence are useful primarily as a **confirmatory tool** (yielding evidence to confirm that a known suspect is the actual person) as opposed to one that makes an initial identification.

DNA. Deoxyribonucleic acid, or DNA, is a form of trace evidence that has perhaps received that most attention in recent years. This evidence entails the ability to compare human cells found at a crime scene to either an individual suspect or to a database of DNA evidence. Since no two individuals (except identical twins) have identical DNA, its use is desirable in all cases where it is available.

The FBI administers the **Combined DNA Index System (CODIS)**, which contains DNA profiles from individuals and cases that have been collected by jurisdictions and agencies across the country. All states participate in CODIS and share data with the FBI system. The DNA database currently has almost 14 million offender profiles, and CODIS has provided assistance in over 440,000 cases (FBI 2019). Every state determines which arrestees, if any, are required to submit DNA samples for inclusion in databases for future search. Felonies are the most common crimes that require the collection of DNA profiles, although some misdemeanor offenses trigger collection in some states.

While DNA evidence is considered a prime investigative tool, its collection and analysis must conform to strict scientific standards and training. The typical detective does not have the necessary training and skills for DNA analysis. The investigator's role is limited mainly to collection of evidence that may have DNA materials attached. Those items are submitted to a forensic laboratory for testing. The forensic scientists will conduct the analyses and produce a report for the investigator.

Drug Testing. Drug enforcement is a major concern for law enforcement, and it is common for even moderate police departments to have a drug investigation unit. As with other investigatory functions, drug investigations have benefited from new tools. The identification of illicit substances is particularly problematic in the field. Most substances require laboratory testing in order to correctly identify the substance and to proceed with an arrest and prosecution. This is particularly true in a time of constantly changing chemical compounds and the introduction of designer drugs.

One useful investigative tool is a field drug testing kit. The kit enables one to conduct a **presumptive drug test**, which simply establishes the presence or absence of different drugs. These tests do not provide information on the exact nature of the drug or the quality/concentration of the drug. The officers and investigators in the field can act based on the presumptive test. The drug will undergo a **confirmatory test** in a laboratory, which will supply more detailed information on the substance/drug.

A second tool used in drug investigations, and one that receives a great deal of attention in the media, is drug dogs. These dogs are more formally known as **drug detection K-9s** or sniffer dogs. Drug detection dogs use their keen sense of smell to search for drugs. (Sniffer dogs are also used for explosives, cadavers, blood, and many other items.) Dogs are used to find drugs in many situations, such as traffic stops (especially on interstate highways that are known drug routes), and at border crossings, post offices, schools, and suspected drug sales locations. The US Supreme Court in *Florida v. Harris* (2013) ruled that a certified drug dog that alerts to a drug is sufficient to establish probable cause for a full search. This ruling and the use of drug dogs allows for more thorough investigation and expedites investigative searches.

Crime Analysis

Crime analysis has become a key component of modern law enforcement. **Crime analysis** involves the gathering of different types of crime data, problems in the community, information about the community, and other information to provide insight on the commission of crime and disorder and to identify crime patterns and possible responses. Crime analysis is at the core of **intelligence-led policing (ILP)**. ILP relies on real-time (i.e., immediate or temporally proximate) analysis of data and identification of responses. This does not mean that all responses will be implemented immediately. Some analyses will suggest long-term interventions and responses that will require logistical changes that may take some time. The key in crime analysis is to recognize that the investigation of problems and the identification of responses is an ongoing process.

Crime analysis and ILP are not the sole purview of investigators. Indeed, many police departments have established units devoted to crime analysis, and many of the people working in these units may not be sworn police officers. In many cases, departments will hire individuals solely as crime analysts. At the same time, it is common for these units to rely on current and former investigators because of their expertise and experience.

Crime analysis typically relies on a range of different tools. Perhaps the key tool is the use of crime mapping. The mapping of when and where crimes occur

---

Web Activity

Many police departments make their crime data available to the public in a form the allows people to explore it in some detail. Whereas in the past, communities would run their own mapping sites, most police departments today use a third-party service to house and make their crime data available to the public. Two of these are Crime Reports, at https://www.crimereports.com/; and LexisNexis Community Crime Map, at https://communitycrimemap.com/. Investigate these sites and create your own maps for your city or other cities of interest to you.

---

is not a new idea but came to prominence in the 1990s with the introduction of CompStat in New York City (NYC). **CompStat**, short for "compare statistics," and was instituted by the NYC Police Department as a process that uses current crime data to analyze crime patterns and quickly allocate patrol resources to address new and emergent problems. In New York City, the CompStat process developed maps on crime, calls for service, police activity, and a range of other things on at least a weekly basis at the precinct level (as well as aggregated to larger geographic levels). This information is used to inform responses and policy for addressing problems. The simplification of crime mapping programs and techniques has resulted in its spread to police departments across the United States and in other countries.

It is important to note that crime analysis is not all about the creation of maps. Beyond identifying spatial and temporal crime patterns (largely a mapping function), crime analysis seeks to identify the **modus operandi** (i.e., the way that something is done), understand the behavior, assess police resource needs, and evaluate interventions. These functions may be aided by crime mapping, but they require crime analysts to be open to new ideas and to be inquisitive and creative when approaching problems.

Changing Role and Strategies

Law enforcement remains a key role for policing, but both the public expectations and the complexities of modern society have brought about shifts in how the police respond to crime and community demands. The shifts in law enforcement are directly related to the changing nature of crime, society, and emerging methods for combatting problems. Changes in crime since the 1970s include the great growth in the number of crimes, the seemingly endless drug war and the changing nature of drugs, the movement toward online/internet crimes, and the growth of international crimes and terrorism. Societal changes include the growing diversity of the population, the widening gap between the socioeconomic classes, the outward spread of cities, the abandonment of the inner cities, and the shift from a manufacturing to a service economy. At the same time, police have new tools to use in fighting crime and societal problems, such as emerging forensic and digital techniques. These lists of changes are a small sample of those that could be considered.

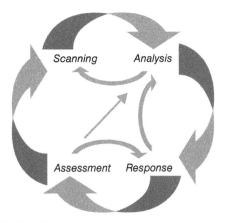

Figure 3.1 SARA and Its Feedback Loops
SOURCE: R. V. Clarke and J. E. Eck (2005). *Crime Analysis for Problem Solvers in 60 Small Steps.* Washington, DC: Office of Community Oriented Policing Services.

Two major strategies adopted by police departments to address the changing landscape of what they face and concerns over their ability to handle the problems alone are **problem-oriented policing (POP)** and **community-oriented policing (COP)**. While these are not identical approaches, they share some major similarities. First, and foremost, both POP and COP rely on in-depth analysis of crimes and factors that may contribute to crime and that lead to evidence-based interventions for dealing with crime and underlying factors. Crime analysis is a critical component of these approaches. One major analysis tool used by POP and COP is Eck and Spelman's (1987) **SARA** (scanning, analysis, response, and assessment) approach. In simple terms, using SARA requires police to identify the problem to be addressed, analyze data on the problem to uncover contributing and/or causal factors, pick out and employ a response that has the potential to deal with the problem, and evaluate/assess the impact of the response (see Figure 3.1 for a visual representation of SARA and its feedback loops).

Second, both approaches target specific crime problems that typically can be identified by a place, time, modus operandi, or other information that provides a basis for analysis. In essence, POP and COP deal with smaller, identifiable components of the crime problem rather than try to tackle all crime in the community at the same time through a one-size-fits-all approach. These approaches recognize the diversity in crimes, offenders, times, locations, and other factors that are potentially unique to smaller parts of the global crime problem.

A third common factor in POP and COP is the central role of the police. The police are critical to the process—from providing essential data to finding potential solutions to implementing responses. It is important to note that the responses to the crime problem may include other agencies and groups outside of the police. The determination of participants rests on the outcome of the SARA (or similar) process. No matter what agency takes the lead in the response, the police are important contributors to the entire process.

There are some identifiable differences between POP and COP. The major difference is mostly one of emphasis. POP tends to emphasize more mainline police responses and the centrality of the police in interventions, and to focus on crime to the exclusion of other factors. A good example of a POP problem and response would be addressing crime hotspots. The recognition of crime clustering in place and time has led to **hotspot policing**. Hotspots of crime often suggest the need for targeted police patrol and enforcement. In COP, the emphasis is on a more collaborative effort between the police and the community with a recognition that the police may need to take a secondary role to other agencies, depending on the problem. A key to COP is community empowerment through close police–citizen interaction. The police may or may not be central to responses.

An example of a POP approach is Boston's **Operation Ceasefire**, which targeted gun crime and youth homicides (Kennedy et al. 2001). Begun in 1996, the project featured the creation of an interagency working group consisting of the police, probation, parole, and district attorney's office. The program developed a plan aimed primarily at gangs and gang members that implemented a strict enforcement policy for all individuals and groups involved directly or indirectly in gun violence. Dubbed "**pulling levers**," the project would take any and all actions possible against violators. That meant that any gun violence would result in the immediate arrest and full prosecution of violators. Probation and parole violators were vigorously prosecuted for any violation of the conditions of their release. Social service and federal agencies (such as Immigration and Naturalization, which was used to deport noncitizen offenders) were also included in the project.

Evaluations of Operation Ceasefire in Boston and replications in other cities show overwhelmingly positive results. Braga et al. (2001) report a 63 percent drop in monthly juvenile homicides after initiation of the project. Similarly, calls to the police about shots being fired decreased by 32 percent, and there was a corresponding drop of 25 percent in assaults with guns (Braga et al. 2001). In Los Angeles, Tita et al. (2005) note that violent crime fell as a result of the enforcement tactics, while a small change was found in gun and gang crime. Corsaro and McGarrell (2009, 2010) and McGarrell et al. (2006), reporting on implementation in Indianapolis, claim significant reductions in homicides, gang-related homicides, and homicides among 15- to 24-year-olds. Throughout these projects, the police were a leading component of the planning and implementation. The results show that this "pulling levers" approach can be effective.

An example of a major COP program is the **Chicago Alternative Police Strategy (CAPS)**. CAPS is perhaps the best example of successfully implementing a community-oriented policing approach. Chicago moved its entire police force into community policing beginning in 1993 (Hartnett and Skogan 1999). Key aspects of the program included assigning officers to permanent neighborhood beats, involving residents in the identification of problems and potential solutions, and relying on other agencies (both public and private) to address identified issues. Citizen interaction is the cornerstone of the program, and the police met with neighborhood residents to engender meaningful interaction and identify local problems (including gangs, drugs, graffiti, burglary, and physical and social disorder) (Skogan and Hartnett 1997).

As expected under community policing, CAPS responses varied from neighborhood to neighborhood. Improved police enforcement appeared throughout the project and often focused on drug problems. Efforts to clean up problem locations and generally improve the physical conditions of neighborhoods epresented major initiatives in the program. Mobilizing residents to provide surveillance, work with one another, call the police, and take other actions also appeared throughout the project (Skogan and Hartnett 1997). These actions successfully reduced the signs of physical decay, impacted the extent of visible gang and drug activity, reduced area crime rates, and improved resident's attitudes and assessments of the police and the city (Skogan and Hartnett 1997). The success of CAPS shows that COP can be effective. Most COP programs are not as wide-ranging as that in Chicago.

POP and COP are just two examples of the changing roles and approaches in policing for enforcing the law. Programs like Operation Ceasefire and CAPS have received a great deal of attention and have led other communities to try to replicate the ideas and approaches. At the same time, there are numerous new and emerging police programs and approaches appearing in communities around the world. Most of the innovative changes in policing do not receive widespread attention and go unheralded.

Law Enforcement Deferred

Not all crimes to which the police respond end in an arrest and formal criminal justice system processing. The police hold a great deal of discretion over when to make an arrest. The decision will depend on the offense under question, facts of the case, public opinion about the type of crime, police resources, departmental policies, and many other things. The decision not to arrest does not necessarily mean that the offender is simply released. Release is one possibility among many. It is also possible that officers will issue a summons to appear in court. Police may also refer the offense and the offender to some alternative intervention or program.

Police work with youthful offenders is a good example of law enforcement deferred. Many youthful offenses—such as smoking, drinking, being out after curfew, and truancy—are against the law only for minors. While the police can intervene in such matters, there is a tendency to ignore the acts unless someone calls on them to do something. In many instances, the police will simply talk to the youth or take him or her home to parents or guardian. The youth will not be taken into custody (the juvenile equivalent to an arrest) and processed through the system. The time and effort needed to formally process a youth is considered too much for something that is really not "criminal" and will probably result in little or no punishment. Police do not want to waste time on these types of problems when there is "real" crime taking place that needs to be addressed.

The decision to either arrest or release an offender is not the only option available to police. New strategies also include informal (or semiformal) interventions and programs run by or involving the police. One good example of this is the use of family group conferencing with youthful offenders. **Family Group Conferencing (FGC)** is a form of restorative justice that brings together the offender, family members, close friends, and other support groups of the victim and offender with a facilitator to discuss the problematic behavior and to reach an agreement on how to resolve the problems. In many cases, FGC include criminal justice system personnel, including police officers (Van Ness and Strong 2015). FGC came to prominence in 1989 when New Zealand, responding to the increasing number of Maori youths being handled in the formal justice system, removed all youths ages 14–17 (with only a few exceptions for very serious offenders) from formal court processing and mandated that they be diverted to family group conferencing (Kurki 2000). Conferences can be held either pretrial or post-trial and have become a part of police and pretrial diversion programs in many countries (McGarrell et al. 2000; Moore and O'Connell 1994). McGarrell and Hipple (2007) report on the Indianapolis Police Department's adoption of FGC in lieu of regular court intervention for dealing with first-time offenders. Similar programs have been established in other communities.

The idea of police involvement in FGC and restorative justice is not new or restricted to use with juveniles. Nicholl (1999) offers a guidebook to incorporating restorative justice into COP. The approach emphasizes police involvement in addressing problems outside of formal arrest and system processing. This does not preclude arrest and formal action by the system, although formal processes should not be the first result. Referring individuals to alternative interventions is commonly done in accord with both formal department policies and individual discretion.

ORDER MAINTENANCE

Crime is not the only thing in modern life that can cause concern. All sorts of conflicts can create alarm, concern, fear, or inconvenience. Loud and boisterous groups of teenagers; heated, chest-thumping bar arguments; and noisy arguments over finances between spouses in the next apartment all disturb the peace and tranquility of neighbors. Those who call for police interventions do not necessarily expect the officers to make arrests, as long as they restore order. Though arrests are possible, most incidents are resolved through other means: mediation, referral, or the mere threat of arrest. In some cases, such as a dispute between a landlord and tenant over the rent payment, the police may have no legal authority in the matter (rent disputes are a matter of civil law), but they may serve as referees. Their presence and authority act as a safety valve: Both parties can back down without losing face.

One theoretical basis for maintaining order is **broken windows theory**, which argues that signs of disorder and decline in an area will inevitably lead to crime and further decline, and failure to address the signs will result in increased crime and delinquency (Wilson and Kelling 1982). In essence, signs of disorder actively *promote* criminal activity. The reason for this is that signs of disorder signal that an area or location is not protected and is open to criminal behavior.

Signs of disorder can be both physical and social (Hunter 1978; Skogan 1990; Taylor and Gottfredson 1986; Wilson and Kelling 1982). Signs of physical disorder include broken windows, abandoned buildings, vacant lots, deteriorating buildings, litter, vandalism, and graffiti. Social indicators of disorder include loitering juveniles, public drunkenness, gangs, drug sales and use, harassment (such as begging and panhandling), prostitution, homeless individuals, and a lack of interaction among people on the street. These domains of disorder are not independent. Perkins and Taylor (1996), Taylor et al. (1995), and Spelman (1993) suggest that physical disorder contributes to the growth of social disorder by inhibiting social interaction among residents, thus allowing social disorder to thrive.

A term commonly used in relation to broken windows arguments is incivility. **Incivility** in a neighborhood has been proposed as evidence that the residents are not concerned, or at least are less concerned, about what is happening around them than people in areas not characterized by incivility (Lewis and Salem 1986). Signs of disorder may lead residents to withdraw into their homes and abandon cooperative efforts at improving the neighborhood (Skogan 1990; Taylor 1988). This would leave the neighborhood open to potential offenders. For offenders, signs of incivility are indicative of lower risk (Taylor and Gottfredson 1986). Efforts to minimize disorder and incivility are key to controlling crime and problem behavior.

Police respond to a wide array of calls that seek help with signs of physical and social disorder and incivility. Disputes between citizens, public drunkenness, disturbing the peace, prostitution, gangs in the neighborhood, and similar calls for assistance hold the potential for an arrest or criminal citation, and often that is the expectation of the complainant. Police are also called about abandoned cars, trash dumped in the neighborhood, broken glass in the street, graffiti, and other physical signs of disorder. Most of the time there is no clear crime and no known offender. The police cannot make an arrest in most of these cases, even if they were disposed to doing so. Instead of invoking the criminal law, officers will respond in different ways. In disputes, they may attempt to mediate between the parties or refer them to other sources for assistance. In the case of physical signs of disorder, the police can make note of the problem and pass it on to another agency or provide the complainant with contact information for other agencies and sources of assistance. Two examples in which police have been proactively involved in order maintenance are neighborhood crime prevention and domestic violence cases.

Neighborhood Crime Prevention

The fact that the police are called on to address incivility, disorder, and order maintenance issues in neighborhoods has prompted police departments to take a more proactive approach to the problems rather than simply reacting to calls for assistance. Police are often active in addressing signs of physical and social disorder and any subsequent criminal behavior through their participation in neighborhood crime prevention programs. These programs take a variety of forms and focus on different issues, depending on the needs and problems in the neighborhood (see Lab 2019). Typical activities include neighborhood watch, surveillance, improvement of lighting, graffiti eradication, vacant lot cleanup, general improvement of residences and property, and neighborhood meetings. All of these measures address some component of disorder and incivility. Perhaps the one constant in almost all neighborhood crime prevention initiatives is police participation. Indeed, most programs are established by or with the aid of the police, they receive police funding and support, and many are led by the police.

Police foster crime prevention in many ways. Officers help organize and support community-based self-help activities, like **Neighborhood Watch**, to observe and report suspicious activity in the neighborhood (Garofalo and McLeod 1989; Rosenbaum 1987). Police involvement in community organizing may encompass arranging supplemental **citizen patrols** to give advice on initiating court action against landlords of properties where drug sales take place. A wide range of anti-crime activities take place at the block level, and the police can be both a catalyst and a resource for citizen patrols, **property marking** projects, **safe havens** for children, block watch groups, and block parties to engender neighborhood interaction.

Addressing Domestic Violence

Another example of the police taking a more proactive stance with an order maintenance function involves police response to domestic violence. The decision on whether to make an arrest in a domestic violence situation has long been debated. Police discretion on how to address calls involving domestic violence has long been a matter of debate (see Chapter 7 for more discussion of police discretion and consider the Chapter 1 discussion of policing as multivariate). Many individuals, including police officers, have viewed disputes between spouses as a private matter and tried to avoid making arrests. Victim advocates, however, have long argued that the police need to take a more proactive role in dealing with domestic violence situations. They have called for the authorities arrest offenders, rather than resorting to non-arrest alternatives, based on the assumption that arrest will curb future acts of domestic violence.

In order to test this assumption, the **Minneapolis Domestic Violence Experiment** examined the impact of three different police responses on subsequent domestic violence: (1) an automatic arrest, (2) having one party leave for a "cooling off" period, and (3) counseling or referral to a social service agency (Sherman and Berk 1984). The initial evaluation indicated that arrest appeared to be the most efficient way of preventing more domestic violence between the parties. These results led many jurisdictions to establish pro-arrest/mandatory arrest policies under which police officers must make an arrest whenever possible in domestic violence cases. Other jurisdictions turned to presumptive arrest policies, which assume that an arrest will be made in every case. A decision to not arrest requires a written justification by the officer. In both cases, the discretion of the police is severely curtailed.

The conclusions of the Minneapolis study came under question and prompted several replications. The subsequent studies uncovered little evidence that any intervention was significantly better than another at reducing subsequent domestic violence (Sherman 1992). In Charlotte, North Carolina, for example, arrest did not reduce domestic assaults (Hirschel et al. 1991; Hirschel, Hutchinson, and Dean 1992), and there is some evidence that recidivism increased after arrests (Sherman 1992). Similarly, Dunford, Huizinga, and Elliott (1989) reported no difference in recidivism within six months of the initial police contact in Omaha. Further, Sherman (1992) pointed to evidence of escalating abuse in Omaha at the one-year mark. While these results did not result in the removal of mandatory and presumptive arrest policies, they do suggest that police use of alternatives may be effective in some situations.

Enduring Order Maintenance

The police participation in order maintenance activities is certain to continue. There is little reason to expect any abatement in calls reporting disorder or incivility. The fact that the police are visible, available, and able to apply and enforce laws means that citizens assume they can do something to help them, even when the issue is beyond the police mandate and abilities. Interestingly, the police embrace many order maintenance functions. This is partly because officers assumed a job that provides assistance to the public. Also, their order maintenance functions may directly impact the level of crime in the community.

SERVICE

Service, the third function of the police, takes a wide variety of forms, depending on the location. Common service activities provided by local police and sheriff's deputies include providing directions, giving assistance to disabled motorists, escorting funeral processions, providing emergency medical aid, administering various kinds of permits, transporting emergency relays of blood, checking vacant residences or looking in on vulnerable adults, conducting search and rescue operations, and aiding with traffic control at road construction and emergency scenes. This wide diversity in service delivery requires police to become generalists who can, at a minimum, provide meaningful referral to those asking for assistance.

The service function is largely a reactive one. Citizens call the police for assistance with these tasks for the same basic reasons they call for order maintenance issues—the police are visible and available 24 hours a day, every day of the week. But unlike many order maintenance issues, most service issues do not involve crime, and they hold little potential for invoking the criminal code and taking people into custody. Indeed, most individuals who call for service assistance are not expecting the police to make an arrest. That does not mean, however, that police providing a service will never find that the situation will require them to employ their law enforcement role and turn to making an arrest.

Service activity is mostly reactive: The police respond to calls for assistance that involve mainly non-crime situations. As noted earlier in the chapter, non-crime-related activity comprises 75–80 percent of police time. This does not mean that these activities have no relation to law enforcement (beyond the call itself). Many service functions are related to safety issues. Conducting firearm background checks is a police service that has the potential of keeping weapons out of the hands of criminals and those with mental illness. Directing traffic at road construction sites and escorting funeral processions has the potential to eliminate traffic offenses.

Beyond reactive service, some service functions also take on a more proactive stance. Checking businesses after hours may uncover criminal activity that requires police to assume a law enforcement stance. Similarly, checking abandoned buildings and vacant residences has the potential to deter drug sales, prostitution, and other vice activities. The proactive nature of police service can be illustrated in many activities related to juveniles. Two examples of proactive police service are involvement in the Police Athletic League and the school resource officer programs.

Police Athletic League

The **Police Athletic League (PAL)** is an organization run by local police departments to engage youths in non-delinquent activities such as sports, school activities, and social events for the purpose of giving the youths direction and support. PAL is not a new idea and can be traced back to police efforts in New York City in 1914 that sought to provide youths with a safe place to play and to build good relations between the police and neighborhood youths (Police Athletic League of New York City 2019). PALs provide a range of services to youths in communities across the United States far beyond simple sports and athletics. PAL activities include organized sports teams, after-school care, arts programs, dances, physical fitness, counseling, computer instruction, tutoring and homework assistance, and educational field trips. Today there are over 300 PAL organizations affiliated with the National Police Athletic League (National PAL 2019). The cornerstone of PAL is to prevent juvenile crime and delinquency. PALs use both on- and off-duty police officers. The overall intent of the activities is to keep youngsters safe and to encourage law-abiding activities.

School Resource Officers

School resource officers (SROs) are police officers assigned to schools who are involved in mentoring and referrals, training teachers and parents, and teaching programs. These officers may also perform traditional police functions, but their primary tasks are to work with schools and youths in a non–law enforcement capacity. A 2005 survey of almost 1,400 schools across the United States found that 48 percent had SROs and 76 percent relied on public law enforcement (Travis and Coon 2005). James and McCallion (2013) report that there are over 19,000 police officers and deputies employed as SROs in the United States. More recently, Musu-Gillette et al. (2018) found that SROs are found in 42 percent of schools.

SROs participate in a wide array of service activities in schools, including mentoring students, chaperoning school activities, working with staff and parents, counseling youths, and teaching programs. Two of the most recognizable programs taught by SROs are **Drug Abuse Resistance Education (D.A.R.E.)** and **Gang Resistance Education and Training (G.R.E.A.T.)**. Both of these national programs, taught by police officers, focus on teaching youths the skills to resist peer pressure, recognize high-risk situations and behavior, and avoid participation in dangerous activities (drug use: D.A.R.E.; gangs: G.R.E.A.T.).

The Service Burden

Calls for service and proactive service functions consume a great deal of police time. The service function of policing is not new and can be seen in the earliest policing initiatives. The early Peelian reforms spoke to serving the community and taking actions short of law enforcement (i.e., using "persuasion, advice and warning") to "restore order." The growth of policing since its establishment has been accompanied by growing calls to become involved in more and more service functions. Police departments have embraced service activities, as evidenced by their proactive establishment of and participation in service programs. At the same time, these service functions require resources that some would claim would be better devoted to law enforcement functions.

CHAPTER SUMMARY

The police have several roles and responsibilities falling into three general categories—law enforcement, order maintenance, and service. While the general public assumes that the police spend most of their time and energy enforcing the law, the reality of police work is that they spend 75–80 percent of their time dealing with order maintenance and service. The public calls on the police to fulfill these activities due to the police's visibility, availability 24 hours a day every day of the year, and their ability to invoke the criminal law if necessary. The diversity in roles and responsibilities impose competing demands on police officers and departments.

Critical Thinking Exercise

The police are called on to offer a great deal of order maintenance and service functions by their communities. Much of that activity takes place in direct response to calls for assistance from citizens. Many (if not most) of those calls involve no criminal behavior, and there is no true laws enforcement action possible. Despite this fact the police continue to respond to these calls and offer assistance to those calls, despite the fact that crimes flourish in society and the police typically claim they do not have the resources to deal with all the crime taking place. Some would say it is surprising, therefore, that the police actually take a proactive stance toward many order maintenance and service problems. Besides the examples given in this chapter, what proactive order maintenance and service activities do the police in your community undertake? Question law enforcement personnel in your community about these types of initiatives. Should the police continue to devote resources to this type of activity? Why or why not? What do the law enforcement officers in your community think about undertaking these programs?

KEY TERMS

Automated Fingerprint
Identification System
(AFIS)
backwards law
broken windows theory
Chicago Alternative
Police Strategy
(CAPS)
citizen patrols
Combined DNA Index
System (CODIS)
community-oriented
policing (COP)
CompStat
confirmatory test
confirmatory tool
crime analysis
deterrence
Drug Abuse Resistance
Education (D.A.R.E.)
drug detection K-9s
entrapment

family group conferenc-
ing (FGC)
Gang Resistance Educa-
tion And Training
(G.R.E.A.T.)
hotspot policing
incivility
Integrated Automated
Fingerprint Identifi-
cation System
(IAFIS)
intelligence-led policing
(ILP)
investigation
Kansas City Preventive
Patrol Experiment
law enforcement
Minneapolis Domestic
Violence Experiment
modus operandi
Neighborhood Watch
new media

Operation Ceasefire
order maintenance
Police Athletic League
(PAL)
presumptive drug test
proactive approach
problem-oriented
policing (POP)
property marking
pulling levers
reactive policing
response time
safe havens
SARA
school resource officers
(SROs)
service
sting operation
surveillance
trace evidence
watch and ward

FURTHER READING

Kelling, G., T. Pate, D. Dieckman, and C. Brown (1974). *The Kansas City Preventive Patrol Experiment: A Summary Report.* Washington, DC: The Police Foundation.

Kennedy, D. M., A. A. Braga, and A. M. Piehl (2001). "Developing and Implementing Operation Ceasefire." *In National Institute of Justice, Reducing Gun Violence: The Boston Gun Project's Operation Ceasefire,* 5–53. Washington, DC: National Institute of Justice.

Lab, S. P. (1984). "Police Productivity: The Other Eighty Percent." *Journal of Police Science and Administration* 12, 297–302.

Newman, G. (2007). "Sting Operations: Response Guide No. 6, Center for Problem-Oriented Policing." Retrieved from https://popcenter.asu.edu/content/sting-operations-0

Robinson, M. B. (2011). *Media Coverage of Crime and Criminal Justice.* Durham, NC: Carolina Academic Press.

Skogan. W. G., and S. M. Hartnett (1997). *Community Policing: Chicago Style.* New York: Oxford University Press.

Surette, R. (2015). *Media, Crime and Criminal Justice: Images, Realities, and Policies.* Stamford, CT: Cengage.

Wilson, J. Q., and G. Kelling (1982, March). "Broken Windows." *Atlantic Monthly,* 29–38.

CHAPTER 4

Police Agencies and Organization

CHAPTER OUTLINE

Introduction

Local Police

Municipal Police

County Police

Special Jurisdiction Police

Campus Police

State Police

Tribal Police

Federal Police

Department of Justice

Department of Homeland Security

Private Police

Chapter Summary

After reading this chapter you should be able to:

- Provide information on the size and scope of policing in the United States
- Discuss the diversity in municipal police departments
- Point out the difference between a sheriff's office and county police
- Explain what is meant by special jurisdiction police and give examples
- List and discuss at least three types of state-level police agencies
- Identify at least three federal police agencies that are part of the Department of Justice and explain responsibilities of each
- Identify and discuss at least three Homeland Security police agencies
- Discuss what constitutes private policing and issues related to private policing

INTRODUCTION

Police agencies are organized according to the legal codes they are empowered to enforce and by the geopolitical boundaries they serve in. The legal codes are federal and state law. The geopolitical boundaries tend to be state, county, and local law, all of which fall under state law. Beyond these agencies are those maintained by Native American tribes. In addition, there are some agencies whose powers are defined by their specialized focus (such as fish, game, and forestry) and a small but growing number of private police agencies serving specific clients within the clients' property interests. College and university campus police may be sworn officers under state law, though many are simply private security.

The common thread of the concept of "police" is the right to make arrests on the state's authority, a right bestowed only after satisfactory completion of rigorous training in law and techniques. Private police and security raise an interesting conundrum in light of the growth of such agencies and organizations. Many of these agencies do not require the training received by public police employees, and they carry out many policing functions without the legal power to make arrests. Instead, they are limited to the jurisdiction's defined power of citizens' arrest.

Police agencies typically employ both sworn and civilian employees. Sworn employees are officers who have undergone formal law enforcement training and can enact arrests. Regardless of jurisdiction, all agencies also employ non-sworn personnel for support services of various types: dispatch, supply management, crime or forensic analysis, technical support, record keeping, and the like. Some federal agencies, such as the FBI and the Secret Service, employ a uniformed police division to protect their offices and training facilities. Those officers are covered under a different federal employment system than are the agencies' investigative agents.

LOCAL POLICE

Local police organizations include municipal and county departments. There are more than 15,000 local police agencies (see Table 4.1), of which 80 percent are municipal agencies (Hyland and Davis 2019). In addition to these agencies are special jurisdiction police and campus police departments.

Table 4.1 Employment by State and Local Law Enforcement Agencies in the United States, 2016

TYPE OF AGENCY	NUMBER OF AGENCIES	EMPLOYEES		
		TOTAL	SWORN	CIVILIAN
Total	15,322	1,050,488	701,273	349,214
Local police	12,261	599,548	468,274	131,274
Sheriff's office[a]	3,012	359,843	173,354	186,489
Primary state[b]	49	91,097	59,645	31,452

[a]Excludes sheriffs' offices with only jail and court duties.
[b]Hawaii does not have a primary state law enforcement agency.

Source: Adapted from Hyland and Davis (2019).

Municipal Police

Municipal is used here to designate any police agency that has primary responsibility for a city, town, or village. The size and organization of municipal police departments are directly related to the size and expectations of the communities that they serve. Their police powers are limited to the town or city's corporation limits. The duties that they share in common are to enforce the state laws (both criminal and traffic) and local ordinances; intervene in family and neighborhood disputes to preserve the peace; provide assistance to citizens as needed; conduct routine preventive patrol, in order to monitor traffic and deter potential criminal activity as well as to reassure the citizens.

Some jurisdictions, as noted above, may choose not to fund a local police department. They will rely instead on the county sheriff or state police for the infrequent need for law enforcement. In some states, the older office of constable endures, some with full police powers and others serving as process servers. There is no uniform definition or standard for the office, and it may coexist with local police departments.

Municipal police comprise four out of five of the local police agencies in the United States with almost 600,000 full-time employees. Of these, 78 percent are sworn officers. Most municipal departments are relatively small agencies. Almost half (48 percent) employ 10 or fewer full-time sworn officers (Hyland and Davis 2019). Only 624 agencies (5 percent) employ 100 or more sworn full-time officers, and 1,469 (12 percent) of the agencies have 50 or more full-time sworn officers (Hyland and Davis 2019).

Small towns may have only a chief of police, or a police chief with one or two full- or part-time officers (24 percent of all departments fit this model). The officers may have regular shifts but cannot provide full-time, around-the-clock coverage. Accordingly, they typically share on-call duties at night and on weekends and holidays. Special officers work on demand, covering traffic, special events like carnivals or school events, or construction security. Although special officers will work in police uniforms, they do not carry full police powers unless they have completed a basic state-administered police academy program.

Larger cities and towns have local departments that provide year-round, round-the-clock coverage, with officers working regular hours in **shifts**. The standard shift is an 8-hour tour of duty: three 8-hour shifts covers the 24-hour day neatly, and five 8-hour shifts comprise a standard 40-hour workweek. Some agencies choose to deploy their officers in overlapping 10-hour shifts, four days a week, doubling the police presence in the overlapping periods where the most crime or disorder—and thus the greatest need for police presence—has been documented.

Web Activity

A great deal of information about police personnel is available (more than just the size of police agencies). Investigate the makeup of police agencies by examining the Hyland and Davis (2019) report on the textbook website.

The types of patrol vary. Patrol by police car—equipped with strobe lights, spotlights, "cage" screens to contain transported prisoners, and a wide range of emergency equipment—is the first image that comes to mind, but other patrol types exist. Motorcycle patrol is a lower-visibility means of doing traffic enforcement and also allows for rapid emergency response. Foot patrol is still conducted in densely populated areas and downtown commercial districts, with bicycle patrols allowing an easier transit through parkland, vehicle-restricted housing, and other specialty areas. K-9 patrols tend to be regular patrol cars with beat assignments. They are notable primarily because of the presence of the four-footed police presence augmenting the uniformed officer, but they can also be pulled from routine duties to assist with searches and crowd control duties if the need arises.

Special Response Teams

Special response teams (SRTs, also called by the older term SWAT, for special weapons and tactics) are specialized full-time units in large departments. In smaller agencies, SRT officers conduct routine duties as patrol officers or detectives until they are called upon to respond to emergency situations.

Most medium- and large-size police departments have two basic divisions, uniformed and detective. The latter work in plain clothes and on shifts generally limited to days and evenings (but subject to call-out for serious crimes that occur in the after-midnight hours). Patrol officers are responsible for the preliminary investigation of reported crime unless there is an obvious and complex crime scene. Once the initial report has been filed, follow-up investigation is turned over to the detectives. Even if patrol officers have made an arrest on or near the scene, detectives need to interview witnesses to the crime and alibi witnesses. They conduct further investigation to collect information suggested, but not verified, by the initial report. Reports filed by patrol are first reviewed by their uniformed supervisors, and subsequently are also reviewed by supervising detectives.

In a number of jurisdictions, uniformed officers may be detailed to work in schools, as **school resource officers (SROs)**, or officer safety. Some such posts are created in the wake of criminal events or unrest in the schools; others are an extension of crime prevention duties, presenting a personal and more accessible vision of the police to a vulnerable and impressionistic audience of youth. SROs gather intelligence as well as present a positive face of the department to populations at a stage of life when "testing the limits" may bring them in contact with officers.

Local departments also employ a variety of civilian employees who do not have police training or sworn powers, but whose work is vital to the efficient operation of the agency. Indeed, 22 percent of the full-time personnel are civilian (non-sworn) employees (Hyland and Davis 2019). Such people include secretaries (who sometimes double as dispatchers), vehicle maintenance personnel, and evidence room technicians or custodians, among others. Records clerks may also serve as crime analysts, providing patrol and investigators with information related to crime patterns or linking cases pursued by different officers (based on the information found in long-term review and data entry).

┌────────────────── **Critical Thinking Exercise** ──────────────────┐

Municipal police departments can take a variety of forms with varying components. Think of the police department from your hometown. What does it look like?
Are there things missing that you think it should have? What are they, and why are
they needed? Does it have components that it could do without? Explain.

└──┘

Most attention paid to policing, both popular and professional, focuses on
policing in large municipal areas. Popular police television shows and movies are
primarily set in cities like New York, Los Angeles, Chicago, San Francisco, and
other major metropolitan communities. Similarly, most research on policing is
conducted in large cities. These large communities typically experience more
crime and receive more attention in the national news media. They also deal with
terrorist threats and other events that attract a great deal of attention and concern. However, most police departments have relatively few sworn officers and
exist in smaller communities and rural areas.

Sheriff

Traditionally, county-level law enforcement was provided by the **sheriff**, the
direct descendant of the English *shire-reeve*. It is the oldest American office, and
it is the only office with police powers elected directly by county residents (local
police are appointed by the local political authorities). In many urbanized areas
in the modern era, the sheriff's office has either been supplanted by a county
police force or exists side by side with one. In 2016, there were 3,012 sheriff's offices in the United States, totaling almost 360,0000 full-time employees, of which
over 173,000 were sworn officers/deputies (Hyland and Davis 2019).

Sheriffs hold a somewhat unique position in policing. They exist in all but
three states (Alaska, Connecticut, and Hawaii), and the office is established by
either the state constitution (37 states) or state statute. While the sheriff is an
elected position, the roles and responsibilities of the office are not subject to local
control; rather, they are dictated by the state constitution and/or state statute
(Scott 2019). Most sheriffs' departments (55 percent) have fewer than 25 sworn
deputies/officers (Brooks 2019).

While there are disagreements over whether elected sheriffs are truly police
officers, they have always held police powers. Unlike any other police agency,
however, sheriffs have responsibilities for all three branches of the criminal justice system in their county. They and their deputies have arrest powers and often
patrol the unincorporated areas of the county as the only enforcement agents
available to residents here. They are also responsible for security of the county
courts, and their deputies serve writs and other legal documents on behalf of the
court. Sheriffs also run and maintain county jails.

Sheriffs' offices also provide a variety of services to citizens beyond serving civil
orders, including fingerprinting and background checks for employment. Depending on the demographics and politics of their region, sheriffs offices may also provide regional 911 emergency coordination for police, fire, and ambulance services.

County Police

County police departments tend to be found in densely populated urban areas, and they function much like local municipal police departments, just serving a wider geographical area. They tend to be concentrated in the eastern and southern states (New York, Virginia, Maryland, Pennsylvania, North and South Carolina, and Georgia, among others), though some western states, such as Hawaii, have county police.

These agencies may be either full-service or limited-service departments. Full-service departments operate throughout the county and provide patrol, respond to calls for service, enforce traffic laws, and basically offer the same services as a municipal police department. Limited-service departments provide services primarily to unincorporated areas within the county. Some offer contractual services to special districts and areas. Some states in the Northeast also have county detectives who are attached to county attorney offices; they are considered "county police." The New York Police Department serves as the full-service police force for the five counties surrounding that city.

Some county departments have merged as the population has grown and municipalities have decided to combine some operations to save resources. Based on 2004 Law Enforcement Management and Administrative Statistics data, there were 32 county police departments employing 100 or more full-time sworn officers in 2000 (Reaves and Hickman 2004). Typical units in these county police agencies are drug enforcement; special weapons and tactics (SWAT)/special response teams; police training academies; and specialized units for gangs, child abuse, and juvenile offenders. Examples of these county police departments would be the Charlotte/Mecklenburg Police Department (North Carolina) and the Prince George's County Police (Maryland) (Reaves and Hickman 2004).

Special Jurisdiction Police

Not all police departments/agencies are tied to traditional jurisdictional boundaries of cities or counties. Some operate in relation to specific needs or functions or somewhat unique jurisdictions. These are considered **special jurisdiction police**. Examples of special jurisdiction police agencies are those related to transportation authorities, parks and wildlife, housing authorities, and schools.

One example of a special jurisdiction police department is the Port Authority of New York and New Jersey (PANYNJ) Police Department. The Port Authority is responsible for the airports, bridges, tunnels bus terminals, and other transportation services in the New York/New Jersey metropolitan area. The department employs 1,700 officers (Port Authority of New York and New Jersey 2019). In addition to the Port Authority, the New York Metropolitan Transit Authority (MTA) has its own police force. The MTA is comprised of the bus and train services (including related bridges and tunnels) in 12 New York and two Connecticut counties. The MTA police employs over 600 sworn police officers and has plans to almost double its size (Rivoli 2019). Transit police operate in a number of other areas, including Washington, DC; Cleveland, Ohio; the Massachusetts Bay area; Minneapolis/St. Paul, Minnesota; and 23 counties in Maryland.

A second broad category of special jurisdiction police deals with parks and wildlife. The title of these officers varies from state to state but includes police officer, park police, wildlife officer, game warden, among others. While these officers are generally charged with enforcing gaming laws and wildlife laws and/or patrolling parks, in most every case the officers hold arrest powers and can enforce a wide range of criminal laws. The size of the agencies varies a great deal. Two of the largest are the Florida Fish and Wildlife Conservation Commission, with over 850 officers (Florida Fish and Wildlife Conservation Commission 2019), and the California Department of Parks and Recreation, with over 500 officers (State of California 2019). Other states typically employ fewer officers, such as Ohio (approximately 300) (Ohio Department of Natural Resources 2019), North Carolina (230) (North Carolina Wildlife Resources Commission 2019), and Washington State (140) (Washington Department of Fish and Wildlife Enforcement 2019).

Special jurisdiction police often transcend more common jurisdictional boundaries. Whereas more police departments are responsible for the area within municipal/city boundaries and sheriff's departments operate within county (boroughs in Alaska and parishes in Louisiana) boundaries, many special jurisdiction police agencies cross city, county, and even state boundaries.

Campus Police

The most recent Survey of Campus Law Enforcement Agencies (2011–12) reveals that campus police are a common feature of colleges and university in the United States. Reaves (2015a) reports that roughly two-thirds of the four-year college campuses with 2,500+ students have campus police with full arrest powers. The almost 900 campuses with police departments have approximately 15,000 full-time sworn officers and another 11,000 non-sworn security officers. The average campus police department employs 24 sworn officers (Reaves 2015a).

Campus policing has received increased attention since the late 1970s. This is attributable to crime on college campuses. The passage of the **Clery Act** in 1990 mandated that colleges and universities make certain crime statistics readily available to the public. The shootings at Virginia Polytechnic Institute and State University in 2007 and other campuses raised the concern over campus crime. The first campus police force began at Yale University in the late 1800s. Most campus law enforcement operations existed as public safety forces until the 1970s, when social and student unrest on college campuses presaged the move to campus police agencies (International Association of Campus Law Enforcement Administrators 2019).

Web Activity

Go to your college/university website. Does it have a campus police department or campus safety office? If so, what information can you find about the department, its makeup, and its operations? If it does not have campus police, investigate another school's department.

Campus police operations mirror municipal police in most respects. Officers typically carry firearms and have full arrest powers (Reaves 2015a). Most campus police departments (81 percent) patrol campus and areas immediately adjacent to campus. Community policing is a key component on college campuses and relies on problem analysis and prevention services. This approach is found in 8 out of 10 college police departments (Reaves 2015a) and reflects the growth from campus safety to campus policing.

STATE POLICE

There are three basic types of state-level police agencies: state police, state patrol, and state investigative agencies (in Ohio it is the Bureau of Criminal Investigation, or BCI). The first two are uniformed and generally are called troopers (both forms are organized in troops); the third generally is not. These agencies are not mutually exclusive. In many states, the investigative agency works in concert with either a state police or a state patrol. Every state except Hawaii has some form of state police agency. These agencies employ a total of over 92,000 full-time employees, of whom almost 60,000 (65 percent) are sworn employees (Hyland and Davis 2019).

State police have broad, general enforcement powers throughout the state. They do traffic enforcement as well as criminal investigations and may have their own forensic laboratory facilities to support investigations. Headquarters and training facilities tend to be in or near the state capital, but troops have their own regional headquarters throughout the state. They provide backing and support to sheriffs' offices, county police, and local police when requested, and in emergency situations.

In many states, the state police maintain the basic law enforcement certification academies. Troopers generally undergo more extensive training than local officers. They tend to patrol alone and cannot count on nearby backup.

State patrols have a more limited jurisdiction, focusing primarily on traffic enforcement on the interstate and state highways. Because traffic enforcement cannot be separated from other criminal enterprises, the troopers have powers similar to state police. The patrol may take primary responsibility for enforcing some state codes. State patrol has a more limited area of responsibility.

Criminal investigations bureaus/agencies have statewide responsibilities that vary according to the statutory mandate in the individual state. Eight states have investigation organizations that are either independent or under the direction of the state attorney general's office. The remainder are divisions within their respective state police or state patrol organizations. In addition to their own investigations, they provide support to other law enforcement agencies within the state.

The Ohio BCI operates under the authority of the state attorney general's office and provides three specific services (Ohio Attorney General's Office 2019). The *Identification Division* is the state's repository for criminal records, including juvenile records. It provides background checks for state and private entities, focusing on criminal records and fingerprint checks that are linked to national databases. The *Investigations Division* has several interconnected entities, including crime scene investigation, child protection, a cybercrime unit, environmental enforcement, a variety of drug-related investigation units, and a Special Operations Unit that covers other crimes. The incorporated Investigation Services Unit handles criminal intelligence, polygraphs, missing persons, Interpol liaison, and other information-sharing functions. The *Laboratory Division* has three science laboratories for processing evidence. Drugs, DNA, firearms analysis, fingerprints, trace evidence, and questioned documents all fall within the labs' purview, servicing all state agencies that submit evidence.

TRIBAL POLICE

Tribal police hold a unique place in US law enforcement. There are over 300 federally recognized American Indian reservations in the United States, and they are considered sovereign nations within the country. The legal jurisdiction over crimes on these lands may involve a variety of agencies. Tribes have the authority to establish and operate their own police agencies, but in order to perform police duties, tribal officers must complete a basic law enforcement training course designated by the Director of the Bureau of Indian Affairs (BIA) (Legal Information Institute, n.d.a). In addition, the federal and state governments may also handle policing matters for some crimes committed on tribal lands in accord with federal statutes. **Public Law 83-280** (PL-280) allows the federal government to cede jurisdiction over major crimes to the state in 16 states. In an additional 10 states, the law allows the state to establish jurisdiction. In 19 states, the federal government maintains jurisdiction (Bureau of Justice Statistics 2019).

Despite the tribal police's nominal status as "sovereign," its power is defined and constrained by whether the perpetrator and victim are Indians. Tribal jurisdiction holds sway only when the crime is not a major crime and the persons involved are all Indians. For all major crimes designated by the Major Crimes Act (1885), federal jurisdiction is mandated regardless of the status of those involved. For non-major crimes, if either victim or perpetrator is not an Indian, federal jurisdiction applies under the General Crimes Act. A more detailed description of the application of federal, state, and tribal jurisdictions and criminal codes may be found on the website for the Tribal Law and Policy Institute (Tribal Court Clearinghouse, n.d.). Another piece of legislation, 18 U.S. Code § 1153, defines "Offenses committed within Indian Country" (Legal Information Institute, n.d.b). Tribal judges have the authority to issue warrants for searches on tribal lands under the Code of Federal Regulations 25 CFR § 11.305.

A complete census of tribal police departments does not exist at this time. The Bureau of Justice Statistics is currently gathering data from the 229 known tribal police departments for the first such census (Bureau of Justice Statistics 2019). Based on 2001 data, only 7 tribal departments had 50 or more full-time sworn police officers and 101 (less than 6 percent of the reporting departments) had fewer than 10 sworn officers (Hickman 2003). Tribal police offer the same basis police functions as other law enforcement agencies, including patrolling, responding to calls for service, enforcing traffic, executing warrants, operating jails, and performing other activities. In 2013, tribal police handled 22,920 property crimes and 5,400 violent crimes (Perry 2015).

FEDERAL POLICE

Most federal law enforcement agencies are organized under one of two cabinet-level departments, the Department of Justice or the Department of Homeland Security. Federal officers (often called special agents) do not enforce state laws but are responsible for federal laws specifically delegated to their agency under the United States Code and other specific legislation. In addition, many have mutual aid agreements with state agencies and can assist under specific circumstances, such as disasters, looting, large casualty events, and crimes involving interstate flight.

While the Justice and Homeland Security Departments carry the bulk of the policing responsibility, it is important to note that there are law enforcement units and activities under all of the US cabinet posts. These other policing responsibilities are typically much narrower in scope than those in Justice and Homeland Security and typically operate out of the offices of inspector generals. For example, the Department of Agriculture's Office of Inspector General employs enforcement agents who deal with things like fraud in the Supplemental Nutrition Assistance Program (SNAP) and threats to the health and safety of the public through food processing (U.S. Department of Agriculture 2017). Similarly, the Environmental Protection Agency employs investigators to address environmental laws (Environmental Protection Agency 2018). Therefore, agents employed in cabinet-level offices are required to have or obtain specialized skills that are not part of the more traditional enforcement agents' training. The focus here will be on the agencies that are a part of the Justice and Homeland Security Departments.

Department of Justice

Federal Bureau of Investigations (FBI)

The Federal Bureau of Investigation has perhaps the widest mandate of the federal law enforcement agencies. The FBI was created in 1908 by then-attorney general Charles Bonaparte at a time when crime—particularly bank fraud and political corruption—was on the rise. Christened the Bureau of Investigations, it gave the Justice Department a core group of 34 investigators (rather than depend on the existing Secret Service) to handle various kinds of white-collar and organized crime. The passage of the **Mann Act** in 1910 (which criminalized the transportation of women across state lines for prostitution and human trafficking) and the need to thwart saboteurs at the opening of World War I increased the agency's capacity.

The FBI lists eight priorities:

1. Protect the United States from terrorist attack
2. Protect the United States against foreign intelligence operations and espionage
3. Protect the United States against cyber-based attacks and high-technology crimes
4. Combat public corruption at all levels
5. Protect civil rights
6. Combat transnational/national criminal organizations and enterprises
7. Combat major white-collar crime
8. Combat significant violent crime (FBI, n.d.b)

In order to address these, the FBI divides its investigations into a range of programs. Among those programs as terrorism, counterintelligence, cybercrime, civil rights, organized crime/drugs, and violent crimes. The global scope of those activities has led to the establishment of over 400 FBI offices in the United States and 60 offices (legal attachés) in foreign countries. To carry out its activities, the FBI employs over 35,000 individuals, of whom more than 13,000 are special agents and another 3,000+ are intelligence analysts (Wray 2019).

The FBI has been involved in a wide array of high-profile cases throughout its history. Among these are cases of notorious gangsters like Al Capone and Benjamin "Bugsy" Siegel, the Lindbergh baby kidnapping in 1932, bank robbers like John Dillinger and Bonnie Parker and Clyde Barrow in 1934, espionage during and after World War II (including Alger Hiss in 1950 and Ethel and Julius Rosenberg in 1951), the John F. Kennedy assassination in 1963, the CIA spy Aldrich Ames in 1994, and the September 11, 2001 (hereafter 9/11) terror attacks (FBI, n.d.a). In addition to these high-profile cases, the FBI addresses a wide range of basic criminal cases covered by federal and state laws.

Though best known for its Ten Most Wanted List, the bureau also provides training and forensic analysis to state and local agencies through its facilities in Quantico, Virginia. The FBI also gathers extensive police data from agencies across the United States every year and releases data through the its Uniform Crime Reporting Program. It also issues extensive publications on crime analysis and other information management services, as well as assists local, state, and other federal agencies on cases.

US Marshals Service

The US Marshals Service is the oldest federal law enforcement agency, founded in 1793 when President George Washington appointed the first 13 marshals upon the passage of the Judiciary Act. They were the first US census takers, the first agents to pursue counterfeiters, and they were charged with the enforcement of the 1850 Fugitive Slave Act until the outbreak of the Civil War in 1861. The creation of the Department of Justice in 1870 ended their census duties, but they were soon charged with enforcing the whiskey tax laws in the 1800s, and Prohibition in the 1920s and 1930s. Marshals played a critical role in protecting black students integrating formerly all-white schools during the 1960s; they were also called upon to maintain peace in the Boston busing conflicts in 1975. The passage of the Omnibus Crime Control Act of 1970 led to the creation of the Witness Protection Program under the Marshals' control, and the FBI transferred some fugitive apprehension duties to them in 1979. A court security program and responsibility for the management and disposition of seized assets followed in the early 1980s. Today the US Marshals Service has over 5,000 employees. Approximately 3,600 of these are US marshals or deputy marshals. The remaining employees are administrative and other support staff (U.S. Marshals 2019b).

US marshals have been involved in a number of high-profile crime events in American history, including the 1878 Lincoln County War, the shootout at the O.K. Corral in 1881, the Pullman railroad strike in 1894, the Pentagon antiwar riots in 1967, the Wounded Knee Massacre in 1973, the 1995 Oklahoma City bombing, and the 9/11 attacks on the Twin Towers in New York in 2001 (U.S. Marshals 2019c). A number of famous names have served as marshals, including Frederick Douglass and the Earp brothers (Virgil, Wyatt, and Morgan).

In the modern era, the marshals are charged with security for federal judges and providing security to and from court proceedings for federal prisoners. The US Marshals Service website indicates that they received an average of 700 persons each day in 2017 and escorted more than 800,000 prisoners to courts and to correctional facilities. Prisoner supervision includes medical care when necessary (U.S. Marshals 2019d).

The marshals handle witness security for federal trials, they conduct sex offender investigations under the Adam Walsh Act, and they operate a missing child program that targets child trafficking operations. The marshals also manage the Department of Justice's Asset Forfeiture Program, which held more than $1.8 billion in assets in mid-2017 and involved the distribution of almost half a billion dollars' worth of forfeited assets to crime victims and to participating state and local law enforcement agencies under the 1984 Comprehensive Crime Control Act. "Managing" may simply mean keeping forfeited money in a safe bank account, but it can also extend to the upkeep of property awaiting sale (U.S. Marshals 2019a).

Bureau of Alcohol, Tobacco, Firearms and Explosives (ATF)

Taxes on alcohol are almost as old as the American republic, having been authorized first in 1789. The function was managed under the US Department of the Treasury from 1791 until 1930, when the Bureau of Prohibition (first created in 1927) was transferred to the Department of Justice and became the Alcohol Tax Unit (ATU). The 1934 and 1938 National Firearms Acts instituted federal regulation of the types of weapons favored by the gangsters running the illegal alcohol trade, and in 1941 their enforcement was passed over to the ATU (Bureau of Alcohol, Tobacco, Firearms and Explosives n.d.).

A variety of developments in the 1960s and early 1970s led to the 1972 transfer of ATU duties back to the Treasury Department and the creation of the ATF as an independent bureau. Explosives were included in its mandate under the

1970 Organized Crime Act. Interstate tobacco smuggling was added in 1980, along with additional duties outlined on the department's website (Bureau of Alcohol, Tobacco, Firearms and Explosives n.d.). In the wake of the 9/11 assaults and the creation of the Department of Homeland Security, the licensing and criminal investigations functions of the ATF were transferred back to the Department of Justice in 2003, while tax enforcement remained in Treasury Department as the Alcohol and Tobacco Tax and Trade Bureau (ATTB).

The ATF maintains a yearlong training academy for firearms examiners and a two-year program for agents who will become certified explosives specialists, as well as laboratory facilities to assist in arson investigation. They also maintain a fire research laboratory and produce a number of documents related to arson examination protocols that are available on their website.

The ATF has over 2,600 special agents (Bureau of Alcohol, Tobacco, Firearms and Explosives 2019). In 2018, it investigated almost 36,000 firearms cases, 2,000 arson cases and 1,100 explosives cases. The bureau also recommended almost 16,7000 individuals for prosecution (Bureau of Alcohol, Tobacco, Firearms and Explosives 2019).

Drug Enforcement Administration (DEA)

The Drug Enforcement Agency was created in 1973 by executive order of President Richard Nixon. It consolidated several existing agencies and units under a single command, as part of the national response to the increased drug use of the 1960s and the criminal and medical issues that accompanied it. Illegal narcotics and hallucinogens were the drugs of greatest concern at that time; the opioid crisis is a major concern today (DEA n.d.a).

The DEA employs almost 5,000 special agents (DEA n.d.b). The agency has two primary responsibilities. The first is to oversee and regulate the legitimate production of controlled substances (those with legitimate medicinal purposes, including some opioids). The second responsibility is the criminal investigation and prosecution of illegal drugs. The latter charge includes the illegal markets for opioids, fueled by the over-prescription of painkillers, which some ascribe to a profit-driven push by pharmaceutical companies (DEA n.d.a).

Opioids that have been manufactured legitimately are only part of the problem because once the formula is known, do-it-yourself illegal manufacture becomes possible. As early as 2006, the dangers of methamphetamine labs and the chemicals used in making meth were known (National Drug Intelligence Center 2006). Since then, secondary exposure (skin contact or inhalation) with fentanyl has made headlines, including a viral report of an East Liverpool, Ohio, officer who came in contact with a white powder and collapsed in 2017 but was revived with the opioid-antidote naloxone, known as Narcan (Associated Press 2018). Though there are ongoing debates about the incidence and severity of secondary exposure, as well as the appropriateness of administering Narcan to overdose victims, many police officers now carry Narcan. An officer in a nearby jurisdiction advised us that his department issued it primarily for the protection of its officers (confidential source).

DEA agents work in international posts as well as domestic ones, aiding foreign governments and state enforcement agents. The drug trade is both transnational and interstate in nature, and DEA agents may work in investigations at all levels. Both undercover and overt enforcement roles are involved, and support positions fill roles in forensic analysis, data analysis and interpretation, and public education. In certain areas, crop eradication and crop substitution are also part of the DEA mission. In the modern era, the state-driven movement to legalize medicinal and recreational marijuana has introduced an element of uncertainty into the DEA mandate.

Federal Bureau of Prisons
While not technically a police agency, the Federal Bureau of Prisons (FBP), created in 1930, is responsible for housing persons convicted of federal crimes. Its regular prison population numbers ranged from 13,000 to 25,00 until the 1980s, when the 1984 Sentencing Reform Act abolished federal parole and increased drug and immigration enforcements expanded the number of prisons. Today, that total stands at almost 176,000 inmates in federal, privately managed, and other state facilities. The number of federal prisons has grown from 13 in 1930 to more than 120 today (Federal Bureau of Prisons n.d.). Security and rehabilitation are the institutional mandates.

Department of Homeland Security
The Department of Homeland Security was established in 2002 in the wake of the 9/11 terrorist attacks on the World Trade Center towers in New York City, the Pentagon, and in Pennsylvania (Homeland Security 2018). The entire department includes roughly 240,000 employees in positions that address the safety of the United States.

US Secret Service
Originally founded to investigate counterfeiting after the Civil War, the Secret Service received its current mission to protect the president, vice president, and visiting dignitaries after the assassination of President William McKinley in 1901. It was incorporated into the Department of Homeland Security in 2003, continuing its counterfeiting charge, augmented with a mandate to pursue cyber investigations and other financial crimes. In the public eye, however, the Secret Service's primary mission is the protection of the president and vice president and their families, and presidential candidates during election years.

The Secret Service is divided into two main divisions: Special Agents and the Uniformed Division. There are roughly 3,200 Special Agents who do financial investigations and serve on protective details (U.S. Secret Service n.d.). The Uniformed Division provides protection to specific buildings and complexes such as the White House, Treasury buildings, and foreign diplomatic buildings in Washington, DC. There are 1,3000 officers employed by the Uniformed Division (U.S. Secret Service n.d.).

Customs and Border Protection

Customs and Border Protection (CBP) is charged with "facilitating lawful international travel and trade" while "keeping terrorists and their weapons out of the U.S.," a mandate that combines "customs, immigration, border security, and agricultural protection into one coordinated and supportive activity" (Customs and Border Protection 2019a). Collection of customs charges has been a responsibility since the creation of the Customs Bureau in 1789. Immigration enforcement was added in 1891, and agricultural inspections was added in 1912 in the wake of the passage of the Plant Quarantine Act (Customs and Border Protection 2019b). Its current configuration and its responsibility for the security of the nation's borders was established in 2003.

Today, CBP employs approximately 60,000 individuals. Over 24,000 serve as CBP officers. Another 19,555 are border patrol agents working primarily on the southern border with Mexico (CBP 2019b).

Immigration and Customs Enforcement (ICE)

An agency with parallel duties to those of Customs and Border Patrol, ICE operates within the nation's borders. It is a relatively new organization, founded in 2003 as a part of Homeland Security in the aftermath of the 9/11 terrorist attacks. It identifies, investigates, and takes custody of persons who have eluded border security and are in the country illegally, or those aliens who pose a threat to the security of the nation regardless of their manner of entry. ICE is responsible for their custody, access to legal resources, transportation, and removal from the country under court order (ICE 2018).

ICE has 400 officers with more than 20,000 employees. Enforcement Removal Operations, with 6,000 officers, focuses on apprehending and removing aliens who are deemed a threat to the country. Removal operations results in over 140,000 arrest in fiscal year 2017. Homeland Security Investigation, which has 8,500 investigators and technical enforcement officers, deals with human trafficking, transnational gang activity, and financial crimes (ICE 2018).

Transportation Security Agency (TSA)

After terrorists used commercial airplanes in the 9/11 attacks, the federal government passed the Aviation and Transportation Security Act in November 2001, which created the TSA. The safe and efficient transit of passengers and freight by air and rail facilities, in coordination with other federal intelligence and enforcement agencies, is its primary mission. The TSA employs over 43,000 officers (TSA 2019).

US Coast Guard

Congress authorized 10 cutter ships to protect the new nation's revenue in 1790, charging the new organization (variously called the Cutter Service, Revenue-Marine and the Revenue Cutter Service) with responsibility to suppress privacy and smuggling. Quarantine law enforcement was added to the duties in 1799, along with the maintenance of lighthouses (taken over from the states and cities).

The service became a constant presence and the first line of defense on the nation's seashores. This responsibility was reinforced by the Posse Comitatus Act of 1870. Among other duties, it was charged with enforcing the ban on Chinese immigration and suppressing liquor smuggling during Prohibition. The U.S. Coast Guard name was installed in 1915.

In 1967, the oversight of the Coast Guard was transferred from the Treasury Department to the Transportation Department, with duties including migrant interdiction and supervision of economic traffic and hazardous cargo at sea, in addition to their traditional search and rescue and enforcement duties. That assignment lasted until November 2001, when the Coast Guard became part of the newly created Department of Homeland Security. There are more than 56,000 members of the Coast Guard, of whom almost 41,000 are active-duty Coast Guardsmen (U.S. Coast Guard n.d.).

PRIVATE POLICE

Unlike police in municipal, county, state, specialized, or federal agencies, **private police** are not directly employed by the state. In essence, they are not "public" police. Rather, they serve the private constituency that hires them for specific tasks or operations. These private police operations are often referred to as private security.

There is no single, agreed upon definition of private police. Joh (2004) defines *private police* as "lawful forms of organized, for profit personnel services whose primary objectives include the control of crime, the protection of property and life, and the maintenance of order" (p. 55). The American Society for Industrial Security (ASIS) International states that private security is "the nongovernmental, private-sector practice of protecting people, property, and information, conducting investigations, and otherwise safeguarding an organization's assets" (Strom et al. 2010, 2-2). But one can replace "an organization's assets" with terms reflecting any constituency to fit a broad view of private policing.

Private policing is provided under different guises by different organizations/agencies (Sparrow 2014). Many companies hire employees specifically to serve as security guards, store detectives, or other protection personnel. Companies or residential associations seek private police services for more on-site presence than can be provided by the local municipal or county police. Officers under contracted services work for an hourly wage, generally lower than the time-and-a-half that would be paid to hire off-duty municipal or county police. Private police can be volunteers and/or regular citizens who step forward to provide security and protections. Many private police are contracted by government agencies to protect public events and buildings.

The size of private policing exceeds that of public policing. This is true in the majority of the world's countries, particularly the more industrialized countries (Provost 2017). According to the Bureau of Labor Statistics (BLS), there were roughly 800,000 police officers in the United States in 2016, compared to over 1.1 million private security workers (Provost 2017). The private security figures include investigative and security service personnel (almost 700,000), private detectives and investigators (over 30,000), and other protective service workers (over 140,000) (Bureau of Labor Statistics 2019). These figures do not include unpaid volunteers who undertake policing actions on behalf of the community or at specific events.

Private police serve in a similar capacity to public police without many of the restrictions and regulations imposed on public police. Private police are not bound to the constitutional guidelines/restrictions to which the public police must adhere (Joh 2004; Stoughton 2017). Issues like the Miranda warnings and other guidelines (generally under the Fourth, Fifth, and Sixth Amendments to the Constitution) are not binding on private police. Part of this freedom is a result of private police working on private property rather than public property (Joh 2004). When "arrests" and detentions are enacted by private police, they are typically done on private property. There is a lack of accountability and less attention paid to civil liberties when private police are involved (Sparrow 2014). The focus of private police is more on property and proprietary concerns than on crimes and public transgressions (Joh 2004; Strom et al. 2010).

A good example of private police is railroad police. The railroad police are a long-standing example of a private corporate police force that serves corporate interests rather than broad public ones. The fact that trains traveled through multiple jurisdictions and parked large amounts of goods and services in freight yards created special circumstances that needed to be addressed. Pinkerton agents originally protected passengers and freight on trains until the companies developed their own forces. The interstate nature of the railroad business requires special powers, which are authorized under the Crime Control Act of 1990. Essentially, a railroad police officer certified in one state can exercise his or her powers in any jurisdiction through which the trains travel, or on railroad-owned property in any state. Those powers do not extend beyond railroad property, however.

Private police/security officers benefit from this freedom from constitutional restrictions despite the fact that they are generally registered and licensed by the state (Stoughton 2017). Many private police officers are licensed to carry guns and do so in the regular course of their jobs. This licensing requires criminal background checks. Private police agencies/companies can ask the FBI to conduct criminal background checks on potential employees under the **Private Security Officer Employment Authorization Act of 2004**.

Private policing also has a number of potential societal benefits. Sparrow (2014) points out that it can leverage resources by pooling public and private

---

Critical Thinking Exercise

Private policing and the great growth of private security pose issues and challenges for public policing and safety. Read Joh's (2004) article "The Paradox of Private Policing." Do you believe the growth of private policing is good or a threat to public police and society? Why do you feel this way?

abilities when the need arises. When special skills are required, a private force may be able to respond quicker with more targeted resources than a public entity. There is also a clear element of community policing in private policing since the actions are invariably targeted at particular places and issues instead of focusing on a larger community at the same time (Sparrow 2014).

CHAPTER SUMMARY

The police are a primary element of the effective rule of law and are integral to the peace that citizens enjoy under their jurisdictions. Although the popular media portray them as "law enforcers," almost exclusively hunting down and arresting criminals, their duties and responsibilities include a much wider range of activities. Crime prevention, the most important of these, can be accomplished through deterrence (a visible presence to discourage potential lawbreakers) and the dissemination of crime prevention techniques to various constituents.

No less important, however, are the social contributions the police make, particularly at the local levels that are affected by disorders and individual challenges. They intervene and diffuse potentially violent situations, both on the street and inside the home (domestic conflict). They refer persons in need of special care to the right facilities and provide general guidance to youth as well as more direct guidance to youth showing signs of particular needs, whether directional, emotional, or behavioral. The presence and demeanor of the police help assure citizens that there is a dedicated force looking out for the peace and tranquility of the town, county, state, and country.

Police authority is defined by the jurisdiction(s) they serve. Federal law enforcement agencies have jurisdiction in all US states and territories, over crimes defined by federal law. State, county, and local police have the power to enforce state criminal and trafficking laws written by that state's legislature; county and local police also have powers to enforce ordinances written for the areas they patrol. All police agencies may cooperate with each other in emergencies, in crimes that span multiple jurisdictions, and in developing situations that might threaten the populace. Private police are limited to the property interests of the agencies that employ them but may also interact with and support the public police agencies.

Across the spectrum, evolving social conditions drive innovation and change in policing, from tax enforcement to slavery, to prohibition, to the civil rights movement and the gay rights movement, to the current opioid crisis. Immigration, the onset of the international terrorism, and the development of digital intrusion have led police to take on new skills and responsibilities, and more developments are expected in the future.

Police will continue to adapt, with or without the support of their political overseers. They will add new skills, new perspectives, and new equipment insofar as it is practical. Police constantly strive to live up to, and advance, their ever-present slogan: "To Protect and Serve."

KEY TERMS

Clery Act

County police

criminal investigations
bureaus/agencies

Mann Act

private police

Private Security
Officer Employment

Authorization Act
of 2004

Public Law 83-280

school resource officers
(SROs)

sheriff

shifts

special jurisdiction police

special response teams
(SRTs)

state patrol

state police

tribal police

FURTHER READING

Hyland, S. S., and E. Davis (2019). "Local Police Departments, 2016: Personnel." https://www.bjs.gov/content/pub/pdf/lpd16p.pdf

Joh, E. E. (2004). "The Paradox of Private Policing." *Journal of Criminal Law and Criminology* 95, 49–131.

Reaves, B. A., and M. J. Hickman (2004). "Law Enforcement Management and Administrative Statistics, 2000: Data for Individual State and Local Agencies with 100 or More Officers." https://www.bjs.gov/content/pub/pdf/lema001a.pdf

Sparrow, M. K. (2014). "Managing the Boundary between Public and Private Policing." *New Perspectives in Policing*. National Institute of Justice and Program in Criminal Justice, Policy and Management. https://www.ncjrs.gov/pdffiles1/nij/247182.pdf

CHAPTER 5

Police Hiring and Training

After reading this chapter you should be able to:

- Discuss the basic requirements to be hired as a police officer
- Distinguish between stress-based and campus-based academies
- Define POST and the minimum training requirements
- List and discuss the found broad categories of POST requirements
- Identify and demonstrate knowledge on issues related to weapons use and the use of force
- Discuss why communication skills are essential for police officers
- Give examples of ethical issues in policing and explain why ethical violations are problematic
- Demonstrate knowledge of field training and the role of FTOs

INTRODUCTION

Personnel are the backbone of policing. Recruiting the proper individuals and providing them with the appropriate training and tools to carry out the roles and responsibility of policing are crucial. This is not a simple task; it involves attention to a wide range of issues. The hiring process calls for identifying the proper individuals who can withstand the rigors and pressures of the job. The training process continues that selection process while equipping the future officers with the skills and knowledge to safely carry out the mandates given to the police.

Three basic types of police training are available to those who serve as police officers: Two are mandatory, and the third elective. The basic recruit academy—whether at state or federal level—must be completed satisfactorily in order for the recruit to assume active duty in the field. Almost every state and agency requires annual in-service training, usually a minimum of 40 hours each year. For individuals wishing to undertake specialized assignments, particular advanced training may be required.

HIRING

The requirements to be hired as a police officer can vary as widely as the types of departments, though state- and federal-level minimums standards almost always apply. There are numerous disqualifiers as well, which constitute rules that apply across the board. These disqualifiers include any felony conviction, any misdemeanor conviction within the three years prior to applying, and any conviction for **driving under the influence (DUI)** or domestic violence. DUI used to be called DWI (driving while intoxicated), but because "intoxicated" was considered by many to refer exclusively to alcohol consumption, DUI has been substituted to include the influence of drugs, both illegal and legal. Some offenses that carry moral implications—including domestic violence, variations of "contributing to the delinquency of a minor" or "indecent exposure," as well as use of illegal drugs within the recent past—may constitute potentially disqualifying moral deficiencies. Organization-specific concerns about "character" are many, and a candidate's background check may delve into many other aspects of their life looking for indicators of possible problems, including financial histories.

Recruitment

In the past, police agencies hired new officers or agents from the cohort of candidates who presented themselves when vacancies were announced. Those cohorts tended to be overwhelmingly white male, but that is no longer the case: In an attempt

---

Web Activity

A list of state-specific qualifications is maintained by LawEnforcementEDU.net. This is a private organization and, although its listings are not exhaustive, they represent a good starting point for individuals who have not already chosen an agency. You can access this material at https://www.lawenforcementedu.net/police-officer/.

---

to ensure that the police reflect the communities they serve, agencies actively recruit people who align with their powerful goal of diversity. Candidates of color, both men and women, are encouraged to apply. Physical strength is no longer the primary sought-after attribute (though it is still important), as the nature of the evolving roles for law enforcement demand skills that tend to be gender- and ethnicity-neutral: the ability to communicate effectively with diverse groups and individuals using words and phrases in a way that they understand, digital analysis skills, and the ability to work with individuals in distress and to deescalate problems and situations.

Recruitment efforts are driven by a recognition of the emerging and developing needs of the community, and they are bolstered by comparable efforts in training and orientation. More and more recruits come from cultures where the older prejudices have been rejected, or have eroded; as they move forward in their careers, we anticipate that the goal of the police representing the communities they serve will become an accepted reality.

Character/Background

Law enforcement agencies must be assured that their recruits bring good character to the job, but the ways of determining or verifying "good character" vary widely. Often, they depend in part on the resources the hosting agency can being to the task. Just contacting references and past employers as part of a background check can require considerable personnel time. The background check can include interviews with grade school, high school, and college teachers, as well as past employers, roommates, and others with whom the applicant has had past contact. The background also looks into financial records and the amount of debt an individual has.

In place of background checks—or to supplement them—agencies may employ standardized written tests, asking applicants to assess and describe their responses to different scenarios. Similar exercises may be conducted in face-to-face interviews. These are particularly appropriate in small-town departments where members of the relevant citizens' council may sit in on the interviews.

Larger agencies tend to do more thorough background checks (Snowden and Fuss 2000). This is partly due to the fact they can draw on more of a well-grounded tax base and may conduct the background checks with their own personnel, contract the process out to private organizations, or employ some process utilizing both. The size of the agency and the number of applicants meeting the minimum advertised standards often play a role in the choice of avenue.

In some cases, the background check is critically important, particularly for applicants who have prior police experience and applicable certification credentials. These individuals can be assigned to duties immediately, without going through training. This represents a great savings to the agency and the political unit funding it. Most certified officers who apply to another agency are in good standing and do so for a variety of reasons. Moving to be closer to family is a significant reason, as is "moving up" in their career track. However, there is a dark shadow that sometimes attends such movement from agency to agency. Those officers may go by the name "gypsy cops."

Gypsy cops generally refers to sworn officers who move from job to job, usually under a cloud of suspicion related to their activities. The general understanding is that they had committed one or more serious improprieties in their former department and they resigned rather than face disciplinary action or firing. "You sign this paper or we sign this one" is the bumper-sticker version of the process. The host agency accepts a resignation rather than go through the process (and expense) of termination proceedings and subsequent lawsuits, and the individual "bad cop" avoids the stigma of discipline or firing on his official record. The officer is free to apply elsewhere, and whatever jurisdiction hires him or her runs the risk of having to deal with similar improprieties. For smaller towns unable to attract suitable candidates otherwise, an already certified officer seeking a job presents a cost-reducing alternative. It is important to note that lateral movement from one police agency to another is not the norm. New recruits/hires typically start at the bottom, regardless of past experience.

Officers who are forced out of their department for a single incident are not necessarily "total losers," however. They may have been adequate, at a minimum, or even better, but were brought down by a single high-profile error. Whether the Cleveland, Ohio, officer who shot Tamir Rice in 2014 represents one such case or not is still open to question. His error was compounded by failure of the 911 dispatcher to provide full details of the call, including the caller's opinion that the gun "was probably a fake." Though his previous background in another Ohio department had suggested "'a dangerous loss of composure' during firearms training" (Haag 2018), he had been hired by Cleveland after a presumably thorough background check and he was subsequently hired by a smaller town in Ohio after a gap in his police employment (Haag 2018).

Web Activity

The New York City Police Department's careers page (https://www1.nyc.gov/site/nypd/careers/careers.page), which outlines candidate requirements and the hiring process, also includes links to web pages on police officer jobs, civilian jobs, and NYPD Cadet Corps opportunities; and a short brief on retirement benefits. The City of Cleveland's Police Division Public Safety web page (http://www.city.cleveland.oh.us/PublicSafetyCareers) hosts links for police, fire, and EMS applications. The Los Angeles Police Department website has an "Opportunities" link, which provides similar information (http://www.lapdonline.org/join_the_team).

Smaller jurisdictions have similar links. Many police departments list open positions using the PoliceApp website (https://www.policeapp.com/Police-Jobs/); the Bowling Green (Ohio) Police Department's recruitment page (http://www.bowlinggreenpolice.org/?page_id=62) gives similar information for larger cities. Many smaller towns and unincorporated districts are served by their county's sheriff's department. The Wood County (Ohio) Sheriff's Department's careers page (http://woodcountysheriff.com/careers/) lists qualifying and disqualifying information; the Sheridan County (Wyoming) Sheriff's Office hosts a more minimal employment page, giving positions, salary ranges, and a general description of benefits (https://www.sheridancounty.com/elected-offices/sheriffs-office/employment-2/).

In the wake of outcry when his hiring was announced, however, he resigned to spare the department and the community any protests or violence resulting from the reaction (Burke 2018).

General Requirements

Most agencies require candidates to be US citizens, between ages 18 and 35 or 37, with a minimum of a high school diploma or a General Educational Development (GED) certificate. A good credit history, lack of a criminal record, and the ability to pass a background check are fairly standard. So are the abilities to pass a minimal physical fitness test and a polygraph examination. For some agencies, a psychological exam is also part of the first-level screening process.

The minimal education qualifications were once nominal, but ever since the crisis of the 1960s and 1970s, many law enforcement agencies have raised their expectations. A college-level associate's degree (two years of college) is now becoming an absolute minimum in many areas, with many places giving preference to a candidate with a bachelor's degree. A growing percentage of larger departments require at least some college coursework for new recruits (Reaves 2015b). Many states have community colleges that offer a police academy training regimen—or part of one—as part of their associate's degree in criminal justice. Four-year colleges and universities generally do not have a training academy, but those agencies requiring a bachelor's degree as an entry-level qualification do not limit their eligibility pool to criminal justice graduates alone. The rapidly expanding nature of criminal activity now requires investigators to have skills in digital forensics, accounting, and other areas that can be subject to illegal manipulation.

Depending on the area in which an applicant seeks to work, additional skills may represent desirable qualities to advance their candidacy. For federal agencies and many large municipalities, skills in one or more foreign languages are a valuable asset, fostering better understanding of the populations they serve and stronger interactions. Cities like New York, Baltimore, New Orleans, Miami, and San Francisco are the ports of arrival for immigrants and visitors from many countries. Both language skills and cultural understanding advance the interactions between new arrivals and the police. For officers whose career aspirations include investigations, skills in accounting and in digital forensics represent attractive skills to many agencies.

The current crisis at the southern border involves not only Spanish-speaking people seeking asylum, but also those whose main (or only) language is one of

---

Critical Thinking Exercise

The issue of at least a two-year college degree as a requirement to become a police officer is an ongoing one in policing. Investigate the minimum education requirement for police agencies in your locality. Contact local police agencies to ask about the minimum degree held by most recruits. Should the minimum education level be increased? Why or why not?

many indigenous Central American languages, spoken for centuries before the Spanish incursion. Beyond entry-level minimum requirements and on-street contacts, foreign languages and cultural references potentially represent a hidden code for the criminal element, both those who are resident in the United States and those whose reach is international. The broader a police recruit's education and exposure to other cultures, the greater potential they bring to the investigative pursuits their career may require.

BASIC TRAINING

Like soldiers, police officers and law enforcement agents need to have a basic set of skills appropriate to their work, and an understanding of the legal framework in which their work is conducted. Each state sets the minimum standards for all sworn officers enforcing its laws. This includes state, county, and local laws/ordinances. Federal agencies have specific mandates accorded by federal law, but most agents in training acquire their basic investigative skills at the Federal Law Enforcement Training Center (FLETC) in Glynco, Georgia. Additional courses are offered in three satellite centers: Charleston, South Carolina; Cheltenham, Maryland; and Artesia, New Mexico. Two federal agencies—the Federal Bureau of Investigation (FBI) and the Drug Enforcement Administration (DEA)—maintain their own academies, both in Quantico, Virginia.

The most recent national survey of state and local training academies published in 2013 by the Bureau of Justice Statistics (BJS) (Reaves 2016) provides a useful overview on a number of related issues. Drawing upon statistics from 2011 through 2013, BJS reported that an average of 45,000 police recruits attended basic police academies each year during that period and that 86 percent completed their training successfully.

Forty-one states host selective basic training academies for their state police or state patrol agencies. These are almost exclusively regarded as stress academies. **Stress-based academies** are modeled on military boot camp, emphasizing physical fitness and the ability to operate calmly and appropriately in the face of aggressive, demonstrative behavior. Because their troopers work alone, and often far from any backup support, the agencies and the training create stress to enable their recruits to endure it, ignore it, and transcend it with their performance.

Thirty states offer **POST (Peace Officer Standards and Training)** to all agencies in their jurisdiction (Reaves 2016). The nine states without exclusive state police academies have their recruits do basic POST, but they often have

---

Web Activity

You can investigate the Federal Law Enforcement Training Center (FLETC) and the FBI and DEA training at Quantico through their websites: https://www.fletc.gov; https://www.fbi.gov/services/training-academy; and https://www.dea.gov/dea-office-training.

extensions that are specific to the state police/state patrol role following completion of the basic regimen. Almost all POST academies are residential, requiring recruits to live in barracks or dormitories during the week's curriculum, but allowing them to return home for weekends. POST academies also tend to follow the stress model, either full stress or "more stress than not."

Of the remaining 593 academies studied by BJS, the largest number (211) are **campus-based academies** situated in two-year colleges. Another 132 were hosted by "municipal police" departments, but that category is dominated almost exclusively by large city agencies with the personnel and the budget resources to maintain their own academy. Four-year universities and technical colleges each hosted 43 police academies, county agencies (sheriff's offices and county police departments) combined for another 88, and regional or multi-agency academies added another 49. The remainder were special jurisdiction academies (Reaves 2016).

Despite its seeming uniformity, POST standards are determined by each individual state, as are its minimum requirements. The average number of hours across all types in the BJS study was 843 hours, with state POST academies offering the minimum of 650 hours and state police/patrol academies requiring 878 hours on average. Sheriff's offices and technical schools required just over 700 hours each, while two-year college academies averaged 822 hours. The 903 hours required in four-year universities was exceeded by municipal police academies' 936 hours, but county police and special jurisdictions held the upper limit, with 1,029 hours and 1,075 hours, respectively (Reaves 2016). Regardless of the hosting environment, basic law enforcement training academies must offer at least the minimum type and number of hours required by the state's POST board in order for their graduates to earn state certification.

Not every state announces it standards on the web, so phone calls to the appropriate office are often the most direct way to learn the various offerings, including training sites. Connecticut's basic training is 22 weeks and Rhode Island's is 953 hours (almost 24 weeks, including water training appropriate to the state's eastern seaboard). Georgia has an 11-week basic training requirement, for which prospective officers pay tuition. Tennessee requires a minimum of 400 hours (10 weeks). Nevada requires 17 weeks for its Category I officers (regular police officers), with Category II officers doing the first 10 to 13 weeks (to work in school districts, community colleges, and courtrooms as special police officers). Nevada's Category III officers—jail and prison guards—complete the first 8 weeks of the academy (Ley 2014).

Four broad categories of topics comprise the bulk of police academy courses, with variation in hours based on the state's POST requirements: legal education, weapons/defensive tactics/use of force, operations, and a category BJS calls "self-improvement" (Reaves 2016). Legal education is offered by at least 97 percent of all academies, focusing on criminal law (the largest number of hours), traffic law, and juvenile law. "Weapons and tactics" focus on physical self-defense, firearms skills, rules governing the use of force, and in the non-lethal weapons like nightsticks and Tasers that are alternatives to firearms in encounters of a less-than-lethal nature.

Legal Education

The appropriate criminal code (state or federal, depending on the type of academy) forms the basis of legal training, but education in the law requires more than just knowing what conduct is prohibited. The manner of enforcement must respect the individual citizens' rights, and the rules governing police conduct have multiple levels. The basic rule of law, applicable throughout the nation, are the decisions handed down by the US Supreme Court. The cases of *Mapp v. Ohio*, *Gideon v. Wainwright*, and *Miranda v. Arizona* are the staples, but officers must know the variations that have expanded on those basic rights since the groundbreaking decisions were handed down.

The country is divided into 14 federal districts to which court member states can appeal their criminal cases. The decisions of the federal district court establish the rule of law for the member states, unless and until the decision is overturned by a US Supreme Court decision. Most criminal cases occur within the bounds of the individual state, and the rule of law established by that state's supreme court is the one most closely aligned to the peace officers' regular duties. No state may establish rules that are at odds with the federal district's rule or the US Supreme Court decisions, but only a small proportion of appeals rise above the state supreme court level.

Weapons and Tactics

Use of force

Because the police are authorized to use lethal force, and often must confront it, considerable training time is devoted to firearms proficiency and weapons retention. Firearms training with service weapons and others (both sidearms and long-barreled weapons—rifles and shotguns) includes nighttime and low-light conditions, both in physical space and online computerized training systems. More than 20 percent of agencies require training in the weapons carried by officers during off-duty hours.

Firearms training comprises two distinct but integrally related components. The first is accuracy, hitting the target being fired at. That requires a core familiarity with any weapons used: duty sidearm, duty-available long-barrel weapons (usually shotguns, but also rifles), and off-duty weapons. Many officers are proficient with sidearms before they join their department, so they are familiar with the recoil produced by the weapon. Shotguns are deployed much more rarely and have a different "kick" that needs to be accounted for. They also fire two very distinct types of projectiles: slugs and pellets. Slugs may be needed against antagonists wearing bulletproof armor. The large single projectile may not penetrate the armor, but it can produce a much larger impact that stuns the target with hydrostatic shock, or knocks the target down or off balance long enough for other officers to rush in and disarm the person, taking physical control.

For other types of encounters, officers are trained to aim pellet rounds a few feet in front of the target so the multiple small pellets bounce (absorbing some of their kinetic energy) and strike the lower legs. Again, the aim is to incapacitate the target long enough for officers to take physical control of the person.

Firearms training is not just accuracy in hitting a target. Because many cases of disputed police shootings involve fatalities and persons who either were not engaged in criminal activity or were holding a toy weapon, considerable emphasis is placed on "Shoot/Don't Shoot" simulations. Under condition of severe stress, police officers must discern whether a person represents a direct threat or not, and many toy weapons are indistinguishable from their real counterparts at a distance. The 2014 police shooting death of Tamir Rice in Cleveland represents the worst-case scenario for officers responding to a call: A real firearm can be lethal in the hands of anyone, regardless of their age, but children often play with realistic-looking toy guns like the one Rice carried (Ohlheiser 2016). And children do not always respond to police commands as adults might.

A second-level consideration is how many rounds are needed to accomplish the termination of a threat. Police do not "shoot to kill" under any but the most exceptional circumstances. Their use of firearms is restricted (by law) to stopping an immediate threat of deadly action against others, including the police themselves. Several high-profile cases have brought about intense criticism of police in one or another jurisdiction, which the public often generalizes to the police at large. The 2014 shooting of Michael Brown in Ferguson, Missouri, is one recent case. Another is the 2015 shooting of Laquan McDonald in Chicago (discussed in greater detail below) in which 16 shots were fired by a single officer.

One approach to the problem is taught in some training sessions: "Double-tap on center mass, and assess." Translated into English, that means "Two shots to the chest area, pause in your shooting, and see how the target reacts." The chest area is "center mass," where the hydrostatic shock effect of the bullet impact will be greatest, theoretically stunning the target and causing them to drop their weapon. "Assess" is a very quick visual check on how the subject who has just been shot reacts. If they drop their weapon and seem stunned, they are not an immediate threat. The police then move in with guns still trained on the target to take physical control by seizing any weapon they are still holding and placing them into a position to be handcuffed.

Should the target person be wearing a bulletproof vest, or if only one shot had struck them, producing only a minor flesh wound that left them capable of further resistance, their reaction might signal a need for the police to fire again. Raising a firearm and pointing it at the police would be a clear justification for another volley of shots. Turning and attempting to run away might, or might not, prompt additional shots, depending on other circumstances. If the suspect is still carrying a firearm capable of harming bystanders or pursuing officers, more police shots might be justified, even though shooting to stop an unarmed fleeing suspect would not be. All of these "what if?" scenarios require quick, clear assessments, and many similar types of scenarios are embedded in simulated shooting exercises to develop officers' cognitive abilities and judgment.

The use of force can be subject to abuse and has been addressed by the courts. The seminal case of *Tennessee v. Garner* (471 U.S. 1 (1985)) addressed the police use of deadly force to apprehend fleeing, unarmed suspects. The standard prior to the case was the fleeing felon rule, which allowed the police to use deadly force.

The court ruled in *Garner* that the use of such force violated the Fourth Amendment. The use of deadly force is justified only if the suspect "poses a significant threat of death or serious physical injury to the officer or others" (*Tennessee v. Garner*, 471 U.S. 1). The use of force also considers the reasonableness of non-deadly force. The case *Graham v. Connor* (490 U.S. 386 (1989)) addressed whether officers' force used in an investigative stop was reasonable. The court ruled that police must use an "objective reasonableness" standard when using force of any kind. This standard requires the officer to consider the severity of the crime, whether the subject poses an immediate threat to the officer or others, and whether the suspect is actively resisting arrest or attempting to flee (*Graham v. Connor*, 490 U.S. 386). These two cases set a basis for determining the proper use of force by police officers.

There are two primary categories of abusive use of force. **Wrongful use of force** involves using force for the wrong reason, such as to retaliate against a person for "disrespect" to the officer. **Disproportionate use of force** occurs when the level of force far exceeds the level of resistance or aggression of the subject. The police are also required to protect the life and safety of those they use force against once the situation is brought under control. Police are trained and equipped to employ force in accordance with the **force continuum**, which links the level of police force to the aggressiveness and resistance of the citizen (see Figure 5.1).

The force continuum begins with the authoritative presence of the officer, moves through commanding voice and directions to the first actual application of physical force, a guiding push or firm grip to steer a person away from a

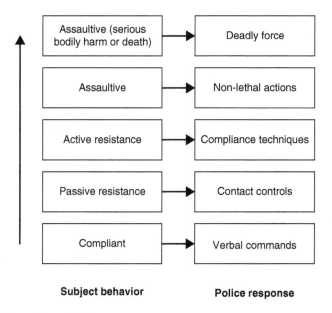

Subject behavior   **Police response**

Figure 5.1 Use of Force Continuum

particular point. Physical resistance from a citizen is required for using higher levels of force, such as pain compliance holds (wristlocks and other pressure-point techniques), devices like pepper spray and electrical shocks from stun guns, and impact weapons like nightsticks. Deadly force is the final step, reserved for a narrowly defined set of circumstances.

Weapons Retention

The retention of one's weapon can be critical in close-order combat, as offenders may try to grab officers' weapons to use against them. Security holsters exist, but their use can be sporadic. If officers have deployed long-barreled weapons, no holster is available, so learning how to fend off aggressors when an officer's weapon is exposed can be vital. Even more complicated is the fact that officers carrying long-barrel weapons are also armed with their duty sidearm, so an aggressor has two targets to choose between, under conditions of the aggressor's choice. The officer must protect both, or become the target of one.

In such an instance, just because an aggressor has discarded a weapon they were carrying when confronted does not mean that they are no longer a threat. Sudden movements as officers move in to take control of the aggressor constitute resistance, and possibly an attempt to grab an officer's weapon to replace the aggressor's discarded one. The assailant could feign an attempt to grab the sidearm and then use the officer's chemical mace instead, an intermediate distracting (and temporarily incapacitating) action while the aggressor makes a second grab for the officer's firearm.

Submission Techniques

Police do not engage in "fair" fights. They must win every conflict they enter. When a police officer moves in alone to make a physical arrest, or to halt an assault against a third person prior to making an arrest, speed and efficiency are paramount. The academy regimen stresses the importance of physical fitness and teaches disarming and submission techniques so that they become automatic reflexes. Both active and passive resistance must be overcome, and with the sudden appearance of weapons after police have engaged with an individual there is a need for both mental awareness and physical skills.

Suspects who are known to be armed as the police approach will be confronted with police weapons drawn, whether the subject's weapon is a firearm, a bladed object, a blunt object like a baseball bat, or some other object (known generally as an "improvised weapon"). The individuals will be ordered to drop the weapon, to step away from it, and to lower themselves to the floor or ground to be handcuffed and searched. Depending on the nature of their refusal, those who fail to comply may be sprayed with chemical mace, shocked with a Taser or similar device, or shot. Any motion that looks like an attempt to bring a gun into firing position, or raise a bladed weapon to be thrown, is almost certain to be met with police gunfire. Police are not paid to take unnecessary chances with their own safety or the safety of the civilians they are protecting.

Operations

Operations focus on patrol operations, since that is where almost all new recruits will begin their careers. An average of 52 hours of instruction in that area is supplemented by an average of 42 hours of instruction in how to conduct criminal investigations (Reaves 2016). Emergency vehicle operations (38 hours), report writing, traffic investigations, and basic first aid and CPR (cardiopulmonary resuscitation) techniques average 23 hours each, and all are offered by 97–99 percent of all academies. A smaller percentage offer at least some hours in computers and information systems—61 percent of academies list those subjects but average fewer than 10 hours of instruction (Reaves, 2016).

Driving Skills

While most police driving is done under normal traffic conditions (except when people tend to slow to or below the posted speed limit when they know a police car is behind them), there are times when officers must respond under emergency circumstances. High speeds, lights and sirens, heavy traffic, and pursuit conditions under gunfire are all possible, and adequate skills must be developed. Closed driving areas allow for high-speed stops, turns, and simulated pursuits (gunfire would be only simulated, too, if employed at all). Vehicles do not really dodge gunfire, but the exercise is practical for keeping one's composure while under fire.

Establishing safety zones while conducting vehicle stops or investigating vehicle accidents is a related skill. Police need to protect persons and evidence, allow clear access for extraction vehicles and ambulances, and ensure a safe, if restricted, flow of traffic. They must also have the awareness to protect themselves, a deepening concern in the era of cellphone-distracted drivers.

Self-Improvement

The self-improvement category is a catch-all that incorporates health and physical fitness, along with communications, ethics and integrity, and professionalism. As noted above, the use of force as an agent of the state is a category that incorporates all of those elements, but individually and collectively they have a far broader reach.

Health and Physical Fitness

The health and physical fitness of officers is an important concern in policing. They are also natural byproducts of the rigorous boot-camp style academy that starts each day with calisthenics and a long run. Many officers and agents do maintain some structured workouts, and some become known as "fitness freaks." The lingering comic presence of the beer-bellied cop, however, is a constant reminder that too many abandon the calisthenics regimen almost as soon as they graduate from the academy. Family obligations, rotating shift work, and the other life demands in general provide all too many reasons and excuses to do less and less. As a distinct course of study, health and wellness is both a cautionary tale and a roadmap of how to remain healthy and physically fit in the unstructured

Critical Thinking Exercise

The topic of health and physical fitness for police officers is one with conflicting points of view. While physical fitness testing is used in recruitment and the police academy, there is typically no ongoing assessment of an officer's fitness through-out their careers. Should officers have to retest for their physical fitness to do the job on a routine basis throughout their careers? Justify your position.

life environments beyond the academy. Officers never know when a seemingly innocuous citizen contact may result in them rolling around in the mud and the blood and the beer, or extricating multiple, overweight citizens from hazardous situations. Maintaining a higher level of fitness is the first key to prevailing in such encounters. Stress prevention and management is also a strong presence, found in four out of five academies.

Communications

The ability to communicate effectively, under a wide variety of situations, is a critical skill for success in law enforcement. It is a combination of effective speaking and effective listening, each of which has multiple subcomponents. Effective speaking and listening can be either enhanced or undermined by the attitudinal cues an of-ficer gives off, both verbally and nonverbally. The basic interview and observation skills taught in the recruit academies vary like most other elements, but time consid-erations tend to limit instructions to some variation of "Just the facts, ma'am."

The "just the facts, ma'am" phrase is commonly, but incorrectly, attributed to the 1950s TV detective Sgt. Joe Friday of the *Dragnet* series. Most sources iden-tify it as originating in a parody of that show, in which the phrase was uttered to cut off a complainant's wild and meandering diatribe. Though experienced offi-cers will doubtless recognize times when they wish they could have done just that, there are occasions when it makes good sense just to let the person ramble. First, the person being interviewed may not know what "just the facts" are. To them, the story is an integrated whole. More importantly, some of those wild rambles may contain clues that are useful to understanding the context or to pursuing a better investigation.

"Just the facts" tends to limit the information solicited to the fill-in-the-blank categories at the top of the offense report form. While those are critical to the proper categorization of the incident (and thus its retrieval, when needed), they constitute only a skeletal picture of the event. "The devil's in the details" is often the better summary quip. The way the person describes events could con-tain important details that link the incident to others or suggest that more is in-volved than the simple definition entry on the first page of the report. In a small number of cases, the expanded narrative may contain contradictory points, sug-gesting the possibility of a false report.

It is recommended to let the complainant, or witness, tell their story first, and then return to ask for clarification when they have concluded. If the story wanders seriously astray—into political commentary, or opinions about popular television shows or phone apps, for instance—gentle reminders to bring the narrative back on point may be needed. The officer's time is valuable for other pursuits beyond being an audience. The skill lies in the gray area between the maximum useful information and simply wasting time being a lonely (or egotistical) person's audience.

When the person speaking is a suspect, there are generally two paths. The first (and probably the most common) is that their resistance is such that their replies are nearly monosyllabic and the officers are reduced to asking yes or no questions (or their equivalent, such as "When did you arrive?" and "Who was here when you came inside?" types of questions). Less common, but often more valuable to investigations, are the egotists who think they are smarter than the police and can control the narrative and the investigation. The more they are allowed to talk, the more information they will reveal, or the more contradictions they will spin into their fantasy narrative.

Interrogation is a special kind of interview, wherein the police ask a suspect a series of questions, for which the police already know the answers, or at least believe they know the answers. Interrogation is often described in police circles as "testing a suspect's responses against known facts," in hopes of obtaining a confession. Naturally, suspects will try to lie, so the art of the interrogation involves letting them do so, and then confronting them with the truth. While interrogation may not always produce a confession, properly administered techniques will produce a series of lies and half-truths that will undermine the suspect's credibility in court.

Taking reports or statements is not the sum total of all communications, of course. Police on the beat are often asked seemingly aimless questions (in addition to requests for directions, etc.), but in each case, a polite response that is as on-task as possible should be given. More difficult questions come in the wake of incidents (local or otherwise) where the police response is brought under question, or in response to scandals that may or may not involve the police. On the surface, any such questions might sound like accusations or challenges to police authority, but it is important that officers respond on a level basis, in a civil tone. Even then, the nature of the reply may have consequences beyond the immediate setting (almost every such exchange will be overheard by persons in the immediate vicinity, and their minds may not be as made up as the questioner's).

"I'm not authorized to talk about that" or "I don't know anything about that" may very well be true responses to the challenging questions, but they easily can be interpreted as rude and dismissive. Rudeness and defensiveness imply guilt, or guilt by agreement. More responsive replies, while avoiding a definite answer to the question, can provide a better image. One way of both recognizing a citizen's viewpoint (without necessarily accepting it) and gently avoiding engaging in the confrontation would be responding with "As you know, we have to let the investigation takes its full course, but I certainly understand your concerns. All of us in the profession are affected when situations like this arise." If the conduct under challenge is especially egregious, answers like that help to separate the individual officer being questioned from the behavior of the accused officer(s). Turning the tables by asking what evidence the citizen might accept as proof of "guilt" or "innocence" (or their civil equivalent) might be a follow-up. It is a way to keep the citizen engaged but on a different footing. As noted above, the person asking the question is not likely to be the only audience. Others observing and overhearing the exchange may not have made up their minds the way the questioner seems to have done, and their judgments will sometimes hinge on how the officer responds.

Direct questions are not the only situations calling for good communications. In many situations it will be an officer who initiates the contacts, sometimes confrontational out of necessity, but in many cases directive out of necessity. At an accident scene, "Stand back!" is a clear directive; "Stand back, please!" is somewhat more palatable, but no less a directive. "Stand back, please! Medical crews need a clear path" is equally directive, but it links the command to a reason linked directly to the visible incident. Similarly, at a fire scene, "Stand back, please! Falling debris can be dangerous" establishes a clear, self-interested reason to comply, no matter how much bystanders might want a close-up view of the action.

Motor vehicle stops for traffic law enforcement are equally directive, with additional purpose. If a motorist pulls over and immediately gets out of the car to come back to the cruiser, they will be ordered to get back in their car. "Please" is unlikely to be part of the order, since the officer does not yet know whether a physical challenge is intended or not. (An officer's hand on his or her sidearm is another nonverbal communication that clearly says to the motorist, "I mean it!") Regardless of the motorist's intentions, their safety on the roadside is also the officer's responsibility.

After stopping a vehicle, the officer approaches the driver's door. (For older model vehicles, with only manual window roll-down capacity, the driver's door is the only alternative. Newer model vehicles, with electronic capacity to roll down any window from the driver's seat, allows the officer to approach the vehicle from the passenger's side. By doing so, the officer remains away from the path of overtaking traffic and has a less obstructed view of the area under the driver's control, allowing sight of any weapons that might be used against him or her.) The next communication (or the first, if the driver had enough sense to remain in the vehicle) is a request for the driver's license and the vehicle registration. It will often be accompanied by the question "Do you know why I stopped you?" (The answer is usually "No," of course, but sometimes the officer gains a verbal admission that the driver knew they had committed an infraction.)

On rare occasions, the driver may be en route to a hospital because of a medical emergency, either as a doctor on call or a citizen transporting a badly injured family member or neighbor. If the officer consents, the motorist will be allowed to proceed after surrendering his license, with the officer either leading or following. The infraction will then be dealt with at the hospital after the emergency is stabilized. Officers may request their dispatcher to call the hospital to confirm that a doctor was called in. It often takes time to do this, but allowing the doctor to proceed to the facility wastes no precious time if the emergency is indeed real. If it is not, the matter can be handled in different fashion.

Whether the officer then chooses to tell the driver the action that will be taken (ticket/citation or a warning) is the officer's choice. Waiting until after a ticket or citation has been written renders rebuttal moot and allows the officer to write the ticket in peace. Otherwise, there is a chance the driver will get out and come to the cruiser as the officer tries to write, complicating the situation. (Not telling the driver the outcome does not necessarily eliminate that problem, of course, but most drivers—and their passengers—conform to the officer's request to "Wait here, please; I will be back in a minute.") On the other hand, if the officer intends to issue a warning, telling the driver that at the outset relieves the inherent tension in the situation.

Other types of confrontational direction will be tense no matter what. Confronting a suspect who may have a weapon requires simple, unequivocal directions, delivered at gunpoint. "Stop! Keep your hands where I can see them. Drop the weapon. Place your hands on the top of your head. Kneel down, with your hands on the top of your head." The exact wording will be dictated by the circumstances, of course, but both the officer's words and the officer's demeanor count as "communication" regardless of the specifics. While it is generally preferred that police officers avoid the use of curse words in dealing with the public, this is one particular type of interaction where the use of profanity may constitute a second level of "I really mean it!" communication to the subject on the receiving end. (Nevertheless, Dirty Harry's "Well, do ya feel lucky *punk!*?" and equivalents should be avoided at all costs.)

Naturally, not everything related to effective communications can be taught in an academy session. Both time and realistic settings are in short supply. Only the basic principles are explored in the recruit academy, as a rule, but the field training part of the new officer's orientation often stresses the communications factors more concisely.

Ethics and Integrity

The respect and cooperation the public gives the police is largely contingent on whether the police are seen as fair and honest. Their loyalty should be to the law and to the communities they serve, and they should show favoritism to none. For the most part, that is an accurate description of the behavior of most individual officers and most police agencies. There are some important exceptions on the positive side, and—unfortunately—many examples in which individuals, groups, or entire agencies have failed to live up to these standards.

"Telling the truth" is one of the nebulous areas, because police will not always tell the truth. In some cases, they will conceal it. In others, they may lie outright. Sometimes that is in in the interest of the communities they serve, but when it is only in the individual interest of the officer (or other officers), it is problematic.

As noted above, for instance, interrogations of criminal suspects take place under circumstances where the police know, or think they know, the facts of the matter. They may not know all of the facts, however, but in order to move a suspect off his or her story, they say that they do. "We have a witness who saw you do it."

"Your fingerprints were found on the weapon: You may have worn gloves at the crime scene, but you handled the gun without gloves before that." This assertion is a bluff—more formally known as a "gambit"—based in the belief of a certain truth and the hope that it will persuade the suspect that the jig is up and he or she might as well confess in order to get the best deal.

There is a dark side to this technique, however, and one that has come to light in far too many cases with the advent of DNA testing. Persistent police lies, in the absence of counsel for the accused, can convince an innocent person to "confess" to a crime he or she did not commit, in order to minimize the sentence that the police say they can bring to bear. While the confessions may be taped, interrogations are less likely to be recorded, so the disadvantage falls on the defendant.

Other ethical breaches include "turning a blind eye" to the misdeeds of companion officers, either out of blind loyalty to the police subculture or because local culture stresses that even a bad officer "may be your backup at a critical time." The Laquan McDonald case (see Box 5.1) is a vivid example of a number of

---

Box 5.1

The Laquan McDonald Case

The following summary of the Laquan McDonald case draws upon numerous publicly available news sources.

McDonald was viewed as a decent and respectful person and an above-average student. His autopsy, however, revealed PCP (phencyclidine, a hallucinogenic drug) in his blood and urine. According to the initial police reports filed after his shooting death by Officer Jason Van Dyke, McDonald was armed with a folding knife and he lunged aggressively at Officer Van Dyke. Van Dyke reportedly fired in self-defense. Van Dyke's report that he had fired in self-defense was supported by reports filed by other officers at the scene, and the initial police investigation ruled it a justifiable homicide.

It was only later that a video recording of the event, made by a dash cam on one of the police vehicles at the scene, revealed a very different story. McDonald was indeed acting erratically, as reported, but he was moving away from Officer Van Dyke rather than confronting him. Van Dyke was in the last police car to arrive at the scene and began shooting six seconds after stepping from the cruiser. None of the other officers at the scene fired their weapons, and they had been observing McDonald's actions for a longer period of time. Van Dyke emptied his 16-shot pistol into McDonald's body, even after McDonald was lying on the pavement: Nine of the 16 rounds entered his back. Further investigation revealed that the dash cams of the other police cruisers at the scene were nonfunctional, for one reason or another, and that five officers had asked to view the surveillance video of a nearby Burger King restaurant. When later investigators attempted to review the Burger King video, they found that 85 minutes had been erased, covering the time of the incident and its subsequent on-scene investigation. After the dash cam video was made public, Officer Van Dyke was discharged from the Chicago Police Department, indicted for second-degree murder and 16 counts of aggravated assault, and subsequently convicted.

police errors, including firing on an unresisting subject, discharging far more shots than were necessary to end the confrontation even if it had been as the officers described, lying about the circumstances by the shooting officer, and lies by other officers at the scene who were backing up the story told by the shooter. An additional level of unethical behavior may have been attempts to prevent the release of videocam recordings of the incident.

The McDonald case indicates a number of procedural and ethical lapses. Seven police units were already on the scene, and the officers were positioned to contain McDonald (whose erratic behavior is not in doubt; PCP has that effect). Officer Van Dyke ignored their presence and challenged McDonald as though he were the first officer at the scene. Emptying his pistol was a tactical mistake even if McDonald had been moving toward him: "Double-tap on center mass and assess," or some equivalent, should have been employed. Shooting a downed subject nine times in the back has no justification under any shooting rules (and supported the murder charge).

Filing a police report containing assertions contrary to the facts was an ethical violation—or a lie—on Van Dyke's part, but when the other officers at the scene supported his version of the event, a far greater ethical violation took place. The rules of the police subculture overruled the social expectations of honesty: Police officers lied to protect "one of their own." Further, they took active steps to disable devices that would have revealed the truth to police investigators (every officer at the scene would have known that a separate investigation would be conducted for any and all police shooting deaths). Private property—the Burger King video—was also destroyed, an ethical violation, if not a criminal one.

There are many other cases similar to McDonald's across the nation and across the years. Although they represent only a small number of incidents, they have an outsized impact on the public trust of the police. Academy training will stress the need to "not do this," but the social pressures each recruit will encounter in their agency may be quite different.

A different type of ethical violation is using the police position for personal enrichment, whether extorting money from civilian clients for "protection" or working sub rosa on behalf of organized crime elements. There is a fine line here. Officers may abstain from bringing well-deserved criminal charges against low-level offenders in return for information about more serious criminal offending. Maintaining "snitches" whose own offenses are relatively minor, but who have access to information about far more harmful crimes, is a long-established and accepted practice. Ignoring more major offenses in return for money or other personal favors from more powerful offenders is not. It is corruption and it is criminal.

These distinctions are part of police training. If the individual who has been hired is inherently dishonest or finds himself or herself in an employment environment that is a complete contradiction of the training lessons, the impact of academy lessons is likely to be small. The system depends on the reinforcement of training lessons by the sponsoring field agencies once the recruit is in the field.

Web Activity

You can view the list of standards set by CALEA for both standard and advanced accreditation at https://www.calea.org/node/11406.

Professionalism

Professionalism is the sum total of all of the elements discussed above, and it requires individual commitment. In some cases, it is an attitude that recruits brought to the training, especially if they are scions of a professional police family. In others, it is an attitude adopted during training and one that survives exposure to less professional elements in the employing agency. A key to professionalism is the extent of training and education that officers receive at the outset of and throughout their careers. Competency in carrying out police duties as they are intended is essential.

The level of police professionalism is not just measured at the level of the individual officer. Professionalism is also an organizational matter. Organizational professionalism can be gauged by the actions of the individual officers but can also be assessed through the standards adopted and established by the organization that direct and guide the activities of the organization and its members. The minimum standards for being a police officer are one element for ensuring professionalism, although it is indeed a "minimum" standard. Standards for police professionalism need to go beyond the minimums for recruitment. They require standards that address the entire operations of police departments, from training to operations to management and administration. The Commission on Accreditation for Law Enforcement Agencies (CALEA) has two levels of accreditation—basic and advanced. The basic accreditation has 181 standards that must be met, while the advanced has 459 standards. These standards cover items related to virtually all elements involved in offering policing services, including hiring, training, organizational structure, and management issues.

FIELD TRAINING

Basic academy training tends to be generic and classroom-focused. Regardless of the agency, newly graduated recruits need an additional layer of training and orientation before starting to work on their own. A **field training period** serves that purpose and may last from several weeks to almost a year, depending upon the agency's needs.

For many uniformed police agencies, the field training stage is comprised of three distinct parts. In the first segment (however long it may be), the rookie rides with a **field training officer (FTO)**, learning the jurisdiction's streets, problem areas, and the agency's expectations while essentially just riding along with the FTO. One thing that a regional academy cannot prepare a recruit for is the sub-communities within the officer's jurisdiction, whether racial, national-origin, or an American subculture. That falls to the FTO, who will hopefully provide a combination of verbal instruction on the background and a personal introduction to major players and leaders of the community. The field training segment is above all mostly an observational period, during which the rookie absorbs additional information about the corporate climate, the community expectations, and how the general lessons of the academy are expected to be applied in the specific jurisdiction.

The second stage of field training has the rookie and the FTO responding to calls and patrolling as equals. Instead of just observing the FTO (and being a visual backup presence), the rookie interacts with citizens, writes some of the reports, and does some of the motor vehicle work, as an independent officer. They are under the watchful eye of the FTO throughout and there may be post-incident evaluations between the FTO and the rookie, examining what was done, and what might have been done.

In the third stage, it is the FTO who is the ride-along, observing and evaluating as the rookie acts as the sole officer handling the calls and assignments. In the cultural vernacular, the FTO is expected to take action "only of the rookie is about to get hurt" or make some other mistake that will bring an expensive lawsuit down on the agency. Those situations rarely occur.

At the conclusion of the FTO session, the field training officer submits a summary report on the rookie's work and attitude, which is part of the agency's assessment to determine whether the rookie will be retained as a full-fledged probationary officer, authorized to assume individual duties independently, or terminated as unfit for the job. The last option does occur but is very rare. Any performance problems observed by the FTO or others are addressed while the FTO period is ongoing. When such problems occur, in most cases the rookie's responses are positive.

ADVANCED POLICE TRAINING

The career aspirations of police recruits are often very different. Some expect to be patrol officers for their entire career. Others desire to become investigators of one sort or another. Naturally, the different options depend on the level and specific charge of the agency that employs them, especially when the agency responds to different levels of court jurisdiction or to specific areas of authorization.

For federal agencies, the FLETC system offers several different types of training. State, local, and tribal law enforcement training is offered at the main FLETC facilities. The International Training Division has a center in Gabarone, Botswana, and also offers programs elsewhere when resources allow. A National Capital Region Training Operations Directorate provides a number of supportive services in Washington, DC; and Los Angeles, California, hosts a Regional Law Enforcement Maritime Training Center. Another center in Orlando, Florida, evaluates new technologies for law enforcement use.

Web Activity

Visit and explore the training available at various federal centers:

> International Training Division at https://www.fletc.gov/international-training-division-itd
>
> National Capital Region Training Operations Directorate at https://www.fletc.gov/washington-operations-wo
>
> Regional Law Enforcement Maritime Training Center at https://www.fletc.gov/los-angeles-california
>
> Training Innovation at https://www.fletc.gov/orlando-florida

---

States and larger agencies provide a wide variety of training courses for officers moving upward in their careers or into specific areas of interest or need. New supervisors need training that sets the ground rules and the legal precepts that define their new responsibilities, powers, and limits. Evidence technicians also need specialized training in the science—and emerging variations and advancements of same—that affects their collection of evidence: It is important that they are aware of what crime laboratories require and what they will do with the evidence taken in the field. That has considerable influence on the field practices of officers who generally are not scientists. In a similar vein, vehicle accident reconstruction skills require more specific knowledge than just doing a basic sketch of the accident scene.

Officers who want to work with dogs (K-9 officers) or horses need special training and information about animal psychology, among other skills. Those who will operate equipment to measure blood alcohol content (BAC) require special certification for their testimony to be admissible in court. Those who investigate child abuse, and some who serve as school resource officers, need a deeper understanding of the psychology of different age cohorts. All of these specific training courses are offered in a limited time frame, usually a short number of weeks, but may be taken in consecutive steps across a broader time frame.

CHAPTER SUMMARY

The recruitment and training of police officers is a crucial part of modern policing. The selection of new officers is a never-ending mission for police agencies. Changes in society and in criminal activity necessitate identifying appropriate individuals to "work the street" and face the public, as well as having the potential to lead future police efforts. While most discussions of police training focus on the initial academy and early field training, modern policing needs to focus on addressing new crimes and criminal activities using new scientific advancements in computer technology, forensic analysis, and other areas. Training needs to be an ongoing activity for all police officers and agencies.

KEY TERMS

campus-based
   academies

disproportionate use of
   force

driving under the
   influence (DUI)

field training officer
   (FTO)

field training period

force continuum

gypsy cop

interrogation

POST (Peace Officer
   Standards and
   Training)

stress-based academies

wrongful use of force

FURTHER READING

Meade, B. (2016). "Recruiting, Selecting, and Retaining Law Enforcement Officers." *Police Foundation Blog*. Retrieved January 20, 2020, from https://www.policefoundation.org/recruiting-selecting-and-retaining-law-enforcement-officers/

Reaves, B. A. (2016). *State and Local Law Enforcement Training Academies*, 2013. Washington, DC: Bureau of Justice Statistics.

Woska, W. J. (2016). "Police Officer Recruitment—a Decade Later." *The Police Chief*. Retrieved from https://www.policechiefmagazine.org/police-officer-recruitment/

CHAPTER 6

Legal Issues

After reading this chapter, you should be able to:

- Understand the rights afforded to citizens under the Fourth Amendment to the US Constitution with regard to searches and seizures
- Define probable cause within the context of government searches and seizures

- Identify and describe the exceptions to the search warrant requirement
- Define a stop and frisk, and explain how police lawfully use it
- Explain the Aguilar-Spinelli test used by courts to discern the lawful use of information from informants
- Distinguish between police interrogations and interviews
- Understand the rights afforded to citizens under the Fifth Amendment to the US Constitution with regard to criminal interrogations
- Describe the ruling in *Miranda v. Arizona* and the case's impact on police procedures
- Define the situational force model and various forms of suspect resistance
- Define the use-of-force continuum and various levels of force used by police
- Explain the limitations of use-of-force continua
- Describe the ruling in *Tennessee v. Garner* and how it influences police decisions to use deadly force

INTRODUCTION AND OVERVIEW

This chapter provides an overview of some of the most important legal issues involved in police work. The chapter proceeds in three main sections. The first section covers specific issues associated with citizen rights under the Fourth Amendment to the US Constitution in relation to police searches and seizures. Searches and seizures are integral to police work and the goals of crime control. The chapter defines requirements to obtain search warrants, as well as the most common exceptions to those warrant requirements. Police officers also commonly conduct "stop and frisks" of criminal suspects. The chapter describes how these situations differ from traditional police searches and the conditions under which police may lawfully stop and frisk citizens. The second section of the chapter covers the topic of police interrogations. The section includes discussions on how police interrogations differ from police interviews, as well as the typical process or procedures involved in the interrogation of criminal suspects. The latter portion of this section of the chapter covers specific issues associated with interrogations and citizen rights under the Fifth Amendment to the US Constitution, including rights against self-incrimination and the suspect's rights to an attorney. The section also includes a detailed discussion of the landmark Supreme Court case *Miranda v. Arizona*. The third section of the chapter covers legal issues associated with police use of coercive force. The section explains the "situational force model," which is designed to guide and constrain officer decision-making, as well as the more traditional use-of-force continuum. The chapter concludes with an overview of situations involving the use of deadly force by police, including the landmark Supreme Court decision in *Tennessee v. Garner*.

SEARCHES AND SEIZURES

One element police use to enforce laws and mitigate crime relates to searches and seizures. Searches within the context of police work involve the search of people and/or property to gather or secure evidence to determine whether a crime has been committed. Items that are commonly the subject of police searches include criminal suspects, contraband (e.g., illegal drugs or weapons), fruits of criminal activity (e.g., stolen property), instruments of a crime (e.g., weapons), or any other evidence that could be reasonably related to a crime.

Police searches are governed by the Fourth Amendment to the United States Constitution. The **Fourth Amendment** sets out the rights of the American people with regard to government searches and seizures, including those conducted by police:

> The right of the people to be secure in their persons, houses, papers, and effects, against unreasonable searches and seizures, shall not be violated, and no warrants shall issue, but upon probable cause, supported by oath or affirmation, and particularly describing the place to be searched, and persons or things to be seized.

The amendment reflects the goals and concerns of the framers of the Constitution during the period of and immediately following the American colonial revolution against Great Britain (1765–83). The colonials vehemently objected to the use of **general writs of assistance**, whereby agents of the British government (i.e., soldiers) were granted authority to enter any house or other place to search for and seize prohibited goods. These general writs also commanded that all British subjects assist in these activities. The idea that citizens should be protected from unreasonable government searches and seizures relates to the notion that "every man's house is his castle," a phrase dating from the early 1600s and English common law traditions. Free citizens should not have to worry about agents of the government—including police officers—storming into their homes and seizing their property absent any evidence of a crime. Some of the newly independent states of the union enacted laws against general writs of assistance in their own state-level constitutions prior to the enactment of the Bill of Rights to the US Constitution in 1787 (Clancy 2011). Thus, the regulation of government searches has a long tradition and is integral to the lawful performance of police duties in the United States.

Searches and the Fourth Amendment

How do courts distinguish between police searches that are defined as reasonable and therefore lawful and searches that are unreasonable and in violation of the Fourth Amendment? Courts recognize that the Constitution grants citizens a **reasonable expectation of privacy** under certain circumstances and protects citizens from government searches and seizures under those conditions. The term encompasses legal definitions important in defining how courts view a particular search as it relates to the rights outlined in the Fourth Amendment. A **search** within the context of the Constitution occurs anytime the police or other government actors intrude into a person's reasonable expectation of privacy. Then, a determination needs to be made as to whether that intrusion was lawful or unlawful. Courts decide each case on its own merits, and the interpretation of whether a particular search is reasonable or unreasonable is based on the particular circumstances of each case. Students need to understand the overarching purpose of the Fourth Amendment in regard to law enforcement searches and seizures: It is not about protecting the "rights" of criminals, but rather the establishment of a check on police authority and protecting the rights of free citizens against government tyranny.

Ways to Lawfully Search

Police may conduct law enforcement searches in one of two ways. First, they may conduct a search after having obtained a valid **search warrant**, which is a legal document authorizing a police officer to enter and search a particular place (or places) (Legal Information Institute 2018). Police obtain lawful search warrants according to a process consistent with the language of the Fourth Amendment. For example, police must demonstrate that **probable cause** exists that justifies the search. The primary issues here revolve around whether the items to be seized as a result of a search are connected to criminal activity, and whether those items will be found within the place to be searched. Police must establish several things in order to effectively demonstrate probable cause. First, they must provide evidence that a crime has been committed. Second, they must show that evidence of that crime exists. Third, they must demonstrate that the criminal evidence exists in the place to be searched. Fourth, they must describe the particular place to be searched and the potential evidence to be seized within that particular place.

Search warrants may be issued only by judges or magistrates. Thus, police officers must demonstrate to these judicial authorities that probable cause exists, and then they must support these points with a sworn statement or affidavit consistent with Fourth Amendment language. This means that police are in effect applying for a warrant through a judge or magistrate who decides whether to issue the warrant. The judge or magistrate will sign and issue the warrant in cases where they determine that police have adequately established probable cause. Students should recall that the purpose of the Fourth Amendment is to check police authority. The warrant process in theory provides that check. Police cannot create search warrants themselves. They need to go through a judge who is presumably neutral in the ultimate process of determining the innocence or guilt of criminal suspects. Searches conducted with a valid search warrant are presumed to be reasonable and lawful by the courts because the process satisfies the requirements and goals of the Fourth Amendment. Thus, it is always best for police to seek and obtain a search warrant prior to conducting any search in cases in which time and circumstances allow.

Of course, circumstances and time do not always allow sufficient opportunities for police to obtain a valid search warrant before they need to conduct a search. Indeed, most searches conducted by police do not involve the issuance of a valid warrant. Courts have ruled that these **warrantless searches** may also comply with the requirements of the Fourth Amendment, so long as the court determines that the search was reasonable under the circumstances (Legal Information Institute 2018). Remember, the Fourth Amendment is not about protecting criminals; it is about checking government tyranny. So courts recognize the reality that police cannot obtain a warrant in each and every case in which a search may be reasonable and justified. Case law has established several circumstances in which courts allow warrantless police searches. These situations are commonly referred to as **exceptions to the warrant requirement**. Warrantless searches are presumed to violate the Fourth Amendment unless the search fits within the context of one or more of these established exceptions to the warrant requirement.

Critical Thinking Exercise

Back to the Future: Police Searches, Mobile Phones, and the Fourth Amendment

This chapter outlines how the US Constitution provides a legal framework within which police officers must operate, including searches and seizures governed by the Fourth Amendment. Students need to be aware of the constantly evolving standards upon which these rules are based. The rules potentially shift as legal issues emerge through new federal court cases. For police, this means that their actions on the street and determinations about what is legal will necessarily change over time. The Bill of Rights was written almost 250 years ago by men who could not have imagined the computer revolution and our information-based society. These changing circumstances give rise to important questions about how our use of technology fits within the intentions of those who wrote the Constitution and the goal of checking police authority to intrude on citizens' privacy.

The US Supreme Court recently considered one of these issues in *Riley v. California*. The case involved the arrest of David Riley during a traffic stop on a weapons charge. Police immediately seized Riley's phone and searched the phone incident to the arrest. Police used the contents of the phone to identify Riley as a member of a criminal gang. They used the information to uncover Riley's involvement in a prior shooting, which eventually led to his criminal conviction.

The issue for the Court was whether the search of Riley's phone was constitutional. Police did not possess a search warrant, so they needed to justify the search under one of the exceptions to the warrant requirement. The Court found that the warrantless search of Riley's phone was unconstitutional. They rejected arguments that the search was lawful incident to his arrest, because the phone could not reasonably be considered a weapon. The Court also rejected arguments that the search was lawful based on exigent circumstances. Justices in the decision emphasized Fourth Amendment goals providing a check on warrantless searches:

> Modern cell phones are not just another technological convenience. With all they contain and all they may reveal, they hold for many Americans "the privacies of life," Boyd supra, at 630. The fact that technology now allows an individual to carry such information in his hand does not make the information any less worthy of the protection for which the Founders sought. Our answer to the question of what police must do before searching a cell phone seized incident to an arrest is accordingly simple—get a warrant. (*Riley v. California*, 28)

Do you believe police should be allowed to conduct warrantless searches of cell phones incident to an arrest? Why or why not? Do you think the decision in Riley will negatively impact police crime control efforts, given the prevalence of cell phones?

Exceptions to the Search Warrant Requirement

The first exception to the warrant requirement is **consent searches**. Consent searches are the most common type of warrantless search. Police may ask citizens to give permission for them to search their property. These types of warrantless searches have been defined as reasonable under the Fourth Amendment because citizens in these cases surrender their rights. As a result, no warrant or probable cause is needed in order for police to conduct a consent search.

The courts have stipulated some rules to determine whether a consent search is reasonable and lawful under the Fourth Amendment. First, consent to search must be voluntarily provided by the citizen. Consent cannot be granted as a result of police use of force, coercion, or duress. Second, the citizen must grant consent intelligently. This means that citizens who ultimately grant consent to search must be aware of the right to refuse consent. Police are not required to inform persons of their rights in this regard, but courts will review the totality of circumstances surrounding a case to determine whether consent was intelligently granted. Third, silence on the part of the citizen to police questions on consent does not constitute consent. Citizens must explicitly give consent. Fourth, citizens are within their rights to revoke consent at any time after they have granted it. The revocation of consent must be explicit and communicated to police. In some circumstances, persons other than the criminal suspect may grant consent to search property. Some examples of these types of situations include spouses with equal property rights to a home, employers who own work-related property provided to an employee, school officials who control access to school lockers, and persons who have been granted permission to borrow property from the owner.

A second exception to the warrant requirement is **searches incident to arrest**. These are searches conducted as part of a lawful seizure or arrest of a criminal suspect by police. Arrests must be based on probable cause to believe that the arrestee has committed a crime; however, a subsequent search incident to the arrest of that person requires no warrant or probable cause. The justifications for a search incident to a lawful arrest are three-fold. First, police are allowed to search persons whom they have arrested in order to protect themselves from harm. They are allowed to search for and seize any weapons possessed by an arrestee incident to an arrest. Second, searches incident to arrest are justified by the need to prevent an immediate escape of the arrestee. Third, searches incident to arrest are justified by the need to prevent the concealment and/or destruction of evidence linking the arrestee to criminal activity.

Courts have outlined two important considerations in regard to determining the reasonableness of particular searches incident to arrest. First, searches defined by police as incident to arrest must occur at the same time or close in time to the arrest. Courts will be increasingly less likely to consider a warrantless search "incident to arrest" as the time elapsed between the arrest and search becomes longer. Searches of an arrestee hours after an arrest would generally need to be based on either a warrant or some other exception to the warrant requirement. Second, searches incident to an arrest must be limited to an area within the arrestee's immediate control. This area of immediate control has been commonly defined as equivalent to a person's "wingspan," or arm's length. This limitation on searches incident to arrest, known as the **Chimel rule**, is based on a case in which police arrested a criminal suspect and then subsequently searched his entire house without a search warrant (*Chimel v. California*, 1969). Courts intend to limit police powers to search incident to arrest consistent with the language and goals of the Fourth Amendment. Police are allowed to search the arrestee and any areas under his or her immediate control for protection and to limit the destruction of evidence; anything beyond that requires either a search warrant or facts that indicate another exception to the warrant requirement is applicable.

A third exception to the warrant requirement is **plain view searches**. Police are allowed to seize items legally subject to seizure that are within their plain view without a search warrant. Courts have determined that citizens do not have a reasonable expectation of privacy for items that are in plain view, so many of the requirements and goals of the Fourth Amendment do not apply. There are three broad rules that govern the lawfulness of seizures under the plain view exception to the warrant requirement known as the **plain view doctrine**. First, the item to be seized must be within the officer's sight or field of vision. He or she must be able to *see* the item rather than just smell, touch, or hear the item. Police can use these other senses to develop probable cause to search, but they cannot use these other senses to justify a seizure based solely on the plain view exception. Second, police must be legally present within the place where a plain view seizure occurs. That is, police cannot do anything illegal to get to the place where he or she views the item to be seized under the plain view doctrine. Third, the item(s) to be seized under the plain view exception must be immediately recognized as subject to seizure, such as illegal weapons, contraband, or instruments of obvious criminal activity. Police need to satisfy all three of these elements in order to legally seize items under the plain view doctrine.

A fourth exception to the warrant requirement is **searches based on exigent circumstances**. Police are permitted to search and/or seize evidence without a warrant in emergency situations that make obtaining a warrant impractical, dangerous, or unnecessary. Police under these circumstances must have established probable cause and some sort of pressing or "exigent" need to preserve evidence that is in danger of being destroyed or corrupted. The most appropriate examples of exigent circumstances under this exception include **hot pursuits**, wherein police enter a premises without a warrant in pursuit of a dangerous criminal suspect whom they reasonably believe is on the premises and/or in response to third parties they know to be in immediate danger inside (e.g., police hear screams for help).

A fifth exception to the warrant requirement is **border searches**. Courts recognize international borders as unique places wherein the government has responsibilities to protect public safety and the entry of contraband into the United States. Border agents are generally allowed to conduct routine searches of luggage or motor vehicles absent either a warrant or probable cause.

Critical Thinking Exercise

Searches and the 100-Mile Border Zone

This chapter identifies border searches as one of the exceptions to the search warrant requirement outlined in the Fourth Amendment to the Constitution. Courts recognize the government's unique responsibilities in securing the national border, so citizens need to have diminished expectations of privacy in these areas and border patrol or other law enforcement officers may conduct routine warrantless searches at border locations.

The manner in which courts have defined "border locations" or "ports of entry," however, has given rise to some controversy on the issue. For example, federal law provides US Customs and Border Protection Officers authority to operate within 100 miles of any US external boundary. Agents within the 100-mile boundary may operate immigration checkpoints wherein vehicles are randomly identified and the occupants asked about their citizenship (American Civil Liberties Union 2018; Kirby and Campbell 2018).

Should US border agents be allowed to conduct such operations 100 miles from any recognized international border? Why or why not? Identify and consider possible situations in which the rights of legal citizens may be threatened by the 100-mile border zone and potential remedies within the context of the Fourth Amendment.

A sixth exception to the warrant requirement is **special needs searches**. This exception covers searches conducted by government employees other than police who perform jobs related to law enforcement. For example, courts have ruled that public school officials do not need either a warrant or probable cause to conduct searches of school lockers if they have "reasonable grounds" to believe that the search will uncover evidence of a violation of law or school rules (*New Jersey v. T.L.O.*, 1985). These warrantless searches are justified under the belief that schools have a "special need" to protect students and school property. Searches conducted by airport screeners also fall under the special needs exception to the warrant requirement. Limited searches of passengers is permitted since the government has a "special need" to protect the safety of airline passengers.

Stop and Frisk

Police have the right to protect themselves during all interactions with citizens. The right to self-protection extends to relatively brief interviews of citizens whom police officers reasonably suspect are involved in criminal behavior. When these brief interviews would cause a reasonable police officer to fear for their safety, the officer is permitted to pat down or "frisk" the subject's outer clothing for any hard objects that might be weapons (Fyfe 2004). Courts allow these **stop and frisk** encounters on the basis of reasonable suspicion. Reasonable suspicion is a legal standard that is less stringent than probable cause but more than a mere "hunch" or guess. Reasonable suspicion must be based on specific and articulable facts or circumstances associated with a specific individual that leads a reasonable police officer to believe, based on their training and experience, that a crime has been or is about to be committed. Reasonable suspicion cannot be based on the subject's membership in a class or some vague sense that he or she "does not belong" within a particular area (Fyfe 2004).

The US Supreme Court defined the parameters under which police may stop and frisk criminal suspects in *Terry v. Ohio* (1968). A plain-clothed police officer on foot observed what he believed to be suspicious individuals who repeatedly walked back and forth looking into the same store window in a way that suggested they were "casing a job, a stick-up." The officer approached the men and asked for their names. The officer confronted John Terry and almost immediately frisked his outer clothing. The officer eventually recovered a pistol from Terry and made an arrest. The Court determined that, based on this brief interaction, the officer had not established probable cause prior to the frisk. The officer obviously did not have a search warrant. The Court, however, ruled that the stop and frisk was not a search under the Fourth Amendment and defined the parameters under which police may conduct brief pat-downs of criminal suspects without probable cause. The Court continued to articulate rules that govern stop and frisks over the next several decades. First, both the "stop" and the "frisk" of the suspect must be based on reasonable suspicion. Second, the stop must be reasonably brief under the circumstances. Third, the frisk is limited to a pat-down of outer clothing for weapons only. In the longer view, the establishment of lawful stop and frisk encounters broadened police powers to protect themselves beyond the language of the Fourth Amendment in cases where police can articulate reasonable suspicion rather than probable cause.

Arrests and the Fourth Amendment

Seizures within the context of the Fourth Amendment involve the seizing of property, but also persons in the form of a formal arrest. Police arrests involve the taking of a person into custody either to compel him or her to answer a criminal charge, or to prevent further criminal activity (Asch 1971). Arrests must be based on probable cause rather than mere suspicion. Police need to be able to demonstrate knowledge of facts and circumstances that are sufficient such that a reasonable person would believe the suspect has committed a crime. Probable cause must exist at the time of the arrest. Arrests may be made with an arrest warrant. Similar to the process that described search warrants, police typically issue a complaint under oath or affirmation that alleges a crime has been committed and there is probable cause to believe that the person named within the arrest warrant committed it (Asch 1971). A judge or magistrate determines whether to issue a valid arrest warrant based on probable cause. Police may also arrest without a warrant if they have probable cause as described above. The lawfulness of a warrantless arrest depends on whether probable cause existed at the time of the arrest. The Fourth Amendment requires a judicial determination of probable cause within a reasonable amount of time subsequent to a warrantless arrest. In most states, these determinations occur at the time of the suspect's initial appearance in court within either a 48- or 72-hour time frame (Olano 1992).

Police can establish probable cause within the context of an arrest in three different ways. First, they can establish probable cause for an arrest on the basis of their own knowledge. Police are allowed to stop and question persons based on reasonable suspicion. From there, they gather information about a suspect and the situation that can be used to establish the more stringent standard of probable cause to arrest. For example, the suspect may admit wrongdoing, fail to answer routine questions, or flee the scene. Police may also use physical cues or the presence of incriminating evidence on scene. They may also conclude that the suspect fits a physical description of the perpetrator provided by dispatch communications or on-scene witnesses. All of these facts can be used as a basis to establish probable cause to arrest a suspect.

Second, police may use information provided by a reliable informant to establish probable cause. Police have historically relied upon information provided by confidential informants and anonymous "tips" in order to identify and arrest criminal suspects, but these practices are controversial because confidential informants are often criminals themselves (del Carmen and Hemmonds 2010). Thus, courts have established intricate rules for the lawful use of informants and confidential "tips." Courts, for example, established the **Aguilar-Spinelli test** based on two Supreme Court cases as a standard to determine the lawful use of confidential informants (*Aguilar v. Texas*, 1964; *Spinelli v. United States*, 1969). The Aguilar-Spinelli test demands that police demonstrate sufficient facts to determine (a) the truthfulness of the information provided and (b) the basis of the informant's knowledge such that he/she was related closely enough to the criminal activity. The Aguilar-Spinelli "two-prong" test, however, made it very difficult for police to establish probable cause on the basis of anonymous tips, so the Supreme Court established a new test in *Illinois v. Gates* (1983). The Court ruled that a warrant based on information from a confidential informant may be used even in cases where both "prongs" of the Aguilar-Spinelli test have not been met. The Court established that probable cause may be established on the basis of information provided by a confidential informant considering the "totality of circumstances" and make a "common-sense decision as to whether there is probable cause" (del Carmen and Hemmonds 2010, 31). The decision made it easier for police to establish probable cause on the basis of information provided by a confidential informant.

Third, police may use information provided by a reliable informant that is also substantially corroborated by police. For example, police may use information provided by a confidential informant about a suspect's criminal activity in cases where police follow up and confirm that information on their own. This avenue to establish probable cause is much less controversial than the second avenue described above because police are not relying solely upon information provided by an informant.

INTERROGATION

Other elements police use to enforce laws and mitigate crime relate to police interrogations. **Interrogation** within the context of police work involves a direct interview with a criminal suspect. Lyman (2002) specifically defines interrogation as "the systematic questioning of a person suspected of involvement in a crime for the purposes of obtaining a confession" (180). The interrogation phase involves many legal considerations that police investigators must be familiar with and adhere to so that information derived from the interrogation—including a confession—may be used in court. One such issue involves legal distinctions between interviews and interrogations.

Interview versus Interrogation

There are several distinctions between police **interviews** and police interrogations. These distinctions are most important within the legal context, since police interrogations more often prompt the application of court precedents on the constitutional rights of suspects. One distinction relates to the goals of the interaction. The goal of interrogation is to secure the truth from the person who is suspected of committing the crime. This goal most often involves producing a confession from the criminal suspect. The goal of an interview, however, is to gather basic information pertinent to the investigation. Another distinction is that interviews are non-accusatory, while an interrogation most often includes the specific accusation that the suspect is the person who committed the crime. The third distinction is that an interview involves a less-structured dialogue, while interrogations are more structured and include a more clearly defined and straightforward question-and-answer format from investigator to the suspect (Blair 2003; Inbau, Reid, Buckley, and Jayne 2011).

Process of Interrogation

Criminal suspects should be removed from more public settings and from other people to facilitate open communication and admissions of truth. Interrogations should occur within a room that is relatively private and specifically dedicated to the interrogation of criminal suspects. Interrogations usually involve two police investigators. One of the investigators will conduct direct questioning, while the other investigator is able to take notes and act as a witness to the statements made by the accused. The two investigators usually also take on different roles and styles of questioning the suspect (Lyman 2002). These include, but are not limited to, the well-recognized "good cop–bad cop" scenario, wherein one investigator adopts a confrontational and argumentative style while the other investigator portrays a more sympathetic and understanding tone toward the suspect. There are no legal restrictions on police investigators with regard to lying or the presentation of false information to criminal suspects. Police quite often communicate that they are in possession of more evidence against the suspect than is actually the case. Police may also describe physical or testimonial evidence against the suspect that does not exist, and they often intimate that the production of a confession will tend to produce more leniency with regard to punishment (Shantz 2011). Investigators are trained in and practice systematic techniques designed to facilitate communication and the eventual admission of guilt. The Reid technique is the most widely used and involves a nine-step, trademarked program that is routinely part of investigator training programs across the nation (Inbau et al. 2011).

Suspect Rights against Self-Incrimination

Police interrogations are in many aspects governed by the **Fifth Amendment** to the United States Constitution. The Fifth Amendment sets out the rights of the American people with regard to several aspects of state power including those that limit police interrogations and citizen rights against **self-incrimination**:

> No person shall be held to answer for a capital, or otherwise infamous crime, unless on a presentation or indictment of a Grand Jury, except in cases arising in the land or naval forces, or in the Militia, when in actual service in time of War or public danger; nor shall any person be subject for the same offense to be twice put in jeopardy of life or limb, nor shall be compelled in any criminal case to be a witness against himself, nor be deprived of life, liberty, or property, without due process of law; nor shall private property be taken for public use, without just compensation.

The phrase "nor shall be compelled in any criminal case to be a witness against himself" has been referred to within legal proceedings as the self-incrimination clause. This clause of the amendment has been interpreted over time to involve the well-recognized right to remain silent while in police custody. The interpretation of the Fifth Amendment in reference to rights against self-incrimination is rooted in English common law traditions that include the exclusion from trial any evidence derived from coerced confessions. Courts long ago recognized that confessions that are coerced—through physical torture, beatings, psychological pressures, or any other circumstances that compel a suspect to confess to police—are not likely to be entirely or at all truthful. Coerced confessions are likewise not consistent with the ideals of due process and a system of justice that is adversarial and fair to criminal defendants (Zalman 2010).

The history of American policing at least through the early decades of the 20th century includes the routine imposition of what has been referred to as the **third degree** by police against criminal suspects. This involved cases of torture, physical beatings, assaults, and psychological pressure designed to coerce confessions from criminal suspects, a phenomenon that was publicly exposed during the 1930s and the Wickersham Commission (Zalman 2010).

The public exposure of police misconduct during interrogations proceeded rulings by the Supreme Court that established standards to determine the constitutionality of confessions known as the due process-voluntariness test (*Brown v. Mississippi*, 1936). The case involved three African-American defendants whose confessions came after being beaten by police with a metal-studded belt along with other forms of physical and psychological coercion. The resulting due process voluntariness test includes consideration of the totality of circumstances that surround a particular confession and whether those circumstances had produced a confession that was involuntary. Courts in this context would take into account factors such as the suspect's age and level of intelligence, and whether police had denied the suspect interaction with an attorney (Justia 2009).

Suspect Rights to an Attorney

The development of laws that govern police interrogations involves legal interpretations regarding suspect rights against self-incrimination rooted in the Fifth Amendment, but also interpretations regarding suspect rights to an attorney derived from the Sixth Amendment. The **Sixth Amendment** sets out the rights of the American people with regard to legal representation:

> In all criminal prosecutions, the accused shall enjoy the right to a speedy and public trial, by an impartial jury of the state and district wherein the crime shall have been committed, which district shall have been previously ascertained by law, and to be informed of the nature and cause of accusation; to be confronted with witnesses against him; to have compulsory process for obtaining witnesses in his favor, and to have the assistance of counsel for his defense.

The phrase "to have assistance of counsel for his defense" had been historically interpreted to involve the suspect's right to an attorney at trial. There is no specific mention in the amendment to any right to an attorney during an interrogation. States historically were not required by law to appoint a trial attorney for indigent offenders. The decision in the Supreme Court case *Gideon v. Wainwright* (1963) required states to appoint a trial attorney to indigent criminal defendants in felony cases (Taylor 2004). Gideon had been a poor defendant who represented himself in court against charges of felony breaking and entering. Florida law at the time required the appointment of counsel only for cases involving the potential penalty of death. The Supreme Court ruled that the Sixth Amendment right to counsel in criminal cases extended to all felony defendants in state courts (Taylor 2004).

The Supreme Court had determined that all criminal defendants in serious cases had the right to an attorney at trial proceedings; however, questions remained as to when suspects had the right to an attorney prior to any court proceedings, including any police interrogations. The issue is obviously crucial since police interrogations are often designed to produce a confession that provides the basis of evidence to ultimately prove the defendant's guilt at trial.

The decision in the Supreme Court case *Escobedo v. Illinois* (1966) involved the extension of suspect's rights to an attorney prior to trial. Danny Escobedo, a suspect in a murder case, was taken into police custody and interrogated over several hours. Escobedo's repeated requests to speak to an attorney during his interrogation were denied by police, and he eventually confessed to the murder and was convicted at trial. The Supreme Court in this case determined that the right to an attorney begins anytime a criminal suspect is in police custody for what the court defined as a **custodial interrogation**. Custodial interrogations are (a) initiated by police, and (b) occur whenever a suspect's freedom is restricted in a significant way. Custodial interrogations obviously include any questioning that occurs post-arrest but also may extend to any situation in which police question someone who reasonably believes that are not free to leave (Taylor 2004). In the longer view, the Supreme Court had more clearly defined laws about what police could and could not do during the interrogation of criminal suspects with regard to both suspect rights against self-incrimination and the right to an attorney. The stage was set for a decision on how these established rights would be protected and ensured within the context of street-level interactions between police and those they determine to be criminal suspects.

Miranda v. Arizona: **The Establishment of Procedural Safeguards**

The case of *Miranda v. Arizona* (1966) is probably the most widely recognized Supreme Court decision among American citizens. Ernesto Miranda was a man with schizophrenia who had been convicted of rape. He was identified in a police lineup, he was questioned by police, and then he confessed to the crime. Based on the facts, his confession had not been coerced. The Supreme Court, however, considered the case within the context of the two constitutional rights covered within this section: the right against self-incrimination and the right to an attorney during a custodial interrogation. The Court was interested in providing law enforcement with "concrete constitutional guidelines" to follow so as to mitigate the potential for Fifth and Sixth Amendment violations (Taylor 2004, 193).

The *Miranda* ruling required police to warn criminal suspects of the following rights under the Fifth Amendment prohibition against self-incrimination:

1. You have the right to remain silent.
2. Anything you say can and will be used against you in a court of law.
3. You have a right to an attorney present during questioning.
4. If you cannot afford an attorney, one will be appointed for you.

The phrases are commonly referred to as the *Miranda* warnings—words that have become part of the popular lexicon through constant repetition within the popular media and particularly television crime dramas. Taylor (2004) refers to the *Miranda* decision as involving the "intersection" of the two separate but complementary constitutional rights covered within this section (182). The first two warnings refer specifically to citizen rights against self-incrimination and the consequences of waiving those rights for criminal suspects. The last two warnings recognize the importance of citizen rights to an attorney during any custodial interrogation. The *Miranda* decision was initially harshly criticized by many police administrators and policymakers on the grounds that it would severely hamper crime control strategies and the utility of police interrogations. Most observers over time came to agree that the decision has served to increase police professionalism and legitimacy within the context of interrogations. Data also suggests that about four-fifths of all criminal suspects waive their rights after they are provided the warnings (Zalman 2010). Students of policing no doubt need to recognize the *Miranda* warnings and their importance in providing procedural safeguards to protect the constitutional rights of criminal suspects and rules for conducting lawful interrogations.

USE OF FORCE

The use of force by police involves some obvious legal issues. In the context of policing, the term *force* is commonly understood by students to be limited to acts of physical violence such as kicks, punches, and the use of deadly and less-than-lethal weapons. Police scholars, however, have often defined it in much broader terms to include threats, verbal commands, and other nonviolent behaviors intended to address situations in which "something ought not to be happening and about which something ought to be done about right now" (Bittner 1970, 249). This broad conceptualization of force is preferred because it describes how police exercise some form of coercion in almost everything they do: traffic control, the settlement of everyday disputes, verbal commands and threats, and escort or leverage techniques used to complete an arrest (Klahm, Frank, and Liederbach 2014, Muir 1977; Rubenstein 1973). These and many other police actions encompass a continuum that ranges from nonviolent acts, intended as some lower level form of coercion, all the way to the most violent of behaviors, including instances in which police shoot to kill a dangerous criminal suspect. This broad definition captures the many ways in which police use some form of coercion to do their job. A broad conceptualization of how police use various levels of coercion also provides a framework for defining and understanding how police must select among various options, depending on the situation, in order to accomplish the goals of their job within legal constraints.

The Situational Force Model

Police may use any level of force that is reasonable and necessary to make an arrest, to overcome suspect resistance, or to prevent an escape. Police may use non-deadly force to protect themselves or others from physical harm, to subdue an individual who resists their attempts to control a situation, and/or to bring a disorderly situation under control. Police may use deadly force within the context of narrowly defined encounters wherein a suspect presents an immediate deadly threat to officers or others. Police officers are commonly trained on the "situational force model," which is intended to guide officer discretion in use-of-force situations. The **situational force model** recognizes that police have a variety of available force options depending on the situation. Police need to select the least violent force option in order to make an arrest, overcome suspect resistance, or to prevent an escape. The option selected by police in any particular encounter depends on many factors, but the most important factor in determining the appropriate force option is the level of resistance offered by the suspect. Police are trained to recognize and act upon various levels of suspect resistance including:

- *No resistance:* The suspect complies with orders and offers no resistance.
- *Resistance/passive:* The suspect refuses to comply or only partially complies but offers no defensive action or active resistance. The most common example is a refusal to move when ordered to do so.
- *Resistance/defensive:* The suspect acts in a way that prevents police from gaining control over them. This is not an attack on the officer, but an action designed to prevent officer control. The most common example is pushing an officer away.
- *Resistance/active:* The suspect acts in a physical or assaultive way against the officer or another person with less than deadly force. The most common examples include grabs, punches, and kicks.

- *Deadly threat:* The suspect performs any action that puts the officer or others at immediate risk of serious bodily injury or death.

Police need to consider other factors beyond the level of suspect resistance in choosing from available force options. These include, but are not limited to, the severity of the suspected crime, whether the suspect is attempting to flee, any potential risks to bystanders and/or third parties on the scene, and any special vulnerabilities of suspects who are young, frail, or disabled. Students should recognize more generally that any decision to use police force is complicated and involves a myriad of factors that need to be considered and decided upon under circumstances that are sometimes exigent.

The situational force model also defines the basis upon which officers choose among the various force options that were defined by the US Supreme Court in *Graham v. Connor* (1989). The Court ruled in this case that the "reasonableness" of a particular use-of-force act must be judged from the perspective of a reasonable police officer at the scene, and that this judgment must allow for the fact that police are often forced to make split-second decisions about the amount of force necessary in a particular situation (Police Executive Research Forum 2016). Students should understand at least two important products of this ruling. First, courts will judge the lawfulness of police actions from the perspective of the police officer on the scene rather than some "reasonable" person who was not directly involved. This means that legal actors must follow the proverbial goal of "putting themselves in the officer's shoes" in order to determine the legality of any particular use-of-force action. Second, courts need to recognize that police must make immediate decisions on force options and they often do not have the luxury of time on their side. It is commonly easy to determine what the most appropriate level of force should have been hours, days, or months after a particular encounter, but police on the scene do not have the luxury of hindsight. The legality of police actions must be judged with recognition of the immediate context within which the decision to use force was made.

The Use-of-Force Continuum

The variety of force options available to police is often defined within police training materials and manuals on policy and procedures as a use-of-force continuum. The **use-of force-continuum** is intended to guide officer discretion in force situations and describes an escalating series of options the officer may take to resolve an encounter (National Institute of Justice 2009). Use-of-force continua vary by agency, but the options described below are typical:

- *Level 1: Police presence.* This is a recognition that an officer can inspire respect and generate cooperation on the basis of their mere presence in an encounter.
- *Level 2: Verbalization.* This is a form of nonphysical coercion and includes the use of both non-threatening commands and increasingly urgent and authoritative verbalized orders. Verbal control may also be in the form of advice or persuasion.

- *Level 3: Escort.* This involves some form of physical maneuvering required to escort or lead an individual from one place to another. These situations involve no significant suspect resistance and are designed to prevent any injury to the suspect.
- *Level 4: Soft empty hand controls.* Empty hand controls involve the use of bodily force to gain control of an encounter. Soft empty hand controls include the use of pressure points, tactical handcuffing, grabs, and holds to restrain a suspect. These controls are commonly used in situations involving suspects who are uncooperative and refuse to be placed into custody, or to control defensive resistance when lesser forms of force have failed or when the officer reasonably believes they will fail.
- *Level 5: Hard empty hand controls.* These are empty hand controls such as punches, counterpunches, and kicks. These techniques are commonly used to control actively aggressive suspects or as a means for officers to defend themselves against a physical assault.
- *Level 6: Less-lethal force.* This includes the use of less lethal devices such as batons, chemical sprays, and/or conductive energy devices more commonly referred to by the public as Tasers. These techniques do not create a substantial risk of causing death or serious bodily injury and are intended to control the suspect's active aggression.
- *Level 7: Deadly force.* Any force used by an officer that may result in serious injury or loss of human life. The most common example is use of the service weapon.

American police agencies have utilized versions of the use-of-force continuum since the late 1980s to guide officer decision-making on when and how to legally use force on the job. These continua provide a useful framework to train officers in the lawful use of force, but clear **limitations associated with use-of-force continua** have emerged over the last 25 years (Aveni 2003; Flosi 2012). First, traditional use-of-force continua such as the one above present the range of force options in a linear manner that moves sequentially, or step by step, from the least coercive level (e.g., police presence) to the most coercive and violent level (e.g., deadly force). Police–citizen encounters do not always proceed in a linear or sequential manner based on the actions of the suspect, however. Reasonable police officers may need to skip some or all of the non-deadly force options to gain control over a particular criminal suspect. For example, a previously compliant suspect may suddenly reach for or grab the officer's service weapon—a situation that may reasonably involve the officer resorting to the use of deadly force against the suspect to mitigate an immediate deadly threat. There is obviously no need for the officer to move sequentially through the various levels of force in order to protect their own life. Traditional linear use-of-force continua do not accurately portray this street-level reality.

Second, traditional use-of-force continua usually do not emphasize the option of de-escalation or even complete disengagement as a viable—and perhaps most reasonable—alternative in some encounters. When any particular

---

Web Activity

The complete use-of-force policy of the San Francisco Police Department is available online at sanfranciscopolice.org/sites/default/files/2018-11/DGO%205.01. pdf. The policy provides a valuable resource for students interested in learning about how the policies of police agencies strive to guide officer decision-making in use-of-force situations. The policy includes specific sections on levels of suspect resistance, force options, and what they agency refers to as the "critical decision-making model" designed to govern officer use of force.

---

level of force is ineffective in gaining control of a resistant or actively aggressive suspect, police are not obligated to maintain and/or increase levels of force. Reasonable police may be able to more effectively gain control of a situation by temporarily "backing off" rather than using immediate and/or sequential escalation. Third, the traditional use-of-force continua present the various force options in ways that fail to recognize the importance of method and degree. That is, legal determinations on whether police used a "reasonable" level of force depend largely on *how* the force was utilized. For example, an officer may use hard empty hand controls, such as a single counterpunch, to gain control of an actively aggressive suspect who had assaulted them. One counterpunch may have been reasonable; however, that does not imply that five counterpunches—the same level of force but a different degree—would necessarily be reasonable in this situation, particularly when one counterpunch would have worked to subdue the suspect. Method and degree often matter more than the level of force utilized when determining whether the officer acted "reasonably" within the context of any particular citizen encounter.

These and other limitations of traditional use-of-force continua have led to the development of other non-linear presentations of the various force options. The Canadian Association of Chiefs of Police, for example, endorsed a continuum that presented the force options in a "wheel" format that placed either the officer or the situation at the center of an evolving or rotating set of circumstances and appropriate force levels intended to more adequately inform officer decision-making and the choice of reasonable alternatives (Aveni 2003; Laucius 2016). The Canadian "wheel of force" largely failed to catch on, but the situational force model described earlier and upon which the "wheel of force" is based has largely been incorporated into police policies, procedures, and training within many American police agencies over the course of the previous decade.

Deadly Force

A series of notorious police shootings has once again underscored the importance of deadly force in the study of policing and more broadly the relationship between police and communities within a democratic society. Recent deadly police–citizen encounters sparked protests in Baltimore, Chicago, New York City, and elsewhere (Gambino and Thrasher 2014; Mathis-Lilley 2015; Wisniewski

====== **Critical Thinking Exercise** ======

The Role of Less-than-Lethal Technologies

Police use-of-force incidents have been increasingly influenced by weapons designed to expand the range of options available to police. These less-than-lethal (LTL) technologies most often involve electronic immobilization devices ("Taser" guns) and chemically based weapons (tear gas, mace, and oleoresin capsicum pepper spray) (Trostle 1990). LTL technologies have been touted as providing a safe and effective non-lethal option for use in incapacitating suspects who may actively resist police attempts to control situations.

Taser guns are a specific brand of electronic immobilization device. They are conducted energy devices (CEDs) that fire a cartridge attached to two small probes. These probes emit an electronic charge that overwhelms the suspect's central nervous system on contact, thus "stunning" them into submission (Nielson 2001). OC pepper spray, the most widely used chemically based LTL technology, is discharged from pressurized canisters as a spray, stream, or fog (Nowicki 2001). OC pepper spray produces temporary blindness and breathing difficulties after it has been sprayed into a suspect's face (National Institute of Justice 2003b).

The use of pepper spray has elicited largely positive reviews within the law enforcement community (National Institute of Justice 1994). Comparisons following the introduction of pepper spray in three North Carolina police departments, for example, concluded that the use of pepper spray decreased both the number of injuries to both police and combative suspects and the number of excessive force complaints filed against police (National Institute of Justice 1994). The U.S. Government Accounting Office (2005) estimated that over 7,000 law enforcement agencies in the United States use the Taser, with over 140,000 units issued. More recent industry sources indicate that as many as 11,500 law enforcement agencies utilize CEDs, with the Taser X26 being the preferred model (Amnesty International 2008).

The adoption of LTL technologies has also introduced a number of significant issues, especially in terms of safety. There appears to be some instances in which LTL technologies can produce unintended fatalities. Pepper spray, for instance, has been cited as a primary cause of death in cases where it was used against suspects who had pre-existing respiratory ailments such as asthma (National Institute of Justice 2003b). In these cases, the use of pepper spray induced asthmatic responses that fatally compromised the breathing ability of targeted suspects. Tasers may also be used excessively and/or inappropriately, particularly when they are used against suspects who are only passively resisting. Popular media accounts provide anecdotal evidence regarding the criminal misuse of Tasers by police, including cases that resulted in significant injuries and even deaths to suspects and others (Stinson, Reynes, and Liederbach 2012). While cases such as these appear to be rare, they provide a vivid reminder that less-than-lethal weapons should not be considered *non*-lethal in all possible scenarios.

Do you think that LTL weapons are most often utilized in appropriate situations, or do weapons such as Tasers and chemical sprays increase, rather than decrease, the incidence and seriousness of force used by police in situations where lesser levels of force would be more appropriate?

and Madden 2015a, 2015b). The protests and public acrimony clearly underscores the degree to which the deadly force issue can impact relations between law enforcement and citizens. Deadly police–citizen encounters carry so much importance for a couple of reasons. The first reason is most obvious—deadly consequences elicit elevated emotional responses from the people most directly impacted by the death; but also, there are legions of citizens who are exposed to the gruesome realities associated with police shootings. Police–citizen interactions that result in consequences much less serious than death simply cannot impact wider police-community relations in the same manner that deadly force encounters often do. The second reason relates more broadly to the societal role of police and how that role is perceived by members of the public. The legitimate use of force is central to the functioning of police in a democratic society. Deadly force encounters uniquely demonstrate and reinforce why we have police in the first place—but only in cases where the public perceives the use of deadly force as legitimate and righteous. Deadly force encounters that are perceived to be unnecessarily brutal or wrong, on the other hand, have the potential to diminish perceptions of police legitimacy and their proper role in a democracy. The conflict and acrimony that sometimes result from a police shooting publicly defined as unjust or brutal can become enduring and extremely difficult to resolve.

The primary goal of this section is to outline the legal restrictions on police use of deadly force. An understanding of the operation of these legal restrictions should, however, coincide with knowledge about when and why police use deadly force, since these realities necessarily go a long way in determining the reasonableness and ultimate effectiveness of legal and organizational restrictions on police use of deadly force. The use of deadly force, by all accounts, is an exceedingly rare occurrence in police work, despite the degree of public and media attention these sorts of encounters produce. Officer surveys indicate that between 1 and 2 police officers per 1,000 shoot at a citizen(s) each year. Firearms are utilized by police in only 0.2 percent of all arrest situations (Adams 1999; Pate and Friddell 1993). These deadly force encounters most often occur in public locations in response to armed robbery crimes or situations in which police have been called on to investigate "person with a gun" situations. Police shootings disproportionately involve young, African-American males who are armed (Geller and Scott 1992).

Scholars have conducted many studies to discern the factors that seem to influence police officers to use deadly force—in particular, situations focusing on the individual characteristics of officers, the race of suspects shot by police, and the features of communities in which police use deadly force. These studies consistently find that police decisions to use deadly force are most directly influenced by the level of risk confronted by the officer who decides to use deadly force. Scholars refer to this factor as **situational risk** (Fyfe 1981; Sherman and Langworthy 1979). Put simply, police are significantly more likely to shoot persons who are armed and/or shoot at police and/or attempt or succeed in assaulting police (Fyfe 1988). These situational risks seem to influence police decisions to shoot more than the characteristics of individual officers, or citizens, or the place in which these shootings occur. The incidence of police shootings obviously varies across communities; police tend to use deadly force in some communities more often than in other communities. However, the communities in which police are most likely to use deadly force are also those that tend to present the most situational risk to officers in terms of suspects who are armed, or shoot at police, and/or attempt to assault them. The importance of situational risk demonstrated in the research does not mean that other factors—such as race, class, gender, or officer experience—cannot influence police decisions to shoot. The research does suggest, however, that we need to account for the level of situational risk in consideration of the relative influence of these other factors.

Americans became increasingly interested in controlling the use of deadly force by police during the 1960s in the aftermath of large-scale urban riots and public criticism of police brutality and discrimination. New legal and organizational restrictions designed to control the use of deadly force by police were enacted during the decades that followed. These efforts included changes to existing state criminal codes and decisions of the US Supreme Court (Liederbach and Taylor 2004).

Most states have laws on the books that define how police may use justified levels of force within the context of their work. The exact terminology varies by state, but these statutes typically demand that police utilize a level of force that is appropriate to the seriousness of the crime and the goal of achieving compliance and control of the situation. Police who use force excessively—particularly in situations that result in the death of a citizen—may be criminally prosecuted for homicide, manslaughter, or assault with a deadly weapon (Cheh 1995).

However, the historical reality is that **state-level criminal prosecutions** of American police officers involving cases in which they use deadly force on the job have been exceedingly rare. Research studies suggest that criminal prosecutions are initiated in approximately one of every 500 cases involving police shootings (Cheh 1995; Kobler 1975). The most recent evidence indicates that from 2005 through 2013, only 41 police officers were charged with murder or manslaughter resulting from an on-duty shooting, and just 21 of those officers were convicted (Stinson 2018).

There are some practical reasons why these prosecutions seem to be so rare. Prosecutors know these sorts of cases would be difficult to win, mostly because citizens tend to assume that police officers who shoot are doing so within the legitimate parameters of their job. Civilians tend to define police as trusted authority figures. Perhaps more important, prosecutors must maintain close working ties with police because they often need them to act as witnesses in order to successfully prosecute other cases. The initiation of even a selected number of criminal cases against police who shoot during the course of their work would threaten the ongoing relationship between prosecutors and police necessary to convict ordinary defendants. Basically, the criminal prosecution of police presents a conflict of interest for prosecutors, even in cases that result in what members of the public perceive to be the "unjust" death of a citizen.

The US Supreme Court has also played a role in defining specific legal restrictions on police use of deadly force. In *Tennessee v. Garner* (1985), the Supreme Court heard arguments regarding the death of an unarmed 15-year-old who was shot by police as he attempted to flee the scene of a burglary. The Court heard the case in order to address inconsistencies among state laws on **fleeing felons** (suspects who fee the scene of felony crimes) to determine whether police could justifiably shoot suspects fleeing the scene of felony crimes in order to subdue them. The Court defined these situations within the context of the Fourth Amendment, which protects citizens against unreasonable seizures. The issue that the Court considered was simple: Is it reasonable for police to shoot felony suspects simply because they flee the scene of the crime? The Court ruled that state-level statutes allowing the use of deadly force against fleeing felons were unconstitutional. The Court further articulated rules to govern the use of deadly force by police more generally. Police may resort to deadly force only in situations in which there is probable cause to believe that the suspect constitutes an imminent or immediate deadly threat to the officer or others. Unarmed felony suspects who are running away from police do not constitute an imminent deadly threat to anyone. The ruling in *Tennessee v. Garner* makes clear that police are allowed to shoot or use any other deadly types of force only if their life or the lives of others are in immediate danger.

The issues decided in *Tennessee v. Garner* also underscore the importance of police agency policies and procedures in controlling the use of deadly force. Many large urban police agencies had already enacted policies consistent with the rules set forth in the *Garner* decision in order to protect themselves from potential civil liability and large monetary awards in cases where police had shot unarmed fleeing felons (Fyfe 1988). Prior to *Garner*, police may have been allowed to shoot unarmed fleeing felons according to criminal codes in some states, but those cases were also likely to open up the agency to civil lawsuits and potentially large damage awards. More broadly, research provides clear evidence regarding the necessity and effectiveness of restrictive department policies in the control of deadly force. Organizational rules and guidelines have been shown to significantly reduce the number of police shootings (Fyfe 1979; Milton et al. 1977). The enactment of strict police organizational rules and the implementation of effective training in the use of deadly force probably provides more effective controls on officer discretion in this area than any state law or Supreme Court decision.

The legal context surrounding police use of deadly force is of course evolving. The police–citizen encounters and associated cases that defined parameters on when and how police may use deadly force were developed under conditions that have been altered by technology. Recent events that have fueled the Black Lives Matter movement and associated protests, for example, have occurred under circumstances that are different from those of the past—circumstances that are now more likely to include evidence derived from police body-worn cameras, street surveillance cameras, and smartphone cameras now carried by virtually every citizen. We noted earlier the immediate impact on department policies and training; it is not unreasonable to expect that either emerging court cases or national police institutions will soon create new definitions and protocols for the use of deadly force.

CHAPTER SUMMARY

This chapter presented an overview of the primary legal issues in policing with three goals in mind. One goal was to present students with information on how to conduct lawful searches and seizures under the Fourth Amendment to the US Constitution. This explanation necessarily involved a description of the requirements to obtain a search warrant, as well as coverage of situations in which courts allow police to conduct warrantless searches. Another goal was to explain to students how laws within the context of police interrogations impact police work. Students were presented with the distinguishing features of police interrogations and an overview of citizen rights, such as the right against self-incrimination and attorney representation during the investigatory process. A third goal was to familiarize the student with how laws and police organizations govern police use of force. This goal necessarily involved coverage of the situational force model and the use-of-force continuum, as well as information on how courts regulate police use of deadly force.

KEY TERMS

Aguilar-Spinelli test
border searches
Brown v. Mississippi
Chimel rule
consent searches
custodial interrogation
Escobedo v. Illinois
exceptions to the warrant
    requirement
Fifth Amendment
fleeing felons
Fourth Amendment
general writs of assistance
Gideon v. Wainwright
hot pursuit
Illinois v. Gates

interrogation
interviews
limitations associated
    with use-of-force
    continuum
Miranda v. Arizona
plain view doctrine
plain view searches
probable cause
reasonable expectation
    of privacy
search
search warrant
searches based on exigent
    circumstances
searches incident to arrest

self-incrimination
situational force
    model
situational risk
Sixth Amendment
special needs searches
state-level criminal
    prosecution
stop and frisk
Tennessee v. Garner
Terry v. Ohio
third degree
use-of-force continuum
warrantless search

CASES CITED

Aguilar v. Texas, 378 U.S. 108 (1964).
Brown v. Mississippi, 297 U.S 278 (1936).
Chimel v. California, 395 U.S. 752 (1969).

Escobedo v. Illinois, 378 U.S. 478 (1966).

Graham v. Connor, 490 U.S. 386 (1989).

Gideon v. Wainwright, 372 U.S. 355 (1963).

Illinois v. Gates, 462 U.S. 213 (1983).

Miranda v. Arizona, 384 U.S. 436 (1966).

New Jersey v. T.L.O., 469 U.S. 325 (1985).

Riley v. California, 573 U.S. 373 (2014).

Spinelli v. United States, 393 U.S. 410 (1969).

Tennessee v. Garner, 471 U.S. 1 (1985).

Terry v. Ohio, 392 U.S. 1 (1968).

FURTHER READING

Bittner, E. (1970). *The Functions of Police in Modern Society*. Weston, MA: Oelgschlager, Gunn, and Hain.

del Carmen, R. V., and C. Hemmonds (2010). *Criminal Procedure and the Supreme Court*. New York: Rowan & Littlefield.

Fyfe, J. (1988). "Police Use of Deadly Force: Research and Reform." *Justice Quarterly* 5(2): 165–205.

Geller, W. A., and M. S. Scott (1992). "Deadly Force: What We Know." In *Thinking about Police: Contemporary Readings*, edited by C. B. Klockars and S. D. Mastrofski, 446–76. New York: McGraw-Hill.

Lyman, M. D. (2002). *Criminal Investigation: The Art and the Science*. 3rd. ed. Upper Saddle River, NJ: Prentice Hall.

CHAPTER 7

Officer Issues

After completing this chapter, students should be able to:

- Define the term *subculture* and explain how this term applies to police work
- Identify several characteristics of the police job that contribute to the formation and maintenance of the police subculture
- Identify the factors that comprise the police working personality and describe how this concept contributes to an understanding of police subculture

- Explain the process by which police officers are socialized into the police subculture
- Define and describe the four stages of police socialization: choice, introduction, encounter, and metamorphosis
- Assess the nature of police subculture in terms of various positive and negative aspects
- Explain how potential dangerous conflicts and the potential for deadly force contribute to police stress
- Explain how on-the-job confrontation contributes to police stress
- Describe the cognitive processes by which police officers utilize perceptual shorthand to identify and deal with potential conflicts and dangerous encounters on the job
- Discuss symbolic assailants in terms of how police define them and how they influence police officer stress
- Define turbulence within the context of police work
- Explain how officers commonly engage in edge control as a means to accomplish the work of policing
- Identify and describe the various ways in which citizens, the police organization, social change, and occupational role conflict contribute to on-the-job police stress
- Explain how police use their personal attitudes, experience, and skills in the course of making discretionary decisions
- Define the impact of closed-circuit television cameras (CCTV) and body-worn cameras (BWC) on the ongoing loss of police anonymity and police attitudes and work behaviors

INTRODUCTION

This chapter is dedicated to the coverage of issues that are important to individual police officers in the course of their work. Previous chapters provided students with a framework for understanding many of the structural features or the context of police work, such as their proscribed responsibilities within the criminal justice system, the nature and character of their employing organizations, and some of the legal constraints within which police must operate. This chapter, however, is closely focused on aspects that directly and more personally impact individual police officers on the job. More specifically, the chapter is divided into three primary sections describing the most important officer issues. The first section describes the police subculture as a means to indicate some of the shared values, attitudes, and beliefs most common to police officers. This section covers how the job works to shape and maintain the police subculture and the various subcultural influences on police socialization processes and how those processes influence the street-level behavior of individual officers. The second section identifies stress as an important issue for police officers. Here, the text describes the nature of police–citizen interactions in terms of their potential for danger and conflict. The section also covers some of the ways in which legal decisions, police organizations, social change, and occupational role conflict act as occupational stressors or sources of police stress. The third section of the chapter focuses on the highly discretionary nature of police decision-making. The text describes how individual officers utilize their personal attitudes, experiences, and skills to make discretionary decisions in the course of their work. This section concludes with a discussion on how some recent technological changes, such as closed-circuit television cameras (CCTC) and body-worn cameras, have contributed to a loss of police anonymity, and how these changes seem to have impacted officer attitudes and behaviors.

POLICE SUBCULTURE

Scholars and others looking at the conduct and attitude of police officers have coined the term *police subculture* to describe what they observe to be shared traits and attitudes. In Merriam-Webster's dictionary, the second definition of **subculture** is as follows:

> An ethnic, regional, economic, or social group exhibiting characteristic patterns of behavior sufficient to distinguish it from others within an embracing culture or society. (Merriam-Webster 2021)

Ironically, the example provided with the definition is "criminal subculture." A more expansive definition of subculture is that found on Wikipedia:

> A subculture refers to a group of individuals characterized by a distinct set of values, beliefs, and behaviors. The police subculture refers to the beliefs, norms, attitudes, and values that characterize members of the police force, which may be distinct from the beliefs expressed by other individuals or social groups. . . . Some of the values often associated with the police culture include bravery, solidarity, masculinity, loyalty, and discretion. As with processes of social learning in other forms of subcultures, these beliefs, norms, attitudes, and values may be transmitted from one generation of police officers to another. (Sullivan 2009, 385)

Police scholars and other observers of the police occupation have for years worked to identify and consider the importance of some of the factors associated with both the formation and maintenance of what they and many others believe to be a distinct subculture made up of persons involved in the occupation of policing. Langworthy and Travis (1999), for example, identified several characteristics of police work that contribute to the formation and maintenance of the police subculture. These **job characteristics** described below do two things. First, they work to separate police officers from those who are not police. Second, they work to bring police themselves closer together as a group. This is how the police subculture—indeed any occupational subculture—is formed and maintained.

The job involves characteristics that both separate workers from the rest of us *and at the same time* bring those in the group closer together so as to develop shared attitudes and norms of behavior.

Culture and the Unique Characteristics of Police Work

The characteristics identified by Langworthy and Travis (1999) include some obvious symbols commonly recognized as part of the occupational culture of policing: distinctive uniforms and badges as well as the most identifiable "tools of the trade" such as the baton or "nightstick," handcuffs, and most obviously the service weapon or gun. These things distinguish police from regular citizens and signal the power and authority police officers may exercise over others. Police collectively share this power and authority over citizens, many of whom resent being potentially controlled or coerced by police. Another obvious job characteristic that both separates police from others and knits them closer together as a group is working hours. Police often work second and third shift hours that force them to conform to odd schedules. Police see a lot of each other as a result; they see much less of anyone who works first shift or more regular hours including non-police friends and members of their own families.

Police officers, as a routine part of their work, are also commonly exposed to some of the more "seedy" or miserable aspects of the human condition: dead bodies, natural disasters, deteriorated living conditions, crimes, and all sorts of human suffering. People who are *not* police commonly respond to these sorts of conditions with sympathy or inconsolable guilt, or even paralyzing fear. But police who are collectively and repeatedly exposed must become in some ways hardened to these conditions if they are to properly do their jobs. Police officers also commonly have difficulty sharing these experiences with others, so they most often confide and trust in other police officers in order to deal with the most difficult conditions of their work. Once again, the unique aspects of police work bind officers together as a group but also separate them from everyone else. This situation promotes shared attitudes, beliefs, and behaviors among police that are indicative of their unique subculture.

Skolnick (1994) describes some of these shared attitudes and beliefs that stem from the characteristics of the job. He identified danger and authority as important job characteristics. Police work is infused with both danger and authority in ways unlike any other job. The exercise of authority naturally makes people uncomfortable around police and generates mistrust and fear; no one like to be told what to do. Everyone knows when a police officer is in the room, and that knowledge tends to make people act differently when police are around. Police must deal with the mistrust of citizens as well as the constant threat of potential danger in their work. They cannot be sure whether the next citizen encounter will be violent. Police officers tend to develop some common attitudes and beliefs because the job involves both danger and the exercise of authority over other citizens.

Police tend to be suspicious and less trusting because of the threat of danger in their interactions with citizens. They also tend to be cynical or pessimistic in their outlook on things, probably due to their common exposure to the "seedy" side of life, the most difficult of circumstances, and interactions with people who are under extreme physical or emotional distress or otherwise not at their best. Skolnick (1994) describes how these and other factors contribute to the formation of a police officer's **working personality** or common patterns of thinking and behavior among police. Common patterns of behavior and thinking comprise some of the core aspects of any subculture.

Culture and Police Socialization

Van Maanen (1973) describes the process by which police recruits are socialized into the police subculture and how seasoned officers learn to accept the realities of the job through their interactions with other police officers. He describes these socialization processes in terms of various **stages of police socialization.** The police socialization process begins with the **choice** to apply for a law enforcement position. This stage of socialization distinguishes those who desire to become police officers based on how potential recruits believe police work to be. Recruits are commonly attracted to policing based on a motivation to serve others, perceived good pay and benefits, and their assumptions regarding the goodwill of citizens and the non-routine and exciting aspects of the job. The socialization process for those who are selected continues with the **introduction** to the job, which is experienced at the police academy. The police academy serves to communicate the formal values, attitudes, and beliefs of the police organization through classroom and scenario-based training that can last up to six months. The police academy experience also commonly includes the communication of anecdotes and "war stories" by seasoned police veterans to the new cadets.

The next stage of the process of police socialization, the **encounter** stage, occurs after the completion of the police academy when rookie officers initially face the realities of police work. Rookie police officers are typically assigned to accompany an experienced **field training officer (FTO)** during the first several months on the job. The FTO often communicates some of the more important but informal values, attitudes, and beliefs shared among street-level officers rather than administrative level police executives. These early on-the-job experiences and associated informal values, attitudes, and beliefs routinely differ from those communicated during police academy training. The on-the-job experiences of rookie police officers also clash with many of the perceptions held by recruits during the earlier stages of socialization. The new police officer learns that the realities of the job are in many ways different from what they believed and what they were told at the academy. Citizens they encounter are more often than not disrespectful and contemptuous rather than happy to see them, and patrol work is oftentimes boring and routine rather than exciting. Differences between what recruits believe and what more seasoned police officers come to know about the job during the "encounter" phase of socialization may contribute to poor performance, personal dissatisfaction, job burnout, misconduct, and the eventual termination of the law enforcement career.

Those who continue on the job often experience what Van Maanen (1973) defines as a **metamorphosis**, in which more experienced police officers eventually adapt to the realities of police work. Officers come to terms with the fact that many citizens will distrust and resent them, and they come to know that some aspects of the job—including regular patrol—can become very routine and boring. Experienced police officers also come to recognize and value those moments when they can and do genuinely help people despite the realities of the work, including encounters in which they provide necessary service, render emergency aid, and successfully resolve some of the tragic and most disturbing problems they routinely encounter on the job. They also come to relish the perhaps less frequent but most satisfying parts of the job such as opportunities to "catch bad guys" and make felony arrests.

In the end, police officers who experience these various stages of socialization will share certain values, attitudes, and beliefs that collectively comprise the police subculture. The next issue to be considered within the context of the police subculture involves some type of assessment or determination as to whether this occupational culture exerts positive or negative influences on officers and the citizens they police.

Assessing the Nature of Police Subculture

For our purposes, the police subculture has two sides, positive and negative, with the positive side corresponding to the founding principles associated with the American republic. Within that view, the police associate themselves in the American public's general support for the military (many officers are themselves veterans): "Most people run from the sound of gunfire; soldiers and police run toward it." Bravery and loyalty to comrades who share the potential dangers of the job and the perceived denigration of the public are prized above almost all other ethical considerations. In this view, the police are the "thin blue line" that stands between innocent civilians and the hordes of criminal actors poised at the mythical borders of polite society. As such, police sometimes expect to be exempt from criticism for any mistakes they make or any weaknesses in their responses and reactions in individual events.

The negative side of police subculture might be characterized as a collective blindness to the larger charges involved with "protecting the public": the necessity of adhering to the broad set of rules protecting all citizens from government intervention in their lives, particularly the concept of due process of law that is more easily discussed in the abstract than useful in individual conflicts. Some of the more problematic aspects of "closing the ranks" against criticism include an unwillingness to acknowledge that some criticism may be legitimate; turning a blind eye to individual and group malfeasance; ignoring change directives until a crisis is reached; and developing a cynical, contagious attitude toward the public in general. In effect, this is the mirror image of how many police believe the public regards them within the context of their work.

Westley (1970) in particular described the ways in which the police subculture may promote the obviously negative influences of extralegal violence and

---

Critical Thinking Exercise

Occupational Socialization: Toward the Alignment of Formal and Informal Police Training

The stages of police socialization described by Van Maanen (1973) highlight some important issues about the differences between formal and informal job training and whether police organizations can more effectively prepare police recruits for the job and lessen the potential for negative outcomes including poor job performance, personal dissatisfaction, and the eventual termination of the law enforcement career.

Think of your own experiences in terms of job training and socialization, even in the case of part-time or seasonal employment. These jobs most often begin with some form of formal training provided by a manager or direct supervisor, either in a classroom setting or on the job site. Your first days (or hours) were probably spent listening to supervisors tell you about the formal goals of the job and how to accomplish them according to certain guidelines or rules. Then, you probably were left to communicate and work directly with your co-workers. These co-workers oftentimes communicate to you the more informal values shared by workers based on the realities of the job, such as the following: We cannot do what the bosses want us to within the allotted time; there are not enough resources to complete the assigned tasks; customers are often unreasonable and disrespectful toward the workers. Perhaps these experiences led you to quit the job and seek other employment.

Your part-time or seasonal work experiences are in some ways comparable to the occupational socialization of police officers. They experience a disconnect between what they thought the job would be before they started, what the bosses tell them about the work, and what they actually experience when they perform the job.

Can police organizations do anything to better align the transmission of formal and informal values, attitudes, beliefs, and behaviors to police officers? What changes would you consider making to the police academy experience and/or the on-the-job training provided through FTOs to better prepare police recruits and inexperienced officers for the realities of police work?

---

police brutality. He traces the origins of extralegal violence and brutality to the often contentious nature of police–citizen encounters, in which officers are tasked with the coercion of citizens who naturally dislike or even resist officers who attempt to enforce criminal codes or maintain public order. Police utilize extralegal violence as a means to maintain not only their authority but also public respect, loosely defined by Anderson (1994) within the context of the urban "code of the street" as being treated "right" or "granted the deference one deserves." The perpetration of extralegal violence by police can be viewed as a subcultural adaptation to problems that commonly arise within their interactions with citizens. Another subcultural trait of police identified by Westley (1970)—secrecy—serves as a means to protect those who engage in brutality. Police who fail to maintain secrecy are defined as "snitches" and ostracized by their fellow officers.

Violence and secrecy are indicative of the subculture that both separates police from other citizens and at the same time bonds them closer together as a group.

In that regard, it is important to note that the vast amount of positive police work goes unnoticed by the general public, except to the degree that individual citizens share their positive experiences with family, neighbors, and friends. That contrasts with the relatively small number of incidents of police malfeasance and malevolence that are instantly and broadly newsworthy: To quote an old bromide, "'Dog bites man' isn't news; 'Man bites dog,' now THAT's news!" More critical are the equally small number of cases in which police judgments made in milliseconds are found to be incorrect upon later, more extensive scrutiny. These almost always involve police shootings, and the large majority seem to involve white officers shooting black citizens.

It is important to stress that the largely negative aspects of police culture described above relate to broad concepts, and do not apply to every police officer, or even to every police department. The overbroad statement above, suggesting a "collective blindness" to the larger charges involved with "protecting the public" may be a widespread perspective, but it is not necessarily a valid description of the majority of police behavior. As a rule, those individuals who choose to become police officers tend to be socially and politically conservative, and therefore are more resistant to the inevitable winds of social change. In their view, their primary charge is to enforce the law, and, as we will see in Chapter 8, the law often lags behind social change. They are also sensitive to court decisions—at both the local and the appellate levels—that seem to undercut or make more difficult their attempts to maintain social order. At the same time, however, those

---

Critical Thinking Exercise

Balancing Negative and Positive Media on Police

There seems to be general agreement that traditional forms of popular media, including network television and print journalism, have tended to focus on some of the negative products of the police subculture such as brutality and various other forms of misconduct. Some would argue that these traditional media outlets ignore positive police work.

These trends, however, are subject to change within the context of the ongoing revolution in information and communication technologies and particularly the rise of social media platforms. Surveys show that the majority of American police agencies now utilize social media platforms to communicate and interact directly with members of the public to notify them of safety concerns (91 percent), engage in public relations (86 percent), and solicit crime tips (76 percent) (KiDeuk et al. 2017). Social media platforms clearly provide police organizations with new opportunities to shape how police are depicted to the citizens whom they police.

Students are encouraged to search popular media platforms to discern the nature of police portrayals. Do they depict the positive or negative side of police subculture? How can police organizations more effectively influence the ways in which police are depicted within traditional and social media outlets?

Web Activity

There are a number of good materials on police subculture and the challenges that it brings to policing. You can read one description at https://leb.fbi.gov/articles/featured-articles/changing-police-subculture and view a presentation on police subculture at https://study.com/academy/lesson/police-subculture-definition-lesson.html.

---

who aspire to policing being a true profession take great pains to acknowledge the criminal law's "presumption of innocence," even as they strive to develop the facts and circumstances will overturn that presumption in court.

Most police officers understand their role and the changing dynamics to which they must adapt. Many would argue that it is a small number of exceptional departures from the norm that inform outsiders' concept of a police subculture. To understand the inherent tensions that give rise to a police subculture (by any definition), it is best to examine the courses of stress that officers encounter on the job.

STRESS AND POLICE WORK

Regardless of the specifics of any particular incident, there is an underlying stress that attends police work. Most notably, the system's response begins with the presumption that the accused offender is innocent, which immediately demands justification of any law enforcement action taken by police on the street. The state is required to prove each element of the offense to a neutral and detached decision maker—a judge or a jury of the defendant's peers—in order to convict the individual of a crime. This emphasis on the presumption of innocence is inherently a contradiction of the immediate knowledge of the police. They were there, they know what the defendant did, and they expect to be believed. While this is true of all police encounters, it is most vivid in the encounters that involve the potential for dangerous conflicts, on-the-job confrontations, and even the use of deadly force by police.

The Potential for Dangerous Conflicts

The proverbial and well-recognized statement "Most people run from the sound of gunfire; soldiers and police run toward it" seems particularly apt in any discussion involving the potential for dangerous conflicts and how that situation influences the collective attitudes and behavior of police officers. The possibility of being confronted with lethal weaponry—guns, explosives, knives, vehicles, and battering objects of all kinds—underlies almost all police training. In current American society, this tends to be personified by the potential for gunfire: Many of the incidents currently fueling national criticism of the American police involve retrospective discovery that the police decision was wrong. These include the shootings of Antwon Rose in Philadelphia (Hassan 2019); Tamir Rice in Cleveland (Ohlheiser 2016); Stephon Clark in Sacramento (Del Real 2019);

and Michael Brown in Ferguson, Missouri (Raice 2019), among many others. In 2020, 1,021 people had been shot and killed by American police, 22 more than in 2019 (*Washington Post* 2021).

The *Washington Post* has been tracking reported shootings by the police since 2015. Its findings are derived from news reports rather than federal records, because the latter are voluntary, and not comprehensive (Mock 2019; *Washington Post* 2016, 2017, 2018, 2019, 2021). The numerical reports are not necessarily representative of the larger issues, which require delving into some of the factors, both immediate and indirect, to each shooting encounter: the proportion of citizens shot relative to their ethnic proportion of the larger population; the relative proportion by race of unarmed shooting victims; the relative proportion of those with prior police contacts, or criminal conviction; and numerous others.

For the police, all of these incidents are attended by an understanding of the need to make a split-second decision to protect the life of the officer and/or the lives of others. For the public, the race of the citizen who was shot tends to define the incident more than other considerations. The different perspectives are one of the reasons police tend to close ranks and be defensive of any officer involved in a shooting incident.

The other side of that coin is personified by the Laquan McDonald shooting (detailed in Chapter 5), in which a much-delayed release of a police car's video camera recording directly contradicted the written account of the incident submitted by the officer, as well as the reports of other officers at the scene who supported the shooting officer's account. Not only was the original claim of a justified shooting eviscerated, but the idea that police "closed ranks" to protect even wrongdoers was verified in the minds of otherwise neutral citizens. In the absence of more comprehensive information, one officer—or in this case, one cohort of officers—comes to represent police generally, without regard for agency or regional differences.

The media spotlight on specific notorious police shootings and associated public controversy has in some ways muted the influence of criminal justice empirical research on the phenomenon. The recent dynamic interplay between the "Black Lives Matter" and "Blue Lives Matter" movements, for example, has arguably been as much about politics and racial identity as specific criminal justice reform (see e.g., Solomon and Martin 2018). Police scholars, however, have spent the last several decades compiling and analyzing data to discern when and why police shoot.

One fact seems to get lost in the context of media scrutiny and political controversy: The use of deadly force by police officers is an exceedingly rare occurrence (Liederbach and Taylor 2004). Officer surveys indicate that somewhere between 1 and 2 officers per 1,000 shoot at civilians each year, and firearms are used in only 0.2 percent of all arrest situations (Adams 1999; Pate and Friddell 1993).

Scholars have also studied the relative influence of different factors on the police decision to shoot, including the race of the suspect shot by police; officer demographics such as race, experience, and duty assignment; and community-level factors such as rates of neighborhood poverty. This line of research has identified **situational risk** as the most important factor in determining when and why police officers shoot. Situational risk refers to the immediate scenario that police confront during a potential deadly force encounter. Specific factors that seem to weigh most heavily on the decision to shoot include whether the suspect was armed and whether the suspect assaulted police. Police are significantly more likely to use deadly force during encounters that involve armed and/or assaultive criminal suspects. Studies attribute the disproportionate shooting of African-Americans to disproportionate situational risk in that African-American criminal suspects were found to be more likely to be armed and to shoot at police (Blumberg 1981; Fyfe 1981, 1989).

Levels of situational risk most directly influence police decisions to shoot. This is not to suggest that nothing else matters, just that levels of situational risk seem to matter most immediately and directly on the decision to shoot. Race remains at the core of any discussion involving police legitimacy, excessive force, community relations, and discretion. Scholars, students, and concerned citizens need to continue to focus on the role of race as a significant but less direct influence, not only on levels of situational risk, but also in wider social, political, and legal contexts in which the decision to shoot occurs. No single factor—such as situational risk levels or race or poverty or particular laws or policies of the police organization—completely explains why police decide to shoot. The decision to shoot is undoubtedly both directly and indirectly influenced by a myriad of factors and needs to continue to be on the front burner of discussion about police and their role in a democratic society.

There are other types of dangers common to patrol work. Of particular importance (but often overlooked) are the dangers associated with motor vehicle accidents. Despite using cars with bright flashing lights that warn traffic of stopped vehicles, a number of officers are injured each year, and some killed, by drivers who fail to yield or even slow for the warning lights. The danger is even higher for state police and state patrol officers working the interstate highways, with their higher speeds.

On-the-Job Confrontations

Below the level of armed resistance, confrontation with resistant or combative citizens is a recurrent theme of police training as well as an obvious source of police stress. Nowhere is this more evident than in calls to domestic disputes. Such disputes often involve intoxicated individuals and reflect ongoing, often long-term problems, all of which the officers may not have any knowledge about when answering the call. Police officers do not have the luxury of retreating from confrontation: They must engage with it, head-on. The only information available to them is the subject's words, actions, and demeanor, perhaps supplemented by some (typically limited background information provided by the complainant and relayed by dispatch). The on-scene officers' attempts to de-escalate the situation are typically not visible to the jury, although that is rapidly changing at least in some instances with the ongoing adoption of body-worn cameras discussed later in this chapter.

Confrontation can be compounded by the presence and attitudes of others, whether family in an indoor scene or neighbors in a more public area. If bystanders' existing opinions of the police are negative—whether from prior personal contacts or simply secondhand or vicarious impressions—verbal insults and threatening attitudes accentuate the conflict for the officer. The potential threat coming from other quarters may inhibit the officer's ability to concentrate on the person who prompted the call or first drew the officer's attention.

In like fashion, turbulent bystander behavior may interfere with good-faith attempts of family or neighbors to provide helpful information about the person who is the primary subject of the encounter. Citizens trying to help may be drowned out by the more belligerent shouters, and possibly even mistaken for one of them.

The repeated experience of confrontational encounters on the job leads to an accumulation of shared attitudes and behaviors among police officers about how to prepare for and deal with these types of citizen interactions. Skolnick (1994) describes how police develop a **perceptual shorthand** for identifying potentially threatening individuals. Perceptual shorthand refers to an officer's ability to quickly discern and analyze a situation and prepare to handle it accordingly. Police develop this perceptual shorthand to quickly discern whether a particular citizen is a threat to them using their previous experiences and the on-scene environmental and behavioral clues available to them. Police on the basis of these clues identify certain citizens as **symbolic assailants**, or people who use particular gestures, language, and/or dress that signals the potential for an impending confrontation and/or violent encounter. These shared attitudes and beliefs among police officers are initially based on suspicion rather than fact, so police must move from definitions based on perceptual shorthand to those based on facts and evidence derived from further investigation. Skolnick (1994) refers to the work of police interrogators to specify some conditions used by police to alert them to the potential for confrontation or violence: persons who do not "belong" where they are observed; businesses opened at odd hours; persons who fit the description of a wanted criminal suspect; persons who loiter about places where children play; automobiles that do not "look right"; known troublemakers near large gatherings; and others.

Crank (2004) also describes how the uncertainties of the job and the potential for confrontation shape police officer's attitudes and behaviors. Police–citizen encounters do not unfold predictably and can potentially involve **turbulence**, a situation analogous to an airplane at altitude traveling through unpredictable and sudden shifts in airflow and wind speed. For police, turbulence refers to lots of activity that occurs within short bursts of time. Police–citizen encounters can turn on a dime from the routine to the unusual. A normal traffic stop can suddenly and unpredictably change if the motorist becomes hostile or aggressive. Routine questioning can become an interrogation when the subject is caught in a lie. Routine patrol can lead to a felony arrest on the basis of some lucky discovery of incriminating evidence. Crank (2004) defines the management of on-the-job uncertainties and turbulence in terms of **edge control**, or the ability of police officers to effectively deal with the conditions of the job, de-escalate and dampen turbulence, and prevent things from "getting out of hand." Police work and the necessary skills to accomplish it can be associated with the experiences of other types of "edge workers," or people who purposively engage in exciting but also unpredictable and risky behaviors and situations (Lyng 1990). According to Crank (2004), police as edge workers who operate in these environments must develop two critical skills: the ability to (1) focus on the task at hand and (2) avoid paralyzing fear in order to accomplish their job.

The Impositions of Law

Most officers do their best to adhere to the requirements of existing law, but they are vulnerable to the consequences of a single error or act of misfeasance by another officer anywhere else in the nation. Court decisions that affirm police actions and powers are invisible to officers as a rule; decisions that change the way officers must conduct searches, arrests, interviews, or interrogations require notice, often retraining sessions to ensure that the new rules are known to and adopted by all. Since the vast majority of such decisions tend to restrict accepted police tactics even further, police rarely receive them with favor. Instead, most police officers tend to regard them as "liberal" judgments that give more rights to the criminals than to the police and the citizens police protect.

Court decisions have the force of law, and they carry implicit penalties for failure to comply with their edicts. Probably the two most important legal decisions in this regard were detailed in Chapter 6. Police officer discretion on when and how much force to use generally is determined by the US Supreme Court decision in *Graham v. Connor* (1989). This decision should generally be viewed as one that affirms police actions and powers. The Court ruled that the lawfulness of police actions in the use of force needs to be judged from the perspective of the reasonable officer on the scene rather than the proverbial reasonable person. This decision also identified the need to judge police actions within the immediate context rather than in hindsight. The decision recognized that police must make life-and-death decisions, sometimes within a split second. A second legal decision most important to street-level police is *Tennessee v. Garner* (1985). This case clearly restricted officer discretion in the use of deadly force, since the Court decided that existing state-level statutes allowing the use of deadly force against fleeing felons were unconstitutional.

Similar constriction of police abilities can come through political decisions as well, though they are more amenable to the give and take of dialogue and local politics. Some political interventions, like the recent California standard that allows the use of deadly force only "when necessary in defense of human life" (Adler 2019; Cowan 2019), may ultimately come under challenge in court, with outcomes that could confirm, negate, or modify the original political changes.

Web Activity

In 2019, the National Institute of Justice published a paper titled "Fighting Stress in the Law Enforcement Community." You can access it at https://nij.ojp.gov/topics/articles/fighting-stress-law-enforcement-community.

Sources of Occupational Stress in Policing

Stress, an important issue for police officers, derives from several related but distinct sources. The most important sources of occupational stress in policing include (a) citizens, (b) the police organization, (c) social change, and (d) occupational role conflict.

Citizens

One important source of occupational stress for police is obviously some of the citizens they encounter during the course of their work, particularly those commonly referred to by officers as "regular customers" who are repeatedly and particularly troublesome. Many of these "regulars" do not respond to positive police attempts to help them—for example, the chronic alcoholic who repeatedly refuses suggestions for change that could mitigate further encounters with street-level police. These and many other types of "regular customers" make no attempt to change their lives for the positive, and police are called upon to deal with them repeatedly. Cynicism and jaundice can set in, especially if the courts take no action to force an attempt at change, or social service agencies seem to be having no effect. The "regulars" come to be treated with "the usual" response. "The usual" can be justified in many cases, but it runs the risk of missing important behavioral cues when one of the regulars is at a point where they would be receptive to change. An important turning point could be lost, and "the usual" behavior drive the regular back into the old, destructive groove.

This is a multigenerational phenomenon in some cases. Almost every region has "the family"—the local Jukes or Kallikaks (Dugdale 1910)—whose members have been "regulars" of police intervention for multiple generations. It is too easy to equate every family member with the worst, however: Of the 29 original "male blood relative" Jukes, only 17 had been arrested, and fewer convicted. Many members of "the family" struggle to escape their name legacy, and police need to be aware, ready, and willing to assist those who strive to do better.

The Police Organization

A second important source of occupational stress for police is the employing police organization. Police officers of all ranks must be responsive to their organization's demands. Some of those new demands reflect changes in the overarching laws, both criminal and procedural. Others, though, may reflect changes demanded by the local politicians, in some cases mirroring the demands of the local electorate, or of a new chief of police or a newly elected sheriff. In some cases, the new approach will meet with acceptance by the agency's officers, because it compares well with their existing understanding and expectations. In others, it may represent a different viewpoint, and require difficult adjustment on the part of the officers themselves.

Regardless of the cause or direction of the changed expectations, local and county agencies especially must represent the expectations of the majority of the citizens who support them. That issue is slightly different at the state and federal levels, of course, because of the wider diversity of the population, geographically and politically. Across the spectrum, though, is the understanding that while the law constitutes the "bottom line" of expectations for the police, local majorities may expect different areas of focus. There is also the possibility that officials higher in the criminal justice system may be more responsive to community expectations than the police.

One of the prime examples of this is the enforcement of criminal prohibition of marijuana use. Community acceptance of "the evil weed" developed much earlier than the changes in the law that recently have legalized, or at least decriminalized, its use. For the police, enforcing the criminal law that forbade possession and use of marijuana remained an enforcement priority. For local and county prosecutors, though, the return on prosecution did not match the drain on resources required to mount it, and they began to send signals to the enforcement communities that "it's not worth it; send us something that's really criminal."

Regardless of their individual preferences, officers work within organizations that must respond to community expectations and pressures. In addition to all the normal tensions that occur between subordinates and supervisors in any corporate enterprise, police organizations have additional ones: Police executives must be responsive to community concerns—and sometimes court orders—that are seen by the rank and file as antithetical to their view of the police mission.

One of the prominent areas of concern, particularly in agencies with unionized personnel, is the distinction between seniority and merit. Broadly speaking, union representation considers all union members as equally empowered. As a consequence, those who have served longest are deemed deserving of the open promotional opportunity (and the pay raise and other perks that accompany it). From the standpoint of management, length of service is secondary to a demonstration of qualities and skills identified as vital to the promotional position, as discussed in Chapter 5. The tension between those two viewpoints is another distinctive characteristic of a police subculture, at least at the organizational level.

Social Change

A third important source of occupational stress for police is social change, or any sort of shift in the larger cultural and/or legal context of police work. The changed approach to marijuana possession and use is a singular and timely example of how social changes affect police work. There are far more social trends at work, however, and they have different influences on policing. One of the most prominent at the time of this writing is the highly politicized issue of immigration. The distinction between "illegal immigration" (by inference a crime) and "undocumented immigration" (usually perceived with greater public sympathy, as in the case of asylum seekers or refugees) lies at the federal level, not the local. But local officers cannot ignore the relative leanings of their communities. More tolerant communities, including "sanctuary cities," tend to have a larger immigrant population. The police ability to gain the trust of those communities for investigating serious crimes is at risk if officers demonstrate an anti-immigrant ethos, even if individual officers tend to agree with more restrictive immigration policies.

An earlier era saw tremendous resistance to accepting woman as police officers. In the current era, we have passed beyond the LGBTQ (lesbian, gay, bisexual, transsexual, and queer) issues of the recent past to face new challenges in the form of transgender manifestations. The issue attends both how police officers treat those who flagrantly exhibit trans characteristics and how to accept transgender individuals into police service. The recent political developments in the United States and other nations that reflect a resurgence of white supremacy, including both Nazis and the Ku Klux Klan, is yet another social change that will test the police. Officers with "conservative leanings" do not necessarily embrace the far-right beliefs of the more radical members of American society, and many officers are aware that they, too, could be targets of right-wing fanatics for defending the rights of all American citizens.

Occupational Role Conflict

A fourth important source of occupational stress for police is role conflict. Occupational role conflict occurs when there are contradictory demands placed on people as part of their job. Those who study the police and work with them in the field have noted another point of division among police: Some officers see themselves as "law enforcers," and others engage themselves in community service broadly, with criminal law enforcement only a necessary role they play. Acknowledging that this duality is an artificial construct with many degrees of distinction, "law enforcers" tend to focus on criminal activity as their primary, if not sole, responsibility. Non-criminal calls are handled as efficiently as possible in order to return to patrol patterns that are devoted to crime detection and suppression through deterrence.

Officers who approach the work as a form of community service tend to focus on building relationships, intent on crime prevention more than crime suppression. That is not to say that they are not committed to effective intervention or criminal investigation of reported crime, only that those are activities that stand on an equal basis with bettering the community through other means. Investigators in particular understand the need to develop good relationships with the various communities within their jurisdiction: Many crimes are solved because someone is willing to work with the police. That willingness is far more a product of respect than the coercive approach depicted in "true crime" series or movies: People are far more willing to trust officers they regard as being respectful of the community than those who appear to huff and puff and threaten the community, or at least regard it with derision. These and other associated role conflicts in police work are in many ways related to the police role as the gatekeepers to the formal criminal justice system, as well as the more specific prevalence of discretionary decision-making in police work detailed in the next section.

DISCRETION

Society endows individual police officers with the power to decide whether an individual's instant conduct is serious enough to require formal intervention and adjudication or can be corrected with a warning or other compensatory measures (i.e., **discretion**). Citizens and the criminal justice system expect that all offenders will be treated equally, but if this were the case, the demands on the system would be overwhelming. The system recognizes, and tacitly approves, of the exercise of police discretion in low-level and borderline criminal actions.

In Chapter 1 we generally outlined the importance of discretion both within the criminal justice system and more specifically in the context of police work using two primary points. First, students need to recognize that police significantly reduce the number of cases handled within the larger system through their exercise of discretion between the points of investigation and arrest. Many crimes do not result in an arrest simply because there is a lack of sufficient evidence of wrongdoing or lack of cooperation on the victim's part. But also, police officers in many cases simply decide that an arrest is not the best course of action to resolve a particular situation, perhaps because an arrest would serve neither the needs of a particular citizen (complainant or suspect) nor the need to maintain order and peace within the community (e.g., crowd control situations). These examples instruct the second larger point made earlier in Chapter 1 on the importance of discretion: Police decisions are multivariate. Discretionary decisions by police to take or not take a particular action—including arrest—depend on many factors, some of which relate to the personal attitudes, skills, and experiences that individual police officers bring to their work. Police quite often determine the best course of action—in other words, use their discretion—primarily on the basis of their personal assessment of the situation.

Officer Attitudes, Experience, and Skills

The rationale for providing police with the discretion to choose whether to formally enter a person into the criminal justice system, or to take some other action, has many elements. In some cases, the officer may have knowledge of the offender's personal history and situation, and he or she will come to the same conclusion that a court would after a far more lengthy, expensive, and potentially counterproductive prosecution. A beat officer may know an alcoholic who has been attending Alcoholics Anonymous regularly and has been making major strides to get their life back on track, only to be beset by a major family traumatic situation. Upon discovering them in a severely intoxicated state, the officer may arrest them to get them off the street—halting their offensive conduct and/or taking them out of danger—but will release them after they have slept off their intoxication. A serious one-to-one discussion often accompanies their release, and perhaps an immediate referral back to AA or to a religious counselor if appropriate may be part of the release, but the officer recognizes that the intoxication is most likely a one-time relapse. A release without charges allows the person the opportunity to regain control over their situation, and if successful, is a positive outcome.

Similar to the discretion needed in encounters involving intoxicated persons, police must also rely on their attitude, experience, and individual skills in other types of police–citizen encounters. Muir (1977) describes how the personal characteristics and job skills of individual officers influence the exercise of discretion within the context of domestic disputes, or what he refers to as the "family beef." Officer responses to these often ambiguous and potentially volatile types of calls vary to a large degree. Some officers ("reciprocators") prefer to mediate and counsel personal disputes without resorting to an arrest, while others ("enforcers") tend to quickly intercede using physical force and arrest. More generally, Muir (1977) identifies two personal attributes crucial to the successful resolution of domestic disputes, whether officers choose to utilize an arrest to resolve them or not. Police must be *both* willing and comfortable with using force when necessary, but also police need to possess the ability to empathize—to place themselves "in the shoes" of the disputants to understand the nature of the situation and the motivations of the participants—in order to decide on the best course of action.

The same is true in the case of juvenile offenders. Officer are aware that "acting out" is a phenomenon identified with certain growth stages; indeed, many officers mention having gone through similar stages in their own lives. They understand that a strong punitive approach can be counterproductive, often spurring continued malfeasance, whereas a more positive approach can help curb the misbehavior earlier. Talking with the juvenile calmly, stressing the negative effects of the behavior, and providing a review of more responsible ways of dealing with whatever is troubling them can yield much stronger and longer-lasting positive results than referral into the juvenile justice system. It is this viewpoint that underlies many SRO assignments in middle and high school systems: The police are not "out there" boogeymen, but partners who reinforce the efforts of the school administration and teachers and are interested in the well-being of all students.

Technology and the Loss of Police Anonymity

Another factor that has increasingly influenced officer decision-making and the exercise of police discretion on the street is technology and the associated loss of police anonymity. Several trends have influenced law enforcement's acquisition of new technologies over time. First, Nunn (2003) identifies an ongoing desire by law enforcement agencies to acquire new technology. Over the course of the last century, we have seen police agencies in the forefront of the acquisition and use of new technologies, from the automobile to forensic technologies. Second, money provided through the US Law Enforcement Assistance Administration (LEAA) during the 1970s revolutionized police departments' use of new technologies. These funds allowed police agencies to increasingly acquire equipment from the military to fight the war on crime. Third, Nunn (2003) believes that the movement toward community policing has also aided these trends. For example, community-oriented strategies emphasize the acquisition of information from the public and proactive attempts to mitigate crime. Finally, the war on drugs has increased local police agencies' use of military technologies, such as SWAT armaments, grenade launchers, automatic weapons, and even tanks.

The rapid expansion of technology is an issue that affects both police and the citizenry at large no matter the source of acquisition. The most immediate impact on street policing is (a) the pervasive presence of closed-circuit television cameras (CCTV) and (b) police body-worn cameras (BWCs).

A **closed circuit television (CCTV)** system typically consists of a video camera, a monitor, and a recorder. Of course, systems can become increasingly sophisticated as the number of cameras controlled within a given system increases. The camera technology can also become more sophisticated when technologies such as night vision and zoom lenses are incorporated. The National Institute of Justice (2003a) discussed the impact of new technologies on individual privacy rights, especially in public spaces. This trend has been particularly pronounced in the United Kingdom and has been gaining momentum in the United States. The increasing use of CCTV to monitor public spaces gives rise to issues related to privacy rights and a loss of anonymity for police who must always assume they are being recorded. Citizens are becoming increasingly wary of law enforcement entities recording their movements on public streets, parks, and public transportation areas.

There are some obvious advantages associated with the implementation of CCTVs from a law enforcement perspective. First, the cameras can observe increasingly vast amounts of public space much more efficiently than police officers can. As these systems become more numerous, CCTV systems can free up officers from patrol duty to engage in more purposive law enforcement tasks, such as crackdowns, directed patrol, and/or local community engagement. Relatedly, the cameras are much more likely to "pick up" and record crimes in progress than are patrol officers. Second, crime data analyses have found that the CCTV systems can initially deter criminal behavior in the area that immediately surrounds the placement of the cameras.

There are also disadvantages and problems related to using CCTV as an aid to law enforcement. First, while studies show an initial decrease in criminal activity as CCTV systems become operational, it appears that these positive impacts eventually fade over time as people become more aware of the cameras and their location. Second, the relative contribution of CCTV systems in reducing crime is often related to the technical quality of the system. CCTV systems vary greatly in terms of image quality. Finally, the impact of CCTV technology depends on the attention and skills of the person viewing the cameras. Cameras and recorders do not catch criminals. Cops catch criminals. If the cameras go unattended and/or the personnel watching the cameras suffer from "surveillance fatigue," then the utility of the CCTV system declines accordingly.

Facial recognition technology extends the power of traditional CCTV to allow recorded footage to be matched against a computerized database of photos. These systems aid law enforcement in identifying suspects from CCTV footage. They match existing footage to computerized databases in different ways. Some systems measure the distance between specific facial features of a suspect and match those measurements to those of faces in an existing database. Other systems use a more holistic scan of facial features to compare against existing "facial archetypes" to narrow the range of suspects. The primary problem with these systems is that they are not always accurate. For example, most of them work well only if the videotape captures a full-frontal image of the suspect. Of course, other conditions such as lighting will also impact the accuracy of facial recognition technology. There can be little doubt, however, that as these systems are refined and become more accurate, they will be increasingly linked to existing CCTV systems to provide law enforcement with more tools to identify and capture suspects—as well as tools to increasingly scan the activities of innocent citizens.

Another technology that increasingly impacts the work of police are **body-worn cameras (BWCs)**. The trend toward BWCs has been largely driven by concerns about police brutality and other forms of misconduct. BWCs can provide video evidence to determine at least some of the actions of police and citizens during an encounter. There is also the implied suggestion that such devices will deter officers who might be inclined to engage in misconduct from doing so, as well as discourage citizens inclined to make false allegations, when they know the entire interaction is being recorded.

On the other hand, the use of BWCs also raises some significant privacy concerns, both for citizens who end up being videotaped but also police who must wear them. Common-sense logic would suggest that police who necessarily lose a certain degree of anonymity through the use of BWCs may dislike these trends. Recent surveys, however, indicate that officers generally support the adoption of body-worn cameras despite the apparent loss of officer anonymity. The surveys show that officers overwhelmingly believed that police agencies should adopt body-worn cameras. They tended to believe that body-worn cameras would improve citizen behavior during police–citizen encounters, and they overwhelmingly concluded that body-worn cameras would not reduce their willingness to respond to calls-for-service (Jennings et al. 2014). Police are perhaps more comfortable than can be expected with the usage of BWC because they know that their job already limits their anonymity. Recall some of the unique job characteristics discussed earlier that fuel the formation of the police subculture. These include the wearing of distinctive uniforms and other "tools of the trade" that already and obviously distinguish police from others on the street. Positive police attitudes toward BWCs may also suggest that the most recent generations of officers may be reflective of a more general shift in societal attitudes whereby we all increasingly accept a loss of privacy and anonymity associated with the digital revolution, the rise in social media, and the creation of publicly available data on individuals.

Web Activity

Investigate emerging technologies in policing. One starting point would be an article by Erik Fritzvold at https://onlinedegrees.sandiego.edu/10-innovative-police-technologies/. What other materials can you find, and what do they suggest about the changing nature of policing?

CHAPTER SUMMARY

This chapter covered some of the issues that are most important to individual police in the course of their work, including the police subculture, stress, and discretion. These most important individual officer issues directly impact the day-to-day street-level behavior of police in ways that are recognizable to citizens and other observers of the police. The police subculture derives from various aspects of the job that both separate police from others and bind them together as a group. As a result, police share certain attitudes and behaviors that make them unique within society but collectively similar to one another. Another common feature of police work is stress. Police work is decidedly one of the most stressful occupations, and that stress directly impacts both the people who choose policing as an occupation and the rest of us who routinely encounter them during the course of their work. Policing is also distinguished in terms of discretion. Police have the authority to choose among various alternatives on the job, a situation that contributes to on-the-job stress but also provides the potential for police to resolve problems and help citizens on an individualized basis. Taken collectively, these officer issues are important for understanding the nature of police work, how certain aspects of the job directly influence police interactions with citizens, as well as how police view their work and themselves.

KEY TERMS

body-worn camera (BWC)	encounter	situational risk
choice	field training officer (FTO)	stages of police socialization
closed-circuit television (CCTV)	introduction	subculture
discretion	job characteristics	symbolic assailant
edge control	metamorphosis	turbulence
	perceptual shorthand	working personality

CASES CITED

Graham v. Connor, 490 U.S. 386 (1989).
Tennessee v. Garner, 471 U.S. 1 (1985).

FURTHER READING

Crank, J. P. (2004). *Understanding Police Culture*. 2nd ed. New York: Anderson.
Frank, J., E. G. Lambert, and H. Qureshi (2017). "Examining Police Officer Work Stress Using the Job Demands–Resources Model." *Journal of Contemporary Criminal Justice* 33(4): 348–67. https://doi.org/10.1177/1043986217724248
Liederbach, J., and R. W. Taylor (2004). "Police Use of Deadly Force." In *Controversies in Policing*, edited by Q. C. Thurman and A. Giacommazzi, 77–91. Cincinnati, OH: Anderson.

Solomon, J., and A. Martin (2018). "Competitive Victimhood as a Lens to Reconciliation: An Analysis of the Black Lives Matter and Blue Lives Matter Movements." *Conflict Resolution Quarterly* 37: 7–31.

Violanti, J. M., L. E. Charles, E. McCanlies, T. A. Hartley, P. Baughman, M. E. Andrew, D. Fekedulegn, C. C. Ma, A. Mnatsakanova, and C. M. Burchfiel (2017). "Police Stressors and Health: A State-of-the-Art Review." *Policing* 40(4): 642–56. https://doi.org/10.1108/PIJPSM-06-2016-0097

CHAPTER 8

Into the Future

After reading this chapter, you should be able to:

- Provide examples of issues of equality under the law
- Discuss how changes in the larger society and the criminal justice system impact policing
- Identify new technology and relate it to policing
- Discuss truth decay and its impact on politics, courts, and the police

Throughout most of recorded history, enforcement agents of the political state have tended to be drawn from, and represent, the dominant majority of the native culture. In the case of the modern police as we know them, they were created to contain elements of social change and maintained that role for almost a century and a half. In the United States, the civil rights movement of 1950s and 1960s began an initially slow, and now more expansive, evolution of the police mission to respond to (if not actually embrace) larger and more overlapping social changes. During the same period, even swifter developments in technology have also played a role in changing police methods and capacity, often merging with social issues and movements at the same time. The following sections describe some of the potential developments that police will have to adapt to or deal with.

EQUALITY OF CITIZENS UNDER THE LAW

For most of American history, the superiority of white citizens was assumed to be a natural law (by whites, at least), with so-called "Negro" inferiority an accepted subtext. Social injustice (most notably in relation to race) has existed in the United States since its inception. The civil rights struggles of the 1950s and 1960s moved the dynamic in a positive direction, to the point where Americans of African descent now occupy political, social, business, and even police positions on a par with their American colleagues of European descent. The idea that some Americans are "second-class citizens" because of their families' geographic origins had been receding, but recent developments on the social front have called it back into question (see below, under "White Power"). The authors acknowledge that "race" is an artificial and ultimately flawed concept, but the term is still widely used in social discourse. The perspective here is that there is but one race—human—and that distinctions made on the basis of geographic origin and skin are fundamentally flawed and reflect cultural prejudices. The events of 2020 have revealed that many issues related to race still remain in American society. How they will be resolved and what it means for policing has yet to be seen.

The same time period saw the rise of women's demands for equal respect and equal opportunities. Often derided as "women's lib(eration)," the concept that females are no less competent than males has finally entered the social consciousness. Women serve as police officers, physicians, politicians, construction laborers, and astronauts. New entrants into formerly presumptively male occupations may still undergo more scrutiny than their male counterparts, but they also still manage to "pass the test."

The next stage of the "equal status" issue has dealt with sexual orientation. The last three decades have seen the acknowledgment and general acceptance of multiple sexual orientations. LGBTQ encompassed lesbians and gays (same-sex attractions), bisexuals, transgender, and generic "queers," but there is a current trend away from any sexual identity. Even the English language is changing, from "him/"her" to "they/them," denoting individuals rather than groups.

The most recent iteration of the citizenship issue, contemporaneous with the current federal administration, is that of "legal" versus "illegal" entry into the United States, regardless of purpose. Most immigrants enter the United States with the appropriate application. The reasons for the immigration largely revolve around Central and South American immigrants fleeing either fascist oppression or gang violence in their home countries. The sharp social divide in American society on whether asylum-seeking migrants are "illegal" or simply "undocumented" has created interesting social and political developments. One of those is the idea of a "sanctuary city" that protects the undocumented/"illegal" from federal interventions.

The recent calls to "defund the police" are indicative of concerns over how the police operate, particularly in relation to different racial and ethnic groups. Calls for alternatives to the use of deadly force have become commonplace since early 2020. There is little doubt that change is coming. What is not known at the time of this writing is what those changes will look like. It appears that the idea of defunding the police will probably not occur, particularly given the comments of US Attorney General Merrick Garland in his confirmation hearing. Instead, it appears more likely that there will be greater funding and training for the police in the areas of de-escalation and the handling of individuals with mental illness, and increased use of other professionals to address social issues.

TRANSFORMATION OF THE CRIMINAL JUSTICE SYSTEM

For all their local autonomy, the police are still part of a larger criminal justice system. Changes in the system have direct and indirect consequences for the police, and attitudes toward the system are constantly changing. The old understandings were fairly straightforward: The police identified and secured social malcontents and deviants and, through the power of arrest, referred them to the judicial branch for assessment and assignment to appropriate corrective actions. The corrections component supervised those corrective actions through **probation** (field monitoring of low-level offenders) and incarceration, often followed by post-release field monitoring.

For many, incarceration was supposed to deter future misbehavior by instilling fear of further loss of liberty by the offender. More recent changes in social attitudes have led to viewing corrections as an opportunity for inmates to receive corrective or therapeutic instructions to help them better manage life's frustrations after their release from jail or prison. A wide range of assumptions undermine both deterrent and rehabilitative views of corrections, and recent cases of jail and prison guard corruption involving such things as smuggling drugs and weapons into their facilities and offering allegiance to the dominant inmates have begun to turn social reformers toward ways to improve that system. **Parole** (post-release monitoring of convicts on the conditions allowing their release) has come under similar scrutiny. Common to all of corrections is the scarcity of needed resources: funds to attract, hire, and retain sufficient numbers of competent officers; realistic training and educational opportunities for those new to the work; funds to provide accessible educational and occupational training for inmates and probationers who express willingness to undergo them; and adequate transitions out of correctional institutions into meaningful prosocial work.

Regardless of the vitality or corruption of the correctional system, however, most clients return to the streets and fall once again under the view of the police. That can be positive, as when police support parole officers in monitoring and guiding former clients in bettering their lives. It can also be negative, as when the police have to deal with the behaviors and crimes of those who did not benefit from the attempts at correction.

The shortcomings of the correctional system have come to the attention of the public, in terms of both the lack of evidence of reform and the high costs of incarceration. In addition, reformers point to the disproportionate presence of minorities and citizens of low socioeconomic status (SES) in the criminal justice system, generally, and in corrections, in particular. In some cases, evidence suggests that the low-SES and criminal occupants of prison (overlapping but distinct constituencies) actually have more control over the activities within the institutions than the guards and administrators. One of the solutions to overcrowding in some states has been to identify disparate sentences and release those who seem to have been unfairly over-sentenced because of their minority or low-SES status.

That trend, unfortunately, intersects with a number of others. Persons released from prison have no real advantage in the job market and thus tend to go back to disadvantaged neighborhoods and cohorts. They intermingle with gangs, anonymous immigrant groups, and the down-and-out casualties of local and regional employment shifts, which include homeless families with young children. The long-term consequences of children growing up in such environments are not yet known, although there are likely some predictable parallels to growing up in extreme poverty and in gang-intense localities, many of which will place new demands on the police, the educational systems, and businesses.

In many cities, in addition to the potential increase in petty crimes (including shoplifting in order to eat, purse-snatching, and the like), news articles now report on citizens complaining about people sleeping on the streets and door stoops, panhandling, and leaving excessive garbage strewn on the streets. All of these conditions become low-level "public nuisance"–type offenses that require police attention and stretch police capacity to respond appropriately.

White Power

Cities and towns across the nation are seeing a resurgence of multiple hate groups under the rubric of "White Power." The movement's name suggests a return to the conditions prior to the civil rights movement, but its manifestations also incorporate troubling echoes of the Nazi rise that led to the Holocaust. The white supremacist march in Charlottesville, Virginia, and the related events are indicative of the continuing issues that need to be addressed. The numerous attacks on Jewish synagogues (such as that on the Tree of Life Synagogue in Pittsburgh), schools, institutions, and individuals around the country over the last few years have not been conclusively linked to White Power, but a collaborative partnership is possible and even probable.

The individual attacks are a normal police matter for crime investigations, of course. The overall assertion of the White Power movement, however, is political, or at least semi-political. In areas where a movement attains substantial political power, there is the potential for pressure on the police to subvert the civil rights of some groups (both racial and religious in regard to White Power), including the current anti-Muslim sentiments being espoused and sometimes acted upon. News reports have demonstrated that, at least at the individual level, a number of police are sympathetic to (if not actual members of) the White Power movement. Whether entire jurisdictions are policed by White Power advocates is unclear at this time.

Gun Control

A broader social discussion, and one definitely coordinated with the White Power issues, lies in the debate over of the wording of the Second Amendment of the US Constitution: "A well-regulated militia, being necessary to the security of a free State, the right of the people to keep and bear Arms, shall not be infringed." As the lethality of modern weapons far exceeds the capacity of the muzzle-loading firearms of the late 18th century (when the Constitution was written) and the carnage of firearms assaults increases, a rising segment of society has begun to argue for more effective gun controls. In general, police officers support the broader right to keep and bear arms as a matter of self-defense.

A 2008 Supreme Court decision (*District of Columbia v. Heller*, 554 U.S. 570) has already undercut one of the gun control advocates' arguments declaring that the absence of a "well-regulated militia" of the 18th century does not negate the broader right to keep and bear arms at the individual level. The right is not universal. Persons convicted of a felony are stripped of the right to bear arms in most states. Certain locations—notably hospitals, educational institutions, and places where elected officials meet—prohibit bringing firearms on the premises. Those who wish to carry a concealed weapon must pass a background check and demonstrate proficiency with the weapon before a permit will be issued.

That said, however, the firearms market is strong enough, and multileveled enough, that felons rarely encounter difficulty getting a firearm if they really want one. Data indicate that these weapons are most often either stolen, the product of unregulated private sales, and/or provided to criminals by someone who legally bought the weapon themselves (i.e., "straw purchases"). Detection technology to support place-specific bans on firearms is far from universal and often limited to public entrances. There are multiple ways to get firearms into supposedly secure facilities by other means. The word "militia" is often adopted by ad hoc antigovernment groups and those opposed to minorities to cloak their potential for violence in the language of the Constitution.

The political debates continue and intensify each time there is a multivictim shooting incident with "military-style weapons" (especially at schools and houses of worship). Incidents involving stolen weapons continue to revive assertions that the right to keep and bear arms also carries an unarticulated responsibility to keep them safely. That issue is most fervent when the victim of a shooting is a child with an unsecured gun. It is the increased capacity of modern weapons, whether military-grade or modified with "bump stocks," that drives the political debate.

Critical Thinking Exercise

The right of people to own firearms is a contentious topic for debate in modern society. The police are placed in a position to protect society and uphold the rights of citizens. The International Association of Chiefs of Police have promulgated a position paper on firearms policy. You can read this paper at https://www.theiacp. org/sites/default/files/2019-05/IACP%20Firearms%20Position%20 Paper_2018%20(1).pdf. What issues do you see in relation to their position? What are the pros and cons of such a position (or parts of their position)?

The police are tasked with taking action when firearms are used, and they must face the competing positions and calls in regard to firearms and the Second Amendment.

CHALLENGES OF RAPIDLY DEVELOPING TECHNOLOGY

The future is being defined across the board by the emergence of new technologies and their secondary uses. As with everything else, there are benefits and potential risks associated with all of them. We begin with the simpler ones that have already demonstrated benefits to the police and the broader criminal justice system and will then move into the effects of new technologies (current and potential) on broader social issues.

Visual and Audio Recording

Some say that we are moving into a "surveillance society," given the seemingly instantaneous deployment of public and private cameras throughout society. Whereas surveillance was once the near-exclusive and active domain of the police and some private investigators, it is now a passive and retroactive investigative tool. Traffic cameras at intersections now are part of an extended network of street cameras recording foot and vehicle traffic in public spaces. While not ubiquitous, more and more families (and landlords) are opting to install cameras that provide a view of who is (or was) at the door or in the corridor in apartment buildings. The old "peephole" in the door now has a permanent digital record.

At the same time, smartphones with digital recording capacities are near ubiquitous and a valuable source of information for the police. Although in many instances the recording function is not activated until the owner is aware of the action—such as the recent video of a teacher forcibly removing a recalcitrant student from a Florida classroom (Hauser 2020)—and thus miss important details about the opening of the incident, all videos can provide strong clues about both known and unknown suspects (and victims). Clothing type and color, hairstyle and color, and actions taken are recorded and often provide a far more accurate account than those of eyewitnesses. With a clear front or side view, the potential for identification through facial recognition software (FRS) is possible. These images can be very useful to the police.

At the same time, however, it is not just suspects who are the subjects of smartphone videos. The police themselves may be monitored by citizens. Unprofessional (and sometimes criminal) police behavior can be captured in digital imagery. The investigative news media are presenting more and more of these events, with impacts on the police as well as the individual malefactor. Objective depictions of actual police behavior eviscerate many of the older police defenses—such as denial, "explanation," and outright lying—that were used to help protect a colleague who might soon be one's backup on a serious call. The constant surveillance is an important issue for police supervisors and administrators, but in the long term it will need to be ingrained into the police subconscious by orientation and training. Ultimately it will need to be embedded at the local or administrative level for all police agencies at all levels.

Facial Recognition Software

Facial recognition software (FRS) covers separate types of analysis: detecting the face, capturing the information in digital form, and matching the data to existing databases. Briefly put, **facial recognition** is based on matching unknown photos against massive databases, comparing physical features in largely similar poses. Facial analysis works with the dynamics of expression and other factors. The current generations of software share, in varying degrees, the same problems: They are are based on data sets that are white and male dominated. Women tend to be misidentified as men in almost one out of five attempts, while black men—and especially black women—are misidentified at even greater levels (Cordeiro and Roulette 2019).

When FRS advances to a greater degree of accuracy and legal decisions determine its acceptable use in investigative decisions, the police should have a tool that will allow them to scan popular media sites, such as Facebook, to help identify unknown suspects. If the unknown suspect lives in the general area of the crime, showing the video or still photo to area residents during an investigation may assist in locating the perpetrator. Attempts to defeat the technology, such as wearing a hood even in good weather or using multicolored artificial (and washable) "tattoos," may be a significant challenge initially. Whether criminals can continue to defy efforts to improve the identification algorithms is an unknown at this point.

Dynamic Hotspots

The promise of FRS has given rise to the concept of "dynamic hotspots." Dynamic hotspots are an extension of the idea of hotspots of crime. **Hotspots of crime** (Braga 2001; Sherman, Buerger, and Gartin 1989), a relatively recent development in police patrol assignments, refer to the relatively few number of small places where disproportionately large numbers of crimes are committed. Hotspots traditionally have been static geographic areas, usually no larger than a block or two, where crimes can be observed and theoretically be deterred by increased police presence. **Dynamic hotspots** refer to mobile individuals who present a high potential for committing crimes of a particular type or a broad array of serious crimes. Experiments on the concept (though not yet based on FRS technology) have been underway for some time and will likely expand in the future. The ability of the police to identify those who comprise a dynamic hotspot would be a valuable tool.

DNA

Deoxyribonucleic acid (DNA) has been hailed as the ultimate tool of criminal investigations. **DNA** is a unique "genetic fingerprint" that points to one and only one individual. The ability to identify the unique DNA fingerprint of individuals has been greatly enhanced since it was first done in the 1980s (YourGenome 2016). Unlike actual fingerprints, DNA can be left at a scene in multiple forms, including spit, sneeze mucus, dried saliva on bottles or utensils, and even cast-off skin cells. The "CSI effect," from popular TV shows and movies, has created unrealistic expectations in the public's mind that every crime can be solved through DNA. The public views the failure to produce such evidence as a failure of the police and prosecution. Far more cases, however, are solved with basic police work than DNA. Most TV episodes are based on real cases, but the editing process that presents a 45-minute depiction tends to be highly selective and compressed.

The advent of familial DNA searches, as seen in the case of the Golden State Killer (Joseph James DeAngelo), has not only expanded criminal investigations, but also enabled law enforcement to reunite missing persons with their families (runaways, absconded children, insomniacs, and the like). Familial DNA searches use genetic profiles of family members whose DNA is similar to the person of interest (Kaiser 2018). In the Golden State Killer case, authorities were able to identify DNA from a database that closely matched the evidence in the original killings. The police were able to identify the killer by matching other evidence to family members for the DNA match. Perhaps equally important, DNA can be used to identify the bodies of missing relatives so that families can reclaim them.

Despite its usefulness, expanded DNA searches have triggered a backlash by the public, particularly those who have provided DNA samples to research their family's history and ancestry. People view their contract with genealogical research companies as a purely private matter, which should not be accessible to the state in the absence of a court order. Such a viewpoint would bar the broad seek-and-ye-shall-find discovery inquiries, thus limiting the use of those databases to confirmation searches. The issue is still being contested in courts across the nation and under different state rules. The resolution of the debate has potential to greatly impact police investigation.

Web Activity

Research materials on the police use of DNA technology. One starting point is an article published by the Pew Trusts, "DNA Databases Are Boon to Police but Menace to Privacy, Critics Say," at https://www.pewtrusts.org/en/research-and-analysis/blogs/stateline/2020/02/20/dna-databases-are-boon-to-police-but-menace-to-privacy-critics-say. What are some key issues you find, and what impact does this have on the police?

Social Media and Policing

The growth of social media has greatly impacted people's ability to communicate with one another and to share information. This is also true for organizations like the police. Law enforcement has had a lengthy relationship with the use of media in general to alert the public of events and solicit input from citizens. Crime Stoppers was begun in 1976 as the initial information line program in policing and continues today in the United States and around the world. Crime Stoppers primarily relies on television, newspapers, and the radio. The Amber Alert system began in 1996 to spread news of missing/abducted children and to solicit tips from the public.

Police departments have expanded their public outreach through YouTube, Facebook, microblogs such as Twitter, blogs, Flickr, web chats, and podcasts to post crime videos and information on unsolved crimes. These postings ask viewers to provide information on the crimes and the offenders featured in the materials (DiBlasio 2012). These outlets reach a wide array of people, particularly due to the ubiquitous nature of smartphones (National Neighborhood Watch 2015). Beyond the dissemination of crime news, police use these forums to post prevention topics (International Association of Chiefs of Police 2017; LexisNexis Risk Solutions 2018). Since 2010, the International Association of Chiefs of Police (IACP) Center for Social Media has conducted surveys of law enforcement agencies on the use of social media. The 2015 survey of 553 agencies across 44 states reveals that 96 percent of the agencies use social media (International Association of Chiefs of Police 2017). Almost 90 percent use social media to investigate crimes, 76 percent use it to solicit tips on crime, 84 percent use it to alert the public about crime and other issues, and 79 percent incorporate it in crime prevention initiatives (International Association of Chiefs of Police 2017).

There is little research on the actual impact of these technologies for solving crimes. The fact that there has been widespread adoption of social media and the national and international attention and support given to its use indicates that law enforcement views it positively. Social media programs are valuable tools for police to gather crime-related information.

THE INTERACTIONS WITH LARGER SOCIAL FORCES

Changes in policing and the adoption of emerging technologies and techniques often raise social concerns. Issues of privacy clash with social media. The needs of protecting society conflict with other desires of the populace. Thus, police oftentimes find themselves in the middle of several emerging and evolving debates.

Privacy versus Surveillance

The irony of the public reacting against "the surveillance society" is that many of those same people, who would not even think of permitting police surveillance or research, are already revealing far more about themselves to a broad, anonymous public. Photos, personal histories, associates (even those who people have "met" only online), sexual and political affiliations and preferences, and hints to even deeper secrets are voluntarily shared across a wide range of social outlets, websites, search engines, and the like without any thought of "privacy." The thought that the police and state agents cannot access publicly available information may seem ludicrous, but the fact that access to those sites takes place through contracts with corporate entities brings the debate into public legal focus.

Depending on a user's preferences and choices, mobile phones contain volumes of information, such as persons who are contacted by calls or by texts, including the time and length of those contacts; the owner's physical location by GPS technology; and apps and other access to broader social media outlet. In terrorism and organized crime cases, those information sources can help reveal or confirm connections to other suspects in organizations and networks. In more individual crime investigations, there is considerable potential to reveal embarrassing facts about the owner's life that are not directly relevant to the crime under investigation, such as multiple adulteries, an expressed or actualized interest in child pornography, bombastic claims about public figures, and the like.

At the time of this writing, Apple's iPhone is once again a test case. After previous cases, Apple produced a new technology that could open an iPhone with a password known only to the owner. The Saudi lieutenant who is alleged to have killed three sailors in Pensacola, Florida, in December 2019 carried two of the new iPhones (Nicas and Benner 2020), which the authorities cannot access. The FBI has requested a court order to make the information in the iPhones available to investigators to determine if there are links to terrorist organizations.

From the state's standpoint, devices that can be unlocked only by the owner places the individual ahead of the state or the public collective. As such, those instruments facilitate terrorism, organized crime, and any manner of fraud and conspiracies. Apple's response is that the technology was created in response to consumer demand. Building a "backdoor" access to individual phones would undercut that relationship to private citizens. A backdoor to one phone would essentially constitute a backdoor to any and all phones. The role of the court-ordered search warrant is largely absent in the early rounds of the debate and ultimately will be resolved by a federal court decision.

Truth Decay

The broad reach of social media has serious implications for society and politics—and, as a result, the police. The Rand Corporation introduced the concept of **"truth decay"** (Kavanagh and Rich 2018), perhaps best summarized as "the triumph of volume over veracity." This is hardly the first period in which the loudest voices tend to attract unworthy support without regard for the accuracy of the claims or the supposed truth that would support them. Statements and claims are made and widely broadcast without evidence to support them, and the information is viewed by many as truthful because of who made the statement and/or how loudly and widely it was said.

Impact on Politics

At the national level, "truth decay" is being practiced by all political sides, it would seem. Whereas facts are dismissed as "fake news," a common pushback is the denigration of the person or groups advocating the "fake news" interpretation. That then turns on itself, and denigration comes to dominate the debate, instead of rational discussions about the factual basis for the competing viewpoints—or, perhaps better, "rational discussions examining which basis has the stronger evidence."

Suggestive interpretation of evidence, both intentional and as a result of upbringing and orientation, is hardly a new element in the practice of politics. Neither is outright lying. What is new is the vast expansion of communication technology, including but not limited to the internet. People's ability to "like" or "dislike" particular viewpoints or assertions adds to the background pressure on those who have not yet decided their beliefs will then lean toward the majority view. This raises the possibility of overt manipulation of one side or both, though more likely by those pushing the particular assertion. The manipulation of "the truth" impacts those working of the criminal justice system, particularly the police.

Impact on Potential Jurors

"Variation" on the truth also has potential impact on the court system, especially through its influence on jurors. The Harvey Weinstein case is perhaps the most visible example of the impact of unrefined and largely uncontested assertions. The potentially prejudicial pretrial publicity surrounding the case, based on his celebrity and that of some of his accusers, is unusual, but it demonstrates the possibilities of this happening in other cases. Local "news" is no longer a newspaper article or some short announcement on the six o'clock television news. Instead, it can be an endless back-and-forth roundabout of opinions about the individual(s) involved that have nothing to do with the facts at hand. Rather, it reflects prior encounters, individual prejudices, and a raft of other possible influences.

At the present time, we are not aware of any actual research on the impact of "social me-me-media" on local court jury selection, but the potential for the publicity prejudice is stronger than ever in the internet age. Even more troubling, at least potentially, is the impact that it may have on police officers, supervisors, and executives, influencing the decisions they make at all levels.

Impact on Police Officers

Social media presentations also can have an impact on policing. A good example of social media presentations of the "truth" and its influence can be seen in the immigration debate and the establishment of sanctuary cities. Fear about criminal immigrants has been fomented on social media, which has led for calls to round up undocumented immigrants for deportation. Some cities have opted not to actively participate in those efforts. The police are in the middle of the debate on whether to enforce the mandates or to even assist other policing agencies (such as ICE) in their efforts.

A second example of technology and social media's impact on policing relates to the growing ability of individuals to assume another person's identity. This may be done to gain access to the property of the legitimate person, to hide from the authorities, or to simply remain anonymous from others. Regardless of the reason, the use of the technology poses obstacles for police investigation and eventual apprehension of offenders.

Social media may also influence police officers' beliefs and opinions about people and groups and the proper role of the police. Unlike average citizens, police officers are trained and socialized to test all of their sources in order to be able to refute contrary claims and interpretations, but there is still the possibility of subliminal influences by overexposure (direct or indirect) to social media opinions. It is an issue that will require external as well as internal observation and assessment. This has not yet been identified as a certain flaw in police work, any more than are personal and secondhand prejudices about individuals, groups, or neighborhoods. As society evolves, however, the influence of social media will remain an open issue for the police officers. The potential of subtle influences on the police cannot be dismissed out of hand.

CHAPTER SUMMARY

This concluding chapter identifies a number of emerging sociocultural and technological trends we believe are important to police work both now and in the future. The trends include continuation of a decades-long but often challenged struggle to promote equality among American citizens, but also the opposed resurgence of hate groups that push a White Power agenda. The trends include the well-worn and uniquely American-style debate regarding our presumed Second Amendment right to arm ourselves to the teeth like soldiers, but also the increasingly organized and determined backlash of those more focused on criminal victimization in the wake of the all-too-familiar mass shooting. The trends revolve around emerging technologies and consideration of their proper place within both our society and personal lives. These technological advancements—such as smartphones, facial recognition software, DNA analysis, and digital surveillance—which are increasingly ubiquitous features of modern American life, are often described simply as double-edged tools to be employed for either harm or benefit. In the longer view, our look "into the future" in this chapter identifies trends that seem to repulse rather than coalesce. The narrative paints a portrait of choppy seas rather than a tidal wave, a society increasingly at odds with and at the mercy of movements pulling us in contradictory directions. For their part, the police—as always—find themselves in the middle of these forces. They remain arbiters of freedom versus order and gatekeepers to the criminal justice system much in the way that they have been for centuries. The trends, technologies, and topics of debate shift over time, but policing remains at the core of these struggles, with law enforcement officers performing the necessary roles and functions we, as a society, require of them.

KEY TERMS

DNA
dynamic hotspots
facial recognition

hotspots of
crime
parole

probation
truth decay

FURTHER READING

De Moor, S., C. Vandeviver, and T. Vander Beken. (2018). "Integrating Police-Recorded Crime Data and DNA Data to Study Serial Co-offending Behaviour." *European Journal of Criminology* 15(5): 632–51. https://doi.org/10.1177/1477370817749499

Kavanagh, J., and M. D. Rich (2018). *Truth Decay: An Initial Exploration of the Diminishing Role of Facts and Analysis in American Public Life.* Santa Monica, CA: The Rand Corporation.

Marshall, E. M., J. L. Groscup, E. M. Brank, A. Perez, and L. A. Hoetger (2020). "Public Surveillance of Cell Phone Location Data: Supreme Courts versus Public Opinion." *Behavioral Sciences and the Law* 37, 751–75. https://doi.org/10.1002/bsl.2442

Sherman, L. W. (1995). "Hot Spots of Crime and Criminal Careers of Places." In *Crime and Place*, pp.35–52 edited by J. E. Eck and D. Weisburd. Monsey, NY: Criminal Justice Press.

Glossary

Aquilar-Spinneli test A guideline for determining the lawful use of confidential informants, it demands that police demonstrate sufficient facts to determine (a) the truthfulness of the information provided and (b) the basis of the informant's knowledge such that he/she was related closely enough to the criminal activity.

Automated Fingerprint Identification System (AFIS) A processing system that identifies potential fingerprint matches warranting a visual inspection by a fingerprint examiner.

backwards law The tendency of the media to focus on rare and more serious crimes rather than the more typical street crime.

body-worn camera (BWC) Small device that provides video evidence to determine at least some of the actions of police and citizens during an encounter.

border searches Routine searches of luggage or motor vehicles absent either a warrant or probable cause.

bounty hunter More formally referred to as a bail enforcement agent or bail recovery agent; this person's job is to locate and apprehend defendants who flee or "bail jump" and do not return for trial.

broken windows theory Position that argues that signs of disorder and decline in an area will inevitably lead to crime and further decline.

Brown v. Mississippi Case that established standards to determine the constitutionality of confessions, which is known as the due process voluntariness test.

campus-based academies Police academies situated in two-year colleges.

case clearance The number of crimes that eventually result in a criminal arrest.

changing patterns of social organization As societies become more complex and specialized in terms of their organization, the need for occupational specialists increases, including the need for specialists in social control or law enforcement.

Chicago Alternative Police Strategy (CAPS) An approach to community-oriented policing that included assigning officers to permanent neighborhood beats, involving residents in the identification of problems and potential solutions, and relying on other agencies (both public and private) to address identified issues; perhaps the best example of successfully implementing a community-oriented policing approach.

Chimel rule Rule that police are allowed to search the arrestee and any areas under his or her immediate control for protection and to limit the destruction of evidence.

choice The first stage of police socialization in which the recruit voluntarily applies to join a police agency.

citizen patrols Volunteers who patrol neighborhoods and provide police with information and advice.

Clery Act Law mandating that colleges and universities make certain crime statistics readily available to the public.

closed-circuit television (CCTV) A system typically consisting of a video camera, a monitor, and a recorder.

coercive force Acts of physical force by police as well as all sorts of behaviors police employ to otherwise accomplish the goals of their work including threats, verbal commands, and other nonviolent behaviors intended to address the wide variety of situations.

Combined DNA Index System (CODIS) A system that contains DNA profiles from individuals and cases that have been collected by jurisdictions and agencies across the country.

community alienation A situation in which the police become separated and disengaged from the citizens they were sworn to protect and serve.

community-oriented policing (COP) era Time period in which people believe that police cannot operate successfully in isolation from the community and citizens.

community-oriented policing (COP) An approach that emphasizes a more collaborative effort between the police and the community with a recognition that the police may need to take a secondary role to other agencies, depending on the problem.

CompStat Short for "compare statistics," this program was developed by the New York City Police Department as a process that uses current crime data to analyze crime patterns and quickly allocate patrol resources to problem areas.

confirmatory test A laboratory test that will supply more detailed information on a substance/drug than found in a presumptive field test.

confirmatory tool An implement that is used to confirm information that is already suspected.

consent searches The most common type of warrantless search in which citizens surrender their rights.

county police tend to be found in densely populated urban areas and they function much like local municipal police departments, just serving a wider geographical area

criminal investigations bureaus/agencies State agencies with responsibilities that vary according to the statutory mandate in the individual state.

crime analysis The gathering of different types of data on crime, problems in the community, information about the community, and other information to provide insight on the commission of crime and disorder and to identify crime patterns and possible responses.

criminal justice funnel A representation of the criminal justice system in which a comparatively large number of individuals or criminal cases enter the system and then the number of individuals or cases is significantly reduced at various points as they progress through it.

custodial interrogation An interrogation initiated by police in which a suspect's freedom is restricted in a significant way.

dark figure of crime The vast number of unreported criminal acts.

decentralized police system System in which police powers are distributed locally throughout the nation rather than subsumed over a single or small number of federal-level agencies.

deterrence The act of discouraging potential offenders from committing crimes; one method involves the presence of police patrolling the community.

discretion Police officers' power to decide whether an individual's instant conduct is serious enough to require formal intervention and adjudication or can be corrected with a warning or other compensatory measures.

disproportionate use of force Using force at a level that far exceeds the level of resistance or aggression of the subject.

DNA Deoxyribonucleic acid; a unique "genetic fingerprint" that points to one and only one individual.

driving under the influence (DUI) Driving a vehicle while affected by alcohol or drugs; this used to be called DWI (driving while intoxicated) but now includes the influence of drugs, both illegal and legal.

Drug Abuse Resistance Education (D.A.R.E.) National program taught by police officers focusing on teaching youths the skills to resist peer pressure, recognize high-risk situations and behavior, and avoid participation in drug use.

drug detection K-9s Dogs that use their keen sense of smell to search for drugs.

dynamic hotspots Mobile individuals who present a high potential for committing crimes of a particular type or a broad array of serious crimes.

edge control The ability of police officers to effectively deal with the conditions of the job, de-escalate and dampen turbulence, and prevent things from "getting out of hand."

elite interests Political leaders, high-ranking military officers, and corporate or business executives who desire maintenance of their societal position and use formalized policing to help do so.

encounter A stage of police socialization occurring after the completion of the police academy when rookie officers initially face the realities of police work.

entrapment The idea that the police enticed or induced an individual to act in a way that he or she would not normally act.

Escobedo v. Illinois Supreme Court decision that extended a suspect's rights to an attorney prior to trial.

exceptions to the warrant requirement Circumstances that allow warrantless police searches.

facial recognition The process of matching unknown photos against massive databases, comparing physical features in largely similar poses.

family group conferencing (FGC) A form of restorative justice that brings together the offender, family members, close friends, and other support groups of the victim and offender with a facilitator to discuss the problematic behavior and to reach an agreement on how to resolve the problems.

field training officer (FTO) Officer with whom a rookie rides to learn the jurisdiction's streets, problem areas, and the agency's expectations.

field training period An additional layer of training and orientation before new officers start to work on their own; may last from several weeks to almost a year, depending on the agency's needs.

Fifth Amendment This amendment to the US Constitution sets out the rights of the American people with regard to several aspects of state power, including those that limit police interrogations and citizen rights against self-incrimination.

fleeing felons Suspects who flee the scene of felony crimes.

foot patrol Officers "walking the beat" in order to deter crime and catch criminals on scene when they are able; it allows police the opportunity to interact with citizens face-to-face and become familiar with their problems and concerns, and it is considered a key aspect of building relationships in community policing.

force continuum A continuous sequence that links the level of police force to the aggressiveness and resistance of the citizen.

formal phase of policing This third phase in the development of modern police involves the creation of organized groups of people who act as full-time professional police officers.

Fourth Amendment This amendment to the US Constitution sets out the rights of the American people with regard to government searches and seizures, including those conducted by police.

freedom versus public order Individual liberty to act as one chooses versus the need for some type of authority or civility in society.

Gang Resistance Education and Training (G.R.E.A.T.) National program taught by police officers focusing on teaching youths the skills to resist peer pressure, recognizing high-risk situations and behavior, and avoid participation in gangs.

gatekeepers One who controls access, such as police officers, who are usually the first point of contact between citizens and the rest of the criminal justice system.

general writs of assistance Court orders that authorized agents of the British government during the American colonial period to enter any house or other place to search for and seize prohibited goods.

Gideon v. Wainwright Supreme Court case that ruled that states must appoint a trial attorney to indigent criminal defendants in felony cases.

gypsy cops A term that generally refers to sworn officers who move from job to job, usually under a cloud of suspicion related to their activities.

hot pursuit An exception to the warrant requirement in which police may enter a premises without a warrant in pursuit of a dangerous criminal suspect whom they reasonably believe is on the premises and/or in response to third parties they know to be in immediate danger inside.

hotspot policing Targeted police patrol and enforcement.

hotspots of crime Very small geographic areas in which 3–5 percent of addresses citywide produce roughly 50 percent of all calls for police service.

hue and cry An example of informal or avocational policing in which citizens who witnessed a crime would make a "hue and cry" or public announcement of the crime and identification of the perpetrator.

Illinois v. Gates Case that ruled that a warrant based on information from a confidential informant may be used even in cases where both "prongs" of the Aguilar-Spinelli test have not been met.

incivility Rude or unsociable behavior that can be seen as evidence that residents of an area are not as concerned about what is happening around them than people in other areas.

informal or avocational phase of policing In this first phase in the development of modern policing, ordinary citizens perform the job of "policing" when they are not engaged in their full-time occupation.

Integrated Automated Fingerprint Identification System (IAFIS) A computerized, national storage system for fingerprints and other related information, such as photographs of individuals, name, and birthdate.

intelligence-led policing Strategies that use real-time crime analysis and incorporate intelligence analysis in the deployment of both specialized units and regular patrol officers.

interrogation A special kind of interview wherein the police ask a suspect a series of questions for which the police already know the answers, or at least believe they know the answers.

interrogation In the context of police work, a direct interview with a criminal suspect.

interviews In the context of police work, non-accusatory talk with an individual to gather basic information pertinent to an investigation.

introduction A stage of police socialization that takes place at the police academy, where one learns the formal values, attitudes, and beliefs of the police organization.

investigation A formal inquiry that involves police officers (generally identified as detectives) who specialize in addressing criminal events that require more attention in order to identify the offender and/or gather the evidence needed for prosecution.

job characteristics In police work, the characteristics that contribute to the formation and maintenance of the police subculture.

Kansas City Preventive Patrol Experiment Study that focused on the impact of routine patrol on levels of crime, arrests, citizen fear, service delivery, traffic accidents, and response time.

kin policing An example of informal or avocational policing in which the responsibility for social control was in the hands of "people" who were responsible for their families or "kin."

law enforcement Ensuring obedience to the law; reflects the public's typical view of the police, specifically responding to situations in which the police apply the criminal code, make an arrest, and do the follow-up necessary for a successful prosecution.

limitations associated with use-of-force continua Developments over the last 25 years that recognize police–citizen encounters do not always proceed in a linear or sequential manner based on the actions of the suspect and officers may need to skip some or all of the non-deadly force options to gain control over a particular criminal suspect.

Mann Act Law passed in 1920 that criminalized the transportation of women across state lines for prostitution and human trafficking.

metamorphosis A stage of police socialization in which more experienced police officers eventually adapt to the realities of police work.

militarization of policing The tendency of local law enforcement agencies to adopt military-style tactics and equipment in order to maintain public order and enforce the law.

Minneapolis Domestic Violence Experiment An experiment that examined the impact of three different police responses on subsequent domestic violence: (1) an automatic arrest, (2) having one party leave for a "cooling off" period, and (3) counseling or referral to a social service agency.

Miranda v. Arizona Supreme Court decision that required police to warn criminal suspects of their rights under the Fifth Amendment prohibition against self-incrimination.

modus operandi The way that something is done.

multivariate Involving two or more quantitative variables; in police work, it refers to a phenomenon in which a multitude of factors may potentially influence decision-making.

Neighborhood Watch Program in which community groups observe and report suspicious activity in the neighborhood.

new media Social media platforms.

nonrandom distribution of crime The geographical dispersion of crime across cities. see also hotspots of crime

O. W. Wilson An advocate for institutionalized police organizational management structures that were highly centralized and focused on crime control as the primary function of modern police.

Operation Ceasefire Program that targeted gun crime and youth homicides in Boston.

order maintenance Regulating the public's behavior and ensuring that rules are obeyed; police can handle these situations through means besides making an arrest and invoking the legal processes.

parole Post-release monitoring of convicts on the conditions allowing their release.

perceptual shorthand In police work, this refers to an officer's ability to quickly discern and analyze a situation and prepare to handle it accordingly.

plain view doctrine Broad rules that govern the lawfulness of seizures under the plain view exception to the warrant requirement: the item to be seized must be within the officer's sight or field of vision, police must be legally present, and the item to be seized must be immediately recognized as subject to seizure.

plain view searches Searches in which police seize items legally subject to seizure that are within their plain view.

Police Athletic League (PAL) An organization run by local police departments to engage youths in non-delinquent activities such as sports, school activities, and social events for the purpose of giving the youths direction and support.

political era of policing Time period that spans from roughly the mid-1800s, with the development of the first American municipal police departments, through the early decades of the 1900s; police departments were organized and operated primarily to satisfy the goals of the dominant political machine.

political machine An organization derived from a political party headed by single leader or "boss" that earns enough votes to control the administrative functions of a city.

POST (Peace Officer Standards and Training) A training program for police recruits; almost all POST academies are residential, requiring recruits to live in barracks or dormitories during the week's curriculum, but allowing them to return home for weekends.

presumptive drug test This type of test establishes the presence or absence of different drugs; it does not provide information on the exact nature of the drug or the quality/concentration of the drug.

private police Police who are not directly employed by the state; they serve the private constituency that hires them for specific tasks or operations.

Private Security Officer Employment Authorization Act of 2004 Law that enables private police agencies/companies to ask the FBI to conduct criminal background checks on potential employees.

proactive approach Taking measures to prepare for a situation; in law enforcement, the police take steps to uncover crimes and to intervene as crimes are taking place.

probable cause A requirement that must be met before police make an arrest, conduct a search, or receive a warrant. For a search, police must establish several things, including evidence that a crime has been committed, evidence of that crime, the place to be searched, and the potential evidence to be seized.

probation Field monitoring of low-level offenders.

problem-oriented policing (POP) An effort to make police more proactive and focused on solving community problems that relies on in-depth analysis of crimes and factors that may contribute to crime and that lead to evidence-based interventions for dealing with crime and underlying factors; emphasis tends to be on more mainline police responses, the centrality of the police in interventions.

professional/reform era Time period in which reformers sought to centralize police operations and increase the power and prestige of the police chief, upgrade the quality of police personnel, and narrow the function of police to focus more exclusively on crime control.

progressive reform movement A response to problems associated with rapid changes to American cities associated with large-scale industrialization, urbanization, and immigration.

property marking A common anti-crime activity in community crime prevention initiatives that involves physically marking personal property so that the property can be traced.

Public Law 83-280 A law that allows the federal government to cede jurisdiction over major crimes to the state in 16 states.

pulling levers Part of Operation Ceasefire, in which police would take any and all actions possible against violators.

reactive policing The practice of police acting on information from the public, usually about crimes that have already occurred.

reasonable expectation of privacy Consideration under the Fourth Amendment that protects citizens from government searches and seizures under those conditions.

response time The speed at which the police can respond to a call for service or a crime.

rising perceptions of criminality Shift toward formalized police forces becomes more likely in societies wherein people feel less safe and believe there is more crime than previously was the case.

safe havens Homes or businesses identified as a place of safety in a neighborhood for youths; a common community crime prevention activity.

SARA A major analysis tool used by POP and COP; stands for scanning, analysis, response, and assessment.

school resource officers (SROs) Police officers assigned to schools who are involved in mentoring and referrals, training teachers and parents, and teaching programs.

search Within the context of the US Constitution, a search occurs anytime the police or other government actors intrude into a person's reasonable expectation of privacy.

search warrant A legal document authorizing a police officer to enter and search a particular place.

searches based on exigent circumstances An exception to the warrant requirement in which police are permitted to search and/or seize evidence without a warrant in emergency situations that make obtaining a warrant impractical, dangerous, or unnecessary.

searches incident to arrest Searches conducted as part of a lawful seizure or arrest of a criminal suspect by police.

self-incrimination Being a witness against oneself.

service The action of helping or assisting the community or individuals.

sheriff Oldest law enforcement office; operates at the county level; office is established by either the state constitution or state statute.

shifts One of two or more recurring periods in which different employees work in turns with one another to supply round-the-clock coverage.

shire-reeve Medieval English office granted with wide-ranging duties such as local law enforcement, tax collection, and heading the local judiciary.

Sir Robert Peel Considered the founder of police, he introduced the legislation that created the Metropolitan Police.

situational force model A policy in which police need to select the least violent force option in order to make an arrest, overcome suspect resistance, or to prevent an escape.

situational risk In police work, the immediate scenario that police confront during a potential deadly force encounter; police decisions to use deadly force are most directly influenced by the level of risk confronted by the officer who decides to use deadly force.

Sixth Amendment This amendment to the US Constitution sets out the rights of the American people with regard to legal representation.

special jurisdiction police Police who operate in relation to specific needs or functions or somewhat unique jurisdictions.

special needs searches An exception to the warrant requirement that covers searches conducted by government employees other than police who perform jobs related to law enforcement.

special response teams (SRTs) Specialized full-time units found in large police departments that are called upon to respond to emergency situations; formerly known as SWAT, or special weapons and tactics.

stages of police socialization The steps or sequence of being socialized into the police subculture, including choice, introduction, encounter, and metamorphosis.

state patrol Police with a more limited jurisdiction, focusing primarily on traffic enforcement on the interstate and state highways.

state police Police with broad, general enforcement powers throughout the state.

state-level criminal prosecution An extremely rare event in which American police officers are prosecuted for cases in which they use deadly force on the job.

sting operation Type of focused/proactive investigative activity in which the police set up an opportunity for offenders to do what they would normally do—only, unwittingly, with law enforcement officers.

stop and frisk An encounter that involves detaining and patting down or "frisking" a subject's outer clothing.

stress-based academies Training academies modeled on military boot camp, emphasizing physical fitness and the ability to operate calmly and appropriately in the face of aggressive, demonstrative behavior.

subculture A group of individuals characterized by a distinct set of values, beliefs, and behaviors.

surveillance Closely monitoring or watching; the basic premise in police work is putting eyes on the street in order to see what is taking place.

symbolic assailant Person who uses particular gestures, language, and/or dress that signals the potential for an impending confrontation and/or violent encounter.

Tennessee v. Garner Supreme Court case that ruled that state-level statutes allowing the use of deadly force against fleeing felons were unconstitutional.

Terry v. Ohio This case defined the parameters under which police may stop and frisk criminal suspects.

third degree The use of torture, physical beatings, assaults, and psychological pressure designed to coerce confessions from criminal suspects.

trace evidence Materials that are left behind or could be transferred from the offender to the victim (or location) during the commission of a crime.

transitional phase of policing In this second phase in the development of modern policing, individuals and/or groups perform the policing function on a part-time or voluntary basis.

Tribal police police agencies established on tribal lands to perform police duties

truth decay "The triumph of volume over veracity"; statements and claims made and widely broadcast without evidence to support them.

turbulence For police, turbulence refers to lots of activity that occurs within short bursts of time.

use-of-force continuum Guidelines for officer discretion in force situations that describe an escalating series of options the officer may take to resolve an encounter.

variable Any one factor that can change from one context to another.

vigilante policing Organized extralegal movements comprised of individuals who take the law into their own hands.

warrantless search A search conducted when circumstances and time do not allow sufficient opportunities for police to obtain a valid search warrant beforehand.

watch and ward A system in which able-bodied men to keep watch over the community at night.

watch system One of America's first known law enforcement systems; it was typically comprised of citizens who served as volunteer "watchmen" who patrolled the streets at night looking for crimes.

working personality In police work, common patterns of thinking and behavior among police.

wrongful use of force Using force for the wrong reason, such as to retaliate against a person for "disrespect" to the officer.

Bibliography

Adams, K. (1999). "What We Know about Police Use of Force." In *Use of Force by Police: Overview of National and Local Data*, by K. Adams et al., 1–14. Washington, DC: U.S. Department of Justice. https://www.ncjrs.gov/pdffiles1/nij/176330-1.pdf

Adler, B. (2019, May 24). "In California, Agreement on New Rules for When Police Can Use Deadly Force." *National Public Radio*. https://www.npr.org/2019/05/24/726500537/in-california-agreement-on-new-rules-for-when-police-can-use-deadly-force

Alpert, G. P., and R. G. Dunham (1988). *Policing Urban America*. Prospect Heights, IL: Waveland Press.

American Civil Liberties Union (2018). "The Constitution in the 100 Mile Border Zone." Available at http://www.aclu.org/other/constitution-100-mile-border-zone

American Society of Addiction Medicine (2016). "Opioid Addiction 2016 Facts & Figures." Available at https://www.asam.org/docs/default-source/advocacy/opioid-addiction-disease-facts-figures.pdf

Amnesty International (2008, December 16). "USA: Safety of Tasers Questioned as Death Toll Hits 334 Mark" [Press Release]. Available at http://www/amnesty.org/en/press-release/2008/12/usa-safety-tasers-questioned-death-toll-hits-334-mark-20081216/

Anderson, E. (1994, May). "The Code of the Streets." *The Atlantic*. https://www.theatlantic.com/magazine/archive/1994/05/the-code-of-the-streets/306601/

Asch, S. H. (1971). *Police Authority and the Rights of the Individual*. 2nd. ed. New York: Arco.

Associated Press. (2018, March 13). "Man Pleads Guilty after East Liverpool Officer's Accidental Fentanyl Overdose." *Fox8News*. https://fox8.com/2018/03/13/man-pleads-guilty-after-east-liverpool-officers-accidental-fentanyl-overdose/

Aveni, T. J. (2003). "The Force Continuum Conundrum." *Law and Order 51*(12): 74–77.

Balko, R. (2014). *Rise of the Warrior Cop: The Militarization of America's Police Forces*. New York: Public Affairs.

Baltaci, H. (2010). *Crime Analysis: An Empirical Analysis of Its Effectiveness as a Crime Fighting Tool*. Doctoral diss., University of Texas at Dallas, Richardson.

Banton, M. (1964) *The Policeman and the Community*. London: Tavistock.

Barrile, L. G. (1980). *Television and Attitudes about Crime*. PhD diss., Boston College.

Bittner, E. (1970). *The Functions of Police in Modern Society*. Washington, DC: National Institute of Mental Health.

Bittner, E. (1978). "The Functions of Police in Modern Society." In *Policing: A View from the Street*, edited by P. K. Manning and J. Van Maanen, 32–50. New York: Random House.

Black, D. (1981). *The Manners and Customs of the Police*. New York: Academic Press.

Black's Law Dictionary (2018). "What Is Police?" Available at http://thelawdictionary.org/police/

Blair, J. P. (2003). "Interview or Interrogation: A Comment on Kassin et al. (2003)." Available at http://www.reid.com/pdfs/blair2003interview.pdf

Blumberg, M. (1981). "Race and Police Shootings: An Analysis in Two Cities." In *Contemporary Issues in Law Enforcement*, edited by J. Fyfe (141-57). Beverly Hills, CA: Sage.

Bopp, W. J. (1977). *O. W.: O. W. Wilson and the Search for a Police Profession*. St. Louis, MO: Kennikat Press.

Bowers, W. J., and J. H. Hirsch (1987). "The Impact of Foot Patrol Staffing on Crime and Disorder in Boston: An Unmet Promise." *American Journal of Police 6*: 17–44.

Braga, A. (2001). "The Effects of Hot Spots Policing on Crime." *The Annals of the American Academy of Political and Social Science 578*: 104–25.

Braga, A. A. (2005). "Hot Spots Policing and Crime Prevention: A Systemic Review of Randomized Controlled Trials." *Journal of Experimental Criminology 1*: 317–42.

Braga, A. A., D. M. Kennedy, A. M. Piehl, and E. J. Waring (2001). "Measuring the Impact of Operation Ceasefire." *In National Institute of Justice, Reducing Gun Violence: The Boston Gun Project's Operation Ceasefire*, 55–71. Washington, DC: National Institute of Justice.

Brooks, C. (2019). "Sheriffs' Offices, 2016: Personnel." Washington, DC: U.S. Department of Justice, Office of Justice Programs, Bureau of Justice Statistics. https://www.bjs.gov/index.cfm?ty=pbdetail&iid=6707

Brown, L. P. (1978). "The Role of the Sheriff." In *The Future of Policing* edited by A. W. Cohen (240-68). Beverly Hills, CA: Sage.

Brown, L. P., and M. A. Wycoff (1987). "Policing Houston: Reducing Fear and Improving Service." *Crime & Delinquency 33*: 71–89.

Brown, R. M. (1969). "The American Vigilante Tradition." In *Violence in America: Historical and Comparative Perspectives*, edited by H. D. Graham and T. Gurr, 121–69. Washington, DC: U.S. Government Printing Office.

Buerger, M. (1994). "A Tale of Two Targets: Limitations of Community Anti-Crime Actions." *Crime and Delinquency 40*(3): 411–36.

Bureau of Alcohol, Tobacco, Firearms and Explosives (2019). "Fact Sheet—Facts and Figures for Fiscal Year 2018." https://www.atf.gov/resource-center/fact-sheet/fact-sheet-facts-and-figures-fiscal-year-2018

Bureau of Alcohol, Tobacco, Firearms and Explosives (n.d.). "ATF History Timeline." Accessed December 19, 2019, from https://www.atf.gov/our-history/atf-history-timeline

Bureau of Justice Statistics (1997). "What Is the Sequence of Events in the Criminal Justice System?" Available at https://www.bjs.gov/content/largechart.cfm

Bureau of Justice Statistics (2019). "Tribal Crime Data-Collection Activities, 2019." https://www.bjs.gov/content/pub/pdf/tcdca19.pdf

Bureau of Labor Statistics (2019). "Occupational Employment and Wages, May 2018." https://www.bls.gov/oes/current/oes339032.htm

Burke, M. (2018, October 11). "Officer Who Fatally Shot Tamir Rice Quits Ohio Police Department Days after He Was Hired." *NBC News*. https://www.nbcnews.com/news/us-news/officer-who-fatally-shot-tamir-rice-quits-ohio-police-department-n919046

Burns, R., and P. Kinkade (2005). "Bounty Hunters: A Look behind the Hype." *Policing: An International Journal of Police Strategies & Management 28*(1): 118–38.

Carter, D. L. (2004). *Law Enforcement Intelligence: A Guide for State, Local, and Tribal Law Enforcement Agencies*. Washington, DC: Office of Community Oriented Policing Services.

Cheh, M. M. (1995). "Are Lawsuits an Answer to Police Brutality?" In *And Justice For All: Understanding and Controlling Police Abuse of Force*, edited by W. A. Geller and H. Toch, 233–60. Washington, DC: Police Executive Research Forum.

Chermak, S. M. (1998). "Predicting Crime Story Salience: The Effects of Crime, Victim, and Defendant Characteristics." *Journal of Criminal Justice 26*: 61–70.

Chermak, S. M., and N. Chapman (2007). "Predicting Crime Story Salience: A Replication." *Journal of Criminal Justice 35*: 351–63.

Clancy, T. K. (2011). "The Framer's Intent: John Adams, His Era, and the Fourth Amendment." *Indiana Law Journal 86*: 979–1060.

Conor, P. (2018). "Police Resources in Canada." *Juristat*. Available at https://www.150.stat-can.gc.ca/n1/pub/85-002-x/2018001/article/54912-eng.htm

Cordeiro, M., and J. Roulette (2019, January 25). "A New Study Suggests Amazon's Rekognition Software Sucks at Detecting Dark-Skinned Women." *The Orlando Weekly*. https://www.orlandoweekly.com/Blogs/archives/2019/01/25/amazons-rekognition-software-sucks-at-detecting-dark-skinned-women

Cordner, G. W. (1981). "Effects of Directed Patrol: A Quasi-Experiment in Pontiac." In *Contemporary Issues in Law Enforcement*, edited by J. Fyfe, 37–58. Thousand Oaks, CA: Sage.

Cordner, G., J. Greene, and T. Bynum (1983). "The Sooner the Better: Some Effects of Police Response Time." In *Police at Work: Policy Issues and Analysis*, edited by R. Bennett (145-168). Beverly Hills, CA: Sage.

Corsaro, N., and E. McGarrell (2009). "Testing a Promising Homicide Reduction Strategy: Rassessing the Impact of Indianapolis' 'Pulling Levers' Intervention." *Journal of Experimental Criminology 5*: 63–82.

Corsaro, N., and E. McGarrell (2010). "Reducing Homicide Risk in Indianapolis between 1997 and 2000." *Journal of Urban Health 87*: 851–64.

Cowan, J. (2019, August 20). "What to Know about California's New Police Use-of-Force Rule." *The New York Times*. https://www.nytimes.com/2019/08/20/us/california-police-use-of-force-law.html

Crank, J. P. (2004). *Understanding Police Culture*. 2nd ed. New York: Routledge..

Crime Prevention Website.com (2019). "The Peelian Principles." Retrieved from https://thecrimepreventionwebsite.com/police-crime-prevention-service—a-short-history/744/the-peelian-principles/

Crosby, H. (1883). "The Dangerous Classes." *The North American Review 136*(317): 345–52.

Customs and Border Protection (2019a). "CBP through the Years." https://www.cbp.gov/about/history

Customs and Border Protection (2019b). "Snapshot: A Summary of CBP Facts and Figures." https://www.cbp.gov/sites/default/files/assets/documents/2019-Nov/CBP-Snapshot-Nov-2019.pdf

Davis, A. C., and S. Velastin (2005). "A Progress Review of Intelligent CCTV Surveillance Systems." Retrieved from https://www.researchgate.net/publication/44113794

DEA (n.d.a). "Mission." Accessed December 19, 2019, from https://www.dea.gov/mission

DEA (n.d.b). "Staffing and Budget." Accessed December 19, 2019, from https://www.dea.gov/staffing-and-budget

del Carmen, R. V., and C. Hemmonds (2010). *Criminal Procedure and the Supreme Court*. New York: Rowan & Littlefield.

Del Real, Jose A. (2019, March 2). "No Charges in Sacramento Police Shooting of Stephon Clark." *The New York Times.* https://www.nytimes.com/2019/03/02/us/stephon-clark-police-shooting-sacramento.html

DiBlasio, N. (2012, July 5). "YouTube: The Latest Crime Solver." *USA Today,* A1.

Dominick, J. R. (1978). "Crime and Law Enforcement in the Mass Media." In *Deviance and Mass Media,* edited by C. Winick (105-130). Beverly Hills, CA: Sage.

Draper, R. (2018). "They Are Watching You—and Everything Else on the Planet." *National Geographic Magazine.* Retrieved from https://www.nationalgeographic.com/magazine/2018/02/surveillance-watching-you/

Dugdale, R. (1910). *The Jukes: A Study in Crime, Pauperism, Disease, and Heredity.* New York: G. P. Putnam's Sons.

Dunford, F. D., Huizinga, D., and Elliott, D. S. (1989). *The Omaha Domestic Violence Police Experiments: Final Report.* Washington, DC: National Institute of Justice.

Eck, J. (2002). "Preventing Crime at Places." In *Evidence Based Crime Prevention,* edited by L. Sherman, D. Farrington, B. Welsh, and D. L. McKenzie, 241–94. New York: Routledge.

Eck, J., and W. Spelman (1987). "Who You Gonna Call? The Police as Problem Busters." *Crime and Delinquency* 33(1): 31–52.

Environmental Protection Agency (2018). "Criminal Investigations." https://www.epa.gov/enforcement/criminal-investigations

Epstein, J. (1978). *Neighborhood Police Team Experiment: An Evaluation.* Winnipeg: Institute of Urban Studies.

Esbensen, F. (1987). "Foot Patrols: Of What Value?" *American Journal of Police* 6: 45–65.

Falcone, D. N., and L. E. Wells (1995). "The County Sheriff as a Distinctive Policing Modality." *American Journal of Police* 14: 123–49.

FBI (2010). "Crime in the United States: Offenses Cleared. U.S. Department of Justice." Available at https://ucr.fbi.gov/crime-in-the-u.s./2010/crime-in-the-u.s.-2010/clearances

FBI (2019). "CODIS-NDIS Statistics." Available at https://www.fbi.gov/services/laboratory/biometric-analysis/codis/ndis-statistics

FBI (n.d.a). "A Brief History." Accessed December 19, 2019, from https://www.fbi.gov/history/brief-history

FBI (n.d.b). "Mission and Priorities." Accessed December 19, 2019, from https://www.fbi.gov/about/mission

Federal Bureau of Prisons (n.d.). "About Our Agency." Accessed December 20, 2019, from https://www.bop.gov/about/agency/

Ferguson, C. J. (2013). *Adolescents, Crime and the Media: A Critical Analysis.* New York: Springer.

Florida Fish and Wildlife Conservation Commission (2019). "About Us." https://myfwc.com/contact/law-enforcement/

Florida v. Harris, 568 U.S. 237 (2013).

Flosi, E. (2012, May 30). "Use of Force: Downfalls of the Continuum Model," *PoliceOne.com News.* Available at https://www.policeone.com/use-of-force/articles/5643926-use-of-force-downfalls-of-the-continuum-model/

Fogelson, R. M. (1977). *Big-City Police.* Cambridge, MA: Harvard University Press.

Fritsch, E. J., J. Liederbach, and R. W. Taylor (2009). *Police Patrol Allocation and Deployment.* Upper Saddle River, NJ: Pearson/Prentice Hall.

Fyfe, J. (1979). "Administrative Interventions on Police Shooting Discretion." *Journal of Criminal Justice* 7: 313–35.

Fyfe, J. (1981). "Race and Extreme Police-Citizen Violence." In *Race, Crime, and Criminal Justice,* edited by R. Mcneeley and C. E. Pope, 89–108. Beverly Hills, CA: Sage.

Fyfe, J. (1988). "Police Use of Deadly Force: Research and Reform," *Justice Quarterly* 5(2): 165–205.

Fyfe, J. (1989). "The Split-Second Syndrome and Other Determinants of Police Violence." In *Critical Issues in Policing: Contemporary Readings*, edited by R. G. Dunham and G. P. Alpert, 465–79. Prospect Heights, IL: Waveland.

Fyfe, J. J. (2004). "Stops, Frisks, Searches, and the Constitution." *Criminology and Public Policy* 3(3): 379–96.

Gambino, L., and S. W. Thrasher (2014, December 14). "Thousands March to Protest against Police Brutality in Major U.S. Cities." *The Guardian.* Available at http://www.theguardian.com/us-news/2014/dec/13/marchers-protest-police-brutality-new-york-washington-boston

Garofalo, J., and M. McLeod (1988). "Improving the Use and Effectiveness of Neighborhood Watch Programs." *NIJ Research in Action.* Washington, DC: National Institute of Justice.

Geller, W. A., and M. S. Scott (1992). "Deadly Force: What We Know." in *Thinking about Police: Contemporary Readings*, edited by C. B. Klockars and S. D. Mastrofski, 446–76. New York: McGraw-Hill.

George, A. (2018). "The 1968 Kerner Commission Got It Right, But Nobody Listened." *Smithsonian Magazine* (March 1). https://www.smithsonianmag.com/smithsonian-institution/1968-kerner-commission-got-it-right-nobody-listened-180968318/

Gerbner, G., L. Gross, M. Jackson-Beeck, S. Jeffries-Fox, and N. Signorielle (1978). "Cultural Indicators: Violence Profile No. 9." *Journal of Communication* 28: 176–207.

Gerbner, G., L. Gross, M. F. Eleey, M. Jackson-Beeck, S. Jeffries-Fox, and N. Signorielle (1977). "TV Violence No. 8: The Highlights." *Journal of Communication* 27: 171–80.

Gerbner, G., L. Gross, N. Signorielle, and M. Morgan (1980). "Television Violence, Victimization, and Power." *American Behavioral Scientist* 23: 705–16.

Gerbner, G., L. Gross, N. Signorielle, M. Morgan, and M. Jackson-Beeck (1979). "The Demonstration of Power: Violence Profile No. 10." *Journal of Communication* 29: 177–96.

Graber, D. (September 1977). "Ideological Components in the Perceptions of Crime and Crime News." *Paper presented at the Meeting of the Society for the Study of Social Problems San Francisco.*

Graber, D. (1980). *Crime News and the Public.* New York: Praeger.

Graham v. Connor, 490 U.S. 386 (1989).

Greenwood, P., and J. Petersilia (1975). *The Criminal Investigative Process: Volume 1: Summary and Policy Implications.* Washington, DC: U.S. Department of Justice.

Greer, C., and R. Reiner (2012). "Mediated Mayhem: Media, Crime, Criminal Justice." In *The Oxford Handbook of Criminology*, edited by M. Maguire, R. Morgan, and R. Reiner (245–278). Oxford: Oxford University Press.

Haag, M. (2018, October 8). "Cleveland Officer Who Killed Tamir Rice Is Hired by an Ohio Police Department." *The New York Times.* https://www.nytimes.com/2018/10/08/us/timothy-loehmann-tamir-rice-shooting.html

Hadden, S. E. (2001). *Slave Patrols: Law and Violence in Virginia and the Carolinas.* Cambridge, MA: Harvard University Press.

Haller, M. (1976). "Historical Roots of Police Behavior: Chicago, 1890–1925." *Law and Society Review* 10(Winter): 303–24.

Hansen, C. (2019). "Slave Patrols: An Early Form of American Policing." Retrieved from lawenforcementmuseum.org/2019/07/10/slave-patrols-an-early-form-of-american-policing/

Hartnett, S. M., and W. G. Skogan (1999). "Community Policing: Chicago's Experience." *National Institute of Justice Journal* (April): 3–11.

Hassan, A. (2019, March 22). "Antwon Rose Shooting: White Police Officer Acquitted in Death of Black Teenager." *The New York Times.*

Hauser, C. (2020, January 9). "Teacher Is Charged with Battery after Throwing Student Out of Class." *The New York Times.* https://www.nytimes.com/2020/01/09/us/buddy-taylor-middle-school-teacher-arrest.html

Hickman, M. J. (2003). "Tribal Law Enforcement, 2000." https://www.bjs.gov/content/pub/pdf/tle00.pdf

Higgins, P. B., and M. W. Ray (1978). *Television's Action Arsenal: Weapon Use in Prime Time.* Washington, DC: U.S. Conference of Mayors.

Hirschel, J. D., I. W. Hutchison, and C. W. Dean (1992). "The Failure of Arrest to Deter Spouse Abuse." *Journal of Research in Crime & Delinquency 29*: 7–33.

Hirschel, J. D., I. W. Hutchinson, C. W. Dean, J. J. Kelley, and C. E. Pesackis (1991). *Charlotte Spouse Assault Replication Project: Final Report.* Washington, DC: National Institute of Justice.

Hofstetter, C. R. (1976). *Bias in the News.* Columbus: Ohio State University Press.

Homeland Security (2018). "History." Accessed December 21, 2019, from https://www.dhs.gov/history

Horn, J., L. Rosenband, and M. Smith (2010). *Reconceptualizing the Industrial Revolution.* Cambridge, MA: MIT Press.

Hunter, A. (1978, November). "Symbols of Incivility: Social Disorder and Fear of Crime in Urban Neighborhoods." Paper presented at the American Society of Criminology Annual Meeting, Dallas.

Hyland, S. S., and E. Davis (2019). "Local Police Departments, 2016: Personnel." https://www.bjs.gov/content/pub/pdf/lpd16p.pdf

ICE (2018). "Fact Sheet: Immigration and Customs Enforcement (ICE)." Accessed December 18, 2019, from https://immigrationforum.org/article/fact-sheet-immigration-and-customs-enforcement-ice/

Inbau, F. E., J. E. Reid, J. P. Buckley, and B. P. Jayne (2011). *Criminal Interrogations and Confessions.* 5th ed. Burlington, MA: Jones & Bartlett.

International Association of Campus Law Enforcement Administrators (2019). "FAQs for the Media." Accessed December 17, 2019, from https://www.iaclea.org/faqs-for-the-media

International Association of Chiefs of Police (2017). "2015 Social Media Survey Results." Retrieved from http://www.iacpsocialmedia.org/wp-content/uploads/2017/01/FULL-2015-Social-Media-Survey-Results.compressed.pdf

James, N., and G. McCallion (2013). *School Resource Officers: Law Enforcement Officers in Schools.* Washington, DC: Congressional Research Service.

Jennings, W. G., L. A. Fridell, and M. D. Lynch (2014). "Cops and Cameras: Officer Perceptions of the Use of Body-Worn Cameras in Law Enforcement." *Journal of Criminal Justice 42*(6): 549–56.

Jewkes, Y. (2011). *Media and Crime.* 2nd ed. Los Angeles: Sage.

Joh, E. E. (2004). "The Paradox of Private Policing." *Journal of Criminal Law and Criminology 95*: 49–131.

Justia (2009). "Confessions: Police Interrogation, Due Porcess, and Self Incrimination." Available at http://www.justia.com/constitution/us/amendment-05/09-confessions.html

Kaiser, J. (2018, October 11). "We Will Find You: DNA Search Used to Nab Golden State Killer Can Home in on about 60% of White Americans." *Science Magazine.* https://www.sciencemag.org/news/2018/10/we-will-find-you-dna-search-used-nab-golden-state-killer-can-home-about-60-white

Kavanagh, J., and M. D. Rich (2018). *Truth Decay: An Initial Exploration of the Diminishing Role of Facts and Analysis in American Public Life*. Santa Monica, CA: The Rand Corporation.

Kelling, G. L., and M. H. Moore (1988). *The Evolving Strategy of Policing*. Washington, DC: U.S. Department of Justice.

Kelling G. L., T. Pate, D. Dieckman, and C. E. Brown (1974). *The Kansas City Preventive Patrol Experiment: Technical Report*. Washington, DC: Police Foundation.

Kennedy, D. M., A. A. Braga, and A. M. Piehl (2001). "Developing and Implementing Operation Ceasefire." *In National Institute of Justice, Reducing Gun Violence: The Boston Gun Project's Operation Ceasefire*, 5–53 Washington, DC: National Institute of Justice.

KiDeuk, K., A. Oglesby-Neal, and E. Mohr (2017, February). "2016 Law Enforcement Use of Social Media Survey: A Joint Publication by the International Association of Chiefs of Police and the Urban Institute." Justice Policy Center. Available at http://www.urban.org/sites/default/files/publication/88661/2016-law-enforcement-use-of-social-media-survey_5.pdf

Kirby, J., and A. F. Campbell (2018, June 21). "Why It's Legal for Border Patrol to Have Checkpoints in the US." *Vox*. Available at http://www.vox.com/2018/6/21/17490904/customs-border-protection-patrol-checkpoints-100-miles-legal

Klahm, C. F., J. Frank, and J. Liederbach (2014). "Understanding Police Use of Force: Rethinking the Link between Conceptualization and Measurement." *Policing: An International Journal of Police Strategies & Management* 37(3): 558–78.

Klockers, C. B. (1985). *The Idea of Police*. Beverley Hills, CA: Sage.

Kobler, A. (1975). "Police Homicides in a Democracy." *Journal of Social Issues 31*: 163–81.

Kraska, P., and L. Cubellis (1997). "Militarizing Mayberry and Beyond: Making Sense of Paramilitary Policing." *Justice Quarterly 14*(4): 607–29.

Kraska, P., and L. Gaines (1997). "Tactical Operations Units: A National Study." *Police Chief 64*(3): 34–38.

Kurki, L. (2000). "Restorative and Community Justice in the United States." In *Crime and Justice: A Review of Research*, vol. *27*, edited by M. Tonry (235-303). Chicago: University of Chicago Press.

Lab, S. P. (1984). "Police Productivity: The Other Eighty Percent." *Journal of Police Science and Administration 12*: 297–302.

Lab, S. P. (2019). *Crime Prevention: Approaches, Practices, and Evaluations*. 10th ed. New York: Routledge.

LaGrange, R. L. (1993). *Policing American Society*. Chicago: Nelson-Hall.

LaGrange, R. L. (1998). *Policing American Society*. 2nd ed. Chicago: Nelson-Hall.

Langworthy, R. H., and L. F. Travis (1999). *Policing in America: A Balance of Forces*. Upper Saddle River, NJ: Prentice Hall.

Larson, R. C. (1975). "What Happened to Patrol Operations in Kansas City?" *Journal of Criminal Justice 3*: 267–97.

Laucius, J. E. (2016, July 25). "Police Use of Force: All Situations Are So Complex." *Ottawa Sun*.

Legal Information Institute (2018). "Search Warrants: An Overview." Cornell Law School. Available at http://www.law.cornell.edu/wex/search_warrant

Legal Information Institute (n.d.a). "Do Indian Country Law Enforcement Officers Complete Any Special Training?" Accessed January 5, 2020, from https://www.law.cornell.edu/cfr/text/25/12.35

Legal Information Institute (n.d.b). "18 U.S. Code § 1153—Offenses Committed within Indian Country." Accessed January 5, 2020, from https://www.law.cornell.edu/uscode/text/18/1153

Lewis, D. A., and G. Salem (1986). *Fear of Crime: Incivility and the Production of a Social Problem*. New Brunswick, NJ: Transaction.

LexisNexis Risk Solutions (2018). "Law Enforcement and Public Safety." Retrieved from https://risk.lexisnexis.com/law-enforcement-and-public-safety

Ley, A. (2014, March 8). "Cops, Bailiffs, and Jail Guards: Dissecting Nevada's Officer Categories." *The Las Vegas Sun*.

Liederbach, J., and J. Frank (2003). "Policing Mayberry: The Work Routines of Small-Town and Rural Officers." *American Journal of Criminal Justice 28*: 53–72.

Liederbach, J., and J. Frank (2006). "Policing the Big Beat: An Observational Study of County Level Patrol and Comparisons to Local Small Town and Rural Officers." *Journal of Crime and Justice 29*: 21–44. https//doi.org/10.1080/0735648X.2006.9721216

Liederbach, J., E. J. Fritsch, D. L. Carter, and A. Bannister (2008). "Exploring the Limits of Collaboration in Community Policing: A Direct Comparison of Police and Citizen Views." *Policing: An International Journal of Police Strategies & Management 31*(2): 271–91.

Liederbach, J., and R. W. Taylor (2004). "Police Use of Deadly Force." In *Controversies in Policing*, edited by Q. C. Thurman and A. Giacommazzi, 77–91. Cincinnati, OH: Anderson.

Liederbach, J., C. R. Trulson, E. J. Fritsch, T. J. Caeti, and R. W. Taylor (2007). "Racial Profiling and the Political Demand for Data: A Pilot Study Designed to Improve Methodologies in Texas." *Criminal Justice Review 32*(2): 101–20.

Lilly, R. (1978). "What Are the Police Doing Now?" *Journal of Police Science and Administration 6*: 51–53.

Lundman, R. (1980). *Police and Policing: An Introduction*. New York: Holt, Rinehart and Winston.

Lyman, M. D. (2002). *Criminal Investigation: The Art and the Science*. 3rd. ed. Upper Saddle River, NJ: Prentice Hall.

Lyng, S. (1990). "Edgework: A Social Psychological Analysis of Voluntary Risk Taking." *American Journal of Sociology 95*(4): 851–86.

Marsh, H. L. (1991). "A Comparative Analysis of Crime Coverage in Newspapers in the United States and Other Countries from 1960–1989: A Review of the Literature." *Journal of Criminal Justice 19*: 67–80.

Mastrofski, S. D., J. B. Snipes, and A. E. Supina. (1996). "Compliance on Demand: The Public's Response to Specific Police Requests." *Journal of Research in Crime and Delinquency 35*(3): 269–305.

Mastrofski, S. D., D. Weisburd, and A. A. Braga (2010). "Rethinking Policing: The Policy Implications of Hot Spots of Crime." In *Contemporary Issues in Criminal Justice Policy*, edited by N. A. Frost, J. D. Freilich, and T. R. Clear, 251–64. Belmont, CA: Cengage.

Mathis-Lilley, B. (2015, August 21). "As of Today, Black Lives Matter Activists *Can* Point to a Thorough Police Brutality Reform Plan." *The Slatest*. https://slate.com/news-and-politics/2015/08/black-lives-matter-coalition-police-brutality-policy-proposals-campaign-zero-launches.html

McGarrell, E. F., S. Chermak, J. Wilson, and N. Corsaro (2006). "Reducing Homicide through a 'Level-Pulling' Strategy." *Justice Quarterly 23*: 214–31.

McGarrell, E. F., and Hipple, N. K. (2007). "Family Group Conferencing and Re-offending among First-Time Juvenile Offenders: The Indianapolis Experiment." *Justice Quarterly 24*(2): 221–46. https://doi.org/10.1080/07418820701294789

McGarrell, E. F., K. Olivares, K. Crawford, and N. Kroovand (2000). *Returning Justice to the Community: The Indianapolis Juvenile Restorative Justice Experiment*. Indianapolis, IN: Hudson Institute.

Merriam-Webster Dictionary (2018). "Police." Available at https://www.merriam-webster.com/dictionary/police

Merriam-Webster Dictionary (2021). "Subculture." Available at https://www.merriam-webster.com/dictionary/subculture

Miller, W. R. (1977). *Cops and Bobbies: Police Authority in New York and London, 1830–1870.* Chicago: University of Chicago Press.

Mills, C. W. (1956). *The Power Elite.* New York: Oxford University Press.

Milton, C., Halleck, J., Lardner, J., and Albrecht, G. (1977). *Police Use of Deadly Force.* Washington, DC: Police Foundation.

Mock, B. (2019). "What New Research Says about Race and Police Shootings." *CityLabs.* https://www.citylab.com/equity/2019/08/police-officer-shootings-gun-violence-racial-bias-crime-data/595528

Moore, D., and T. O'Connell (1994). "Family Conferencing in Wagga Wagga: A Communitarian Model of Justice." In *Family Conferencing and Juvenile Justice: The Way Forward or Misplaced Optimism?*, edited by C. Adler and J. Wundersitz (15-44). Canberra, Australia: Australian Institute of Criminology.

Muir, W. K. (1977). *Police: Streetcorner Politicians.* Chicago: University of Chicago Press.

Musu-Gillette, L., A. Zhang, K. Wang, J. Zhang, J. Kemp, M. Diliberti, and B. A. Oudekerk (2018). *Indicators of School Crime and Safety: 2017.* Washington, DC: National Center for Education Statistics. https://nces.ed.gov/pubs2018/2018036.pdf

National Association of Bail Enforcement Agents (2003). Available at http://nabea.org

National Drug Intelligence Center (2006). "Methamphetamine Laboratory Identification and Hazards: Fast Facts." https://www.justice.gov/archive/ndic/pubs7/7341/index.htm

National Institute of Justice (1994, March). "Oleoresin Capsicum: Pepper Spray as a Force Alternative." Washington, DC: U.S. Department of Justice.

National Institute of Justice (2003a). "CCTV: Constant Cameras Track Violators." *NIJ Journal 249.* https://nij.ojp.gov/library/publications/cctv-constant-cameras-track-violators

National Institute of Justice (2003b). "The Effectiveness and Safety of Pepper Spray." Research for Practice Series. Washington, DC: U.S. Department of Justice.

National Institute of Justice (2009). "The Use of Force Continuum." Available at http://www.nij.gov/topics/law-enforcement/officer-safety/use-of-force/pages/continuum.aspx.

National Law Enforcement Museum (2012). "The Early Days of American Law Enforcement." Retrieved from http://www.nleomf.org/museum/news/newsletters/online-insider/2012/April-2012/early-days-american—law-enforcement-april-2012.html

National Neighborhood Watch (2015). "USAonWatch." http://nnw.org/

National PAL (2019). "About Us." Retrieved from https://www.nationalpal.org/Default.aspx?tabid=784239

National Police Agency (2017). "Police of Japan: Organization and Resources." Available at http://www.npa.go.jp/English/pojcontents.html

National Research Council (2004). *Fairness and Effectiveness in Policing: The Evidence.* Washington, DC: The National Academies Press.

Newman, G. (2007). "Sting Operations: Response Guide No. 6, Center for Problem-Oriented Policing." Retrieved from https://popcenter.asu.edu/content/sting-operations-0

Nicas, J., and K. Benner (2020, January 7). "F.B.I. Asks Apple to Help Unlock Two iPhones." *The New York Times.* https://www.nytimes.com/2020/01/07/technology/apple-fbi-iphone-encryption.html

Nicholl, C. G. (1999). *Toolbox for Implementing Restorative Justice and Advancing Community Policing.* Washington, DC: U.S. Department of Justice, Office of Community Oriented Policing Services.

Nielson, E. (2001). "The Advanced Taser." *Law and Order* (May): 57–62.

North Carolina Wildlife Resources Commission (2019). "About." Accessed December 19, 2019, from https://www.ncwildlife.org/About

Nowicki, E. (2001). "OC Spray Update." *Law and Order* (June): 28–29.

Nunn, S. (2003). "Seeking Tools for the War on Terror: A Critical Assessment of Emerging Technologies in Law Enforcement." *Policing: An International Journal of Police Strategies and Management 26*(3): 454–72.

Office of the Health and Safety Executive (2018). "Organization of Police Services." Available at www.hse.gov.uk/services/police/organization.htm

Ohio Department of Natural Resources (2019). "ODN Office of Law Enforcement." Accessed December 19, 2019, from http://ohiodnr.gov/lawenforcement

Ohlheiser, A. (2016, December 12). "Death of Tamir Rice, 12-Year-Old Shot by Cleveland Police, Ruled a Homicide." *The Washington Post.*

Olano, A. B. (1992). "Determination of Probable Cause for a Warrantless Arrest: A Case Note on County of Riverside v. McLaughlin." *Louisiana Law Review 52*(5): 1311–19.

Oliver, M. B. (1994). "Portrayals of Crime, Race, and Aggression in 'Reality-based' Police Shows: A Content Analysis." *Journal of Broadcasting and Electronic Media 38*: 179–92.

Oliver, M. B., and G. B. Armstrong (1998). "The Color of Crime: Perceptions of Caucasians' and African-Americans' Involvement in Crime." In *Entertaining Crime: Television Reality Programs*, edited by M. Fishman and G. Cavender(19-35). New York: Aldine de Gruyter.

Oliver, W. M. (2017). *August Vollmer: The Father of American Policing.* Durham, NC: Carolina Academic Press.

Parenti, C. (1997). "I Hunt Men." *The Progressive 61* (January): 21–23.

Pate, A. M., and L. A. Friddell (1993). *Police Use of Force: Official Reports, Citizen Complaints, and Legal Consequences.* Washington, DC: Police Foundation.

Perkins, D. G., and R. B. Taylor (1996). "Ecological Assessments of Community Disorder: Their Relationship to Fear of Crime and Theoretical Implications." *American Journal of Community Psychology 24*: 63–107.

Perry, S. (2015). "Tribal Crime Data Collection Activities, 2015." https://www.bjs.gov/content/pub/pdf/tcdca15.pdf

Pierce, G., S. Spaar, and L. Briggs (1988). *The Character of Police Work: Strategic and Tactical Implications.* Boston: Center for Applied Social Research, Northeastern University.

Police Athletic League of New York City (2019). "About Us: History." Retrieved from https://www.palnyc.org/history

Police Executive Research Forum (2016). "Critical Issues in Policing Series: Guiding Principles on Use of Force." Available at http://www.policeforum.org/assets/30%20Guiding%20Principles.pdf

Police Executive Research Forum (2017). *The Unprecedented Opioid Epidemic: As Overdoses Become the Leading Cause of Death, Police, Sheriffs, and Health Agencies Must Step Up Their Response.* Washington, DC: Police Executive Research Forum.

Police Foundation (1981). *The Newark Foot Patrol Experiment.* Washington, DC: Police Foundation.

Port Authority of New York and New Jersey (2019). "PAPD History." https://www.panynj.gov/police/en/about/history.html#History

President's Task Force on 21st Century Policing (2015). *Final Report of the President's Task Force on 21st Century Policing.* Washington, DC: Office of Community Oriented Policing Services.

Provost, C. (2017, May 12). "The Industry of Inequality: Why the World Is Obsessed with Private Security." *The Guardian.* https://pulitzercenter.org/reporting/industry-inequality-why-world-obsessed-private-security

Raice, S. (2019, August 9). "Five Years after Michael Brown's Death, Ferguson Still Shows Scars of Riots." *The Wall Street Journal.*

Ratcliffe, J. H. (2007). *Integrated Intelligence and Crime Analysis: Enhanced Information Management for Law Enforcement Leaders.* Washington, DC: Police Foundation.

Ratcliffe, J. H. (2008). *Intelligence-Led Policing.* Portland, OR: Willan Publishing.

Reaves, B. A. (2015a). "Campus Law Enforcement, 2011–12." https://www.bjs.gov/content/pub/pdf/cle1112.pdf

Reaves, B. A. (2015b). "Local Police Departments, 2013: Personnel, Policies, and Practices." *Bureau of Justice Statistics.* https://www.bjs.gov/content/pub/pdf/lpd13ppp.pdf

Reaves, B. A. (2016). *State and Local Law Enforcement Training Academies, 2013.* Washington, DC: Bureau of Justice Statistics.

Reaves, B. A., and M. J. Hickman (2004). "Law Enforcement Management and Administrative Statistics, 2000: Data for Individual State and Local Agencies with 100 or More Officers." https://www.bjs.gov/content/pub/pdf/lema001a.pdf

Reiner, R. (2002). "Media Made Criminality: The Representation of Crime in the Mass Media." In *Oxford Handbook of Criminology,* edited by M. Maguire, R. Morgan, and R. Reiner (302-337). Oxford, UK: Oxford University Press.

Reiner, R., S. Livingstone, and J. Allen (2000). "No More Happy Endings? The Media and Popular Concern about Crime since the Second World War." In *Crime, Risk and Insecurity,* edited by T. Hope and R. Sparks (107-126). New York: Routledge.

Reiss, A. (1971). *The Police and the Public.* New Haven, CT: Yale University Press.

Rivoli, D. (2019). "MTA Expanding Its Police Force to Curtail Fare Beating." *Spectrum News1NY.* https://www.ny1.com/nyc/all-boroughs/news/2019/09/13/mta-looks-to-curtail-fare-beating-by-ramping-up-police-presence?cid=share_clip

Robinson, M. B. (2011). *Media Coverage of Crime and Criminal Justice.* Durham, NC: Carolina Academic Press.

Rosenbaum, D. P. (1987). "The Theory and Research behind Neighborhood Watch: Is It Sound Fear and Crime Reduction Strategy?" *Crime & Delinquency 33*: 103–34.

Rubenstein, J. (1973). *City Police.* New York: Farrar, Straus, and Giroux.

Rumbaut, R. G., and E. Bittner (1979). "Changing Conceptions of the Police Role: A Sociological Review." *Crime and Justice 1*: 239–88.

Santos, R. B. (2014). "The Effectiveness of Crime Analysis for Crime Reduction: Cure or Diagnosis?" *Journal of Contemporary Criminal Justice 30*(2): 147–68.

Scott, E. J. (1981). *Calls for Service: Citizen Demand and Initial Police Response.* Washington, DC: U.S. Government Printing Office.

Scott, R. (2019). "ROOTS: A Historical Perspective of the Office of Sheriff." *National Sheriffs Association.* https://www.sheriffs.org/about-nsa/history/roots

Shantz, J. (2011). "Interrogation Practices." In *Police and Law Enforcement,* edited by W. J. Chambliss, 69–81. Los Angeles: Sage.

Sherman, L. W. (1992). *Policing Domestic Violence: Experiments and Dilemmas.* New York: The Free Press.

Sherman, L. W., and Berk, R. A. (1984). "The Specific Deterrent Effects of Arrest for Domestic Assault. *American Sociological Review 49*, 261–72.

Sherman, L., M. Buerger, and P. Gartin (1989). *Repeat Call Address Policing: The Minneapolis RECAP Experiment.* Washington, DC: Crime Control Institute.

Sherman, L., and Langworthy, R. (1979). "Measuring Homicide by Police Officers." *Journal of Criminal Law and Criminology 70*: 546–60.

Sherman, L., and D. Weisburd (1995). "General Deterrent Effects of Police Patrol in Crime 'Hot Spots': A Randomized, Controlled Trial." *Justice Quarterly 12*(4): 625–48.

Silver, A. (1965). "The Demand for Order in Civil Society." In *The Police: Six Sociological Essays*, edited by D. J. Bordua (2-24). New York: Macmillan.

Skogan, W. G. (1990). *Disorder and Decline: Crime and the Spiral of Decay in American Neighborhoods*. New York: Free Press.

Skogan, W. G. (2004). *Community Policing: Can It Work?* Belmont, CA: Wadsworth.

Skogan, W. G., and S. M. Hartnett (1997). *Community Policing: Chicago Style*. New York: Oxford University Press.

Skolnick, J. H. (1994). *Justice without Trial*. 3rd ed. New York: Macmillan.

Snowden, L., and Fuss, T. (2000). "A Costly Mistake: Inadequate Police Background Investigations." *The Justice Professional 13*: 359-75.

Solomon, J., and A. Martin (2018). "Competitive Victimhood as a Lens to Reconciliation: An Analysis of the Black Lives Matter and Blue Lives Matter Movements." *Conflict Resolution Quarterly 37*: 7-31.

Sparrow, M. K. (2014). "Managing the Boundary between Public and Private Policing." *New Perspectives in Policing*. National Institute of Justice and Program in Criminal Justice, Policy and Management. https://www.ncjrs.gov/pdffiles1/nij/247182.pdf

Spelman, W. (1993). "Abandoned Buildings: Magnets for Crime?" *Journal of Criminal Justice 21*: 481-296.

Spelman, W., and D. Brown (1981). *Calling the Police: Citizen Reporting of Serious Crime*. Washington, DC: Police Executive Research Forum.

SSI (2016, August 31). "North American Security Camera Installed Base to Reach 62M in 2016, Report Says." Retrieved from https://www.securitysales.com/news/north_american_security_camera_installed_base_to_reach_62m_in_2016_report_s/

State of California (2019). "State Park Peace Officers & Superintendents." Accessed December 18, 2019, from https://www.parks.ca.gov/?page_id=24134

Statista (2018). "Number of Video Surveillance Cameras per Thousand People in 2014, by Country." Retrieved from https://www.statista.com/statistics/484956/number-of-surveillance-cameras-per-thousand-people-by-country/

Stead, P. J. (1983). *The Police of France*. New York: Macmillan.

Stinson, P. M. (2018, September 11). "The Federal Government Doesn't Track Police Violence—but I Do." *The Atlantic*. https://www.theatlantic.com/ideas/archive/2018/09/amber-guyger-fallout-how-common-is-police-crime/569950/

Stinson, P. M., B. W. Reynes, and J. Liederbach (2012). "Police Crime and Less than Lethal Force: A Description of the Criminal Misuse of Tasers." *International Journal of Police Science and Management 14*(1): 1-19.

Stoughton, S. W. (2017). "The Blurred Blue Line: Reform in an Era of Public & Private Policing." *American Journal of Criminal Law 44*: 117-55.

Strom, K., M. Berzofsky, B. Shook-Sa, K. Barrick, C. Daye, N. Horstmann, and S. Kinsey (2010). "The Private Security Industry: A Review of the Definitions, Available Data Sources, and Paths Moving Forward." https://www.ncjrs.gov/pdffiles1/bjs/grants/232781.pdf

Struckhoff, D. R. (2003). *The American Sheriff*. Joliet, IL: Justice Research Institute.

Sullivan, L. E. (2009). "Police Subculture." In *The SAGE Glossary of the Social and Behavioral Sciences*, 385. SAGE Publications, Inc. https://www.doi.org/10.4135/9781412972024.n1903

Surette, R. (1992). *Media, Crime and Criminal Justice: Images and Realities*. Pacific Grove, CA: Brooks/Cole.

Surette, R. (2015). *Media, Crime and Criminal Justice: Images, Realities, and Policies*. Stamford, CT: Cengage.

Surette, R. (2018). "Media, Criminology and Criminal Justice." In *Oxford Research Encyclopedia of Criminology and Criminal Justice.* https//doi.org/10.1093/acrefore/9780190264079.013.473

Swedish Police Authority (2018). "The Swedish Police." Available at https://polisen.se/en/the-swedish-police/

Taylor, J. B. (2004). *Right to Counsel and Privilege against Self-Incrimination: Rights and Liberties under the Law.* Santa Barbara, CA: ABC/Clio.

Taylor, R. B. (1988). *Human Territorial Functioning.* New York: Cambridge University Press.

Taylor, R. B., and S. Gottfredson (1986). "Environmental Design, Crime, and Prevention: An Examination of Community Dynamics." In *Communities and Crime,* edited by A. J. Reiss and M. Tonry (387-416). Chicago: University of Chicago Press.

Taylor, R. B., B. A. Koons, E. M. Kurtz, J. R. Greene, and D. D. Perkins (1995). "Street Blocks with More Nonresidential Land Use Have More Physical Deterioration: Evidence from Baltimore and Philadelphia." *Urban Affairs Review 31:* 120–36.

Tennessee v. Garner, 471 U.S. 1 (1985).

Tita, G. E., K. J. Riley, G. Ridgeway, and P. W. Greenwood (2005). *Reducing Gun Violence: Operation Ceasefire in Los Angeles.* Washington, DC: National Institute of Justice.

Travis, L. F., and J. K. Coon (2005). *The Role of Law Enforcement in Public School Safety: A National Survey.* Washington, DC: National Institute of Justice.

Tribal Court Clearinghouse (n.d.). "General Guide to Criminal Jurisdiction in Indian Country." Accessed January 5, 2020, from https://www.tribal-institute.org/lists/jurisdiction.htm

Trojanowicz, R. C. (1983). "An Evaluation of a Neighborhood Foot Patrol Program." *Journal of Police Science & Administration 11*(4): 410–19.

Trostle, L. C. (1990). "Force Continuum: From Lethal to Less-than Lethal Force." *Journal of Contemporary Criminal Justice 6*(1): 23–36.

TSA (2019). "TSA by the Numbers." https://www.tsa.gov/sites/default/files/resources/tsaby-thenumbers_factsheet.pdf

Turner, K. B., D. Giacopassi, and M. Vandiver (2006). "Ignoring the Past: Coverage of Slavery and Slave Patrols in Criminal Justice Texts." *Journal of Criminal Justice Education 17*(1): 181–95.

U.S. Coast Guard (n.d.). "Workforce." Accessed December 19, 2019, from https://www.uscg.mil/Workforce/

U.S. Department of Agriculture (2017). "OIG Investigative and Law Enforcement Authority." https://www.usda.gov/oig/invest.htm

U.S. Government Accountability Office (2005). "Taser Weapons: Use of Tasers by Selective Law Enforcement Agencies." https://www.gao.gov/products/gao-05-464

U.S. Marshals Service (2019a). "Asset Forfeiture." Accessed December 19, 2019, from https://www.usmarshals.gov/duties/factsheets/asset_forfeiture.pdf

U.S. Marshals Service (2019b). "Facts and Figures." Accessed December 18, 2019, from https://www.usmarshals.gov/duties/factsheets/facts.pdf

U.S. Marshals Service (2019c). "Historical Timeline." Accessed December 18, 2019, from https://www.usmarshals.gov/history/timeline.html

U.S. Marshals Service (2019d). "Prisoner Operations." Accessed December 18, 2019, from https://www.usmarshals.gov/duties/factsheets/prisoner_ops.pdf

U.S. Secret Service (n.d.). "About the United States Secret Service." Accessed December 20, 2019, from https://www.secretservice.gov/about/faqs/#

Van Kirk, M. (1978). *Response-Time Analysis: Executive Summary.* Washington, DC: U.S. Department of Justice.

Van Maanen, J. (1973). "Observations on the Making of Policemen." *Human Organization 32:* 407–18.

Van Ness, D. W., and K. H. Strong (2015). *Restoring Justice: An Introduction to Restorative Justice*. 5th ed. New York: Routledge (Anderson).

Washington Department of Fish and Wildlife Enforcement (2019). "WDFW Enforcement." https://wdfw.wa.gov/about/enforcement

Washington Post (2016). "Fatal Force: 971 People Have Been Shot and Killed by Police in 2019." Accessed October 18, 2019, from https://www.washingtonpost.com/graphics/national/police-shootings-2016/

Washington Post (2017). "Fatal Force: 986 People Have Been Shot and Killed by Police in 2018." Accessed October 18, 2019, https://www.washingtonpost.com/graphics/national/police-shootings-2017/

Washington Post (2018). "Fatal Force: 992 People Have Been Shot and Killed by Police in 2018. Accessed March 31, 2019, from https://www.washingtonpost.com/graphics/2018/national/police-shootings-2018/

Washington Post (2019). "Fatal Force: 689 People Have Been Shot and Killed by Police in 2019." Accessed October 9, 2019, from https://www.washingtonpost.com/graphics/2019/national/police-shootings-2019/

Washington Post (2021). "Fatal Force: 1,004 People Have Been Shot and Killed by Police in the Past Year." Accessed March 14, 2021, from https://www.washingtonpost.com/graphics/investigations/police-shootings-database/

Webster, J. (1970). "Police Task and Time Study." *Journal of Criminal Law, Criminology, and Police Science 61*: 94–100.

Weisburd, D., L. Maher, and L. Sherman (1992). "Contrasting Crime General and Crime Specific Theory: The Case of Hot Spots of Crime." In *Advances in Criminological Theory*, edited by F. Adler and W. S. Laufer, 4: 45–69. New Brunswick, NJ: Transaction Press.

Welsh, B. C., and D. P. Farrington (2009). *Making Public Places Safer: Surveillance and Crime Prevention*. New York: Oxford University Press.

Westley, W. A. (1970). *Violence and the Police: A Sociological Study of Law, Custom, and Morality*. Cambridge, MA: MIT Press.

Willman, M., and J. Snortum (1984). "Detective Work: Negative Effects on Organizational Performance in Policing." *Policing: An International Journal of Police Strategies and Management 24*: 115–27.

Wilson, J. Q. (1968). *Varieties of Police Behavior*. New York: Harvard University Press.

Wilson, J. Q., and G. Kelling (1982, March). "Broken Windows." *Atlantic Monthly*, 29–38.

Wisniewski, M., and J. Madden (2015a, December 10). "Hundreds March in Chicago a Day after Mayor's Apology." *Reuters*. https://www.reuters.com/article/us-usa-race-chicago/hundreds-march-in-chicago-a-day-after-mayors-apology-speech-idUSK-BN0TT2B120151211

Wisniewski, M., and J. Madden (2015b, December 18). "Chicago Protestors Call for Mayor to Step Down over Police Brutality." *Reuters*. Available at http://www.reuters.com/article/us-usa-race-chicago/Chicago-protesters-call-for-mayor-to-step-down-over-police-brutality-idUSKBN0U12AU20151218.

Wray, C. (2019). "FBI Budget for Fiscal Year 2020." https://www.fbi.gov/news/testimony/fbi-budget-request-for-fiscal-year-2020

YourGenome (2016). "What Is a DNA Fingerprint?" https://www.yourgenome.org/facts/what-is-a-dna-fingerprint

Zalman, M. (2010). "Miranda v Arizona." In RV del Carmen and C. Hemmonds (Eds.) *Criminal Procedure and the Supreme Court: A Guide to the Major Decisions on Search and Seizure, Privacy, and Individual Rights* 239-254. New York: Rowan and Littlefield

Index

Note: Page numbers followed by *f* or *t* refer to figures or tables found on that page.